T0115162

CHRIST AND THE HINDU DIASPORA

Paul Pathickal

WestBow
PRESS
A DIVISION OF THOMAS NELSON

WestBow Press books may be ordered through booksellers or by contacting:

WestBow Press
A Division of Thomas Nelson
1663 Liberty Drive
Bloomington, IN 47403
www.westbowpress.com
1-(866) 928-1240

Because of the dynamic nature of the Internet, any web addresses or links contained in this book may have changed since publication and may no longer be valid. The views expressed in this work are solely those of the author and do not necessarily reflect the views of the publisher, and the publisher hereby disclaims any responsibility for them.

Certain stock imagery © Thinkstock.
Any people depicted in stock imagery provided by Thinkstock are models, and such images are being used for illustrative purposes only.

Scripture taken from the Holy Bible, New International Version®. Copyright © 1973, 1978, 1984 Biblica. Used by permission of Zondervan. All rights reserved.

Some of the contents of Chapter 11: 'Witnessing to Diaspora Hindus- Friendship Evangelism' is used by permission from 'Service Evangelism' by Richard S. Armstrong.

Some of the content in Chapter 12: 'A Positive Presentation of the Gospel' has been adapted from Evangelism Explosion International and is part of their comprehensive training for personal witness. You can find out more about EE by visiting their website at www.eeinternational.org. All rights reserved including translations. Content used by permission.

ISBN: 978-1-4497-5000-8 (sc)
ISBN: 978-1-4497-5002-2 (hc)
ISBN: 978-1-4497-5001-5 (e)

Library of Congress Control Number: 2012907699

Printed in the United States of America

WestBow Press rev. date: 07/31/2012

DEDICATION

In remembrance of my beloved parents, Mr. and Mrs. Joseph Pathickal, who taught me the basics of the evangelical faith through their words and deeds, and have gone on to glory, this book is dedicated for the glory of God and for the advancement of his kingdom.

CONTENTS

Dedication v

Preface. ix

Introduction. xi

Chapter 1.   The Hindu Diaspora. 1

Chapter 2.   Origin and Development of Hinduism 11

Chapter 3.   Scriptures and Gods of the Diaspora 19

Chapter 4.   Karma, Caste, and Liberation in Diaspora Hinduism . 33

Chapter 5.   Survey of Diaspora Hindus 53

Chapter 6.   Hindu Likings in Christianity. 73

Chapter 7.   Hindu Prejudices Against Christianity. 81

Chapter 8.   Defense of Hinduism 93

Chapter 9.   Christ and Diaspora Hindus. 111

Chapter 10.   A Biblical Approach to Witnessing. 123

Chapter 11.   Witnessing to Diaspora Hindus: Friendship
Evangelism 133

Chapter 12.   A Positive Presentation of the Gospel. 145

Chapter 13.   Answering Common Objections 167

Conclusion 183

Appendix 189

Bibliography. 193

Glossary of Select Hindu Words. 213

Index 217

PREFACE

INDIA, THE TRADITIONAL HOMELAND of the Hindus, is closed to foreign missionaries today. Although the constitution of India guarantees freedom of religion to all its citizens, several States and Union territories forbid preaching and witnessing openly, even by local ministers and evangelists. However, God in his wisdom foresaw what was going to take place and brought fifty million Hindus from India to the outside world. The Hindu Diaspora is scattered from Hong Kong, Indonesia, and Australia in the East to the United States, Canada, and West Indies in the West.

This study is an attempt to consider ways and means to witnessing to the vast Hindu Diaspora spread all over the world. An overseas Hindu is different from his counterpart in India in various ways. For one thing, he is not inhibited by the local customs, manners, and restrictions imposed on him by his extended family, clan, and caste. The old pantheistic thought cannot survive in the foreign soil to which he has migrated. Something else will have to take its place. The secular and humanistic ideas, however enlightened they may be, cannot satisfy the inner yearning of the Hindu for truth, value, and meaning in life.

Hindus are a highly spiritual people. They have been yearning for truth and meaning of life for the last four thousand years since their ancestors, the Aryans, set foot on Indian soil around 2000 BC. Jesus Christ alone will be able to satisfy this spiritual craving for truth and the ultimate meaning of life. Therefore, it is the responsibility of every committed Christian to befriend his Hindu neighbors and point out the true Savior not merely by words but also through deeds.

I wish to express my heartfelt gratitude to the many individuals and organizations for their help and support. I am indebted to the professors of Westminster Theological Seminary, Philadelphia, Pennsylvania, especially to the late Harvie M. Conn for his valuable guidance, to Dr. Timothy J. Keller for his critical insights, and to Dr. Roger Greenway for his suggestions. I am also grateful to International Missions, Inc. for fieldwork during the summer training program in New York City and to Missionary Internship in Dearborn, Michigan, for insights during the pre-field orientation program for missionaries.

I also wish to thank my wife, Mary; my children, Lovely and her husband, Mathews Vadaketh, and Betsy and her husband, Daniel Varghese; and my grandchildren, Jessica, Jonathan, and Caleb for their love, patience, and prayers, as well as my parents, the late Joseph and Mariamma Pathickal, for their prayers and letters of encouragement from faraway Kerala, India, while they were on this side of the curtain. I also thank my nephew, Bobby John, and his wife, Renu, for their help in reading over the manuscript and computer applications. Above all, I am grateful to my Lord and Savior, Jesus Christ, for enabling me to undertake this study. To Him be glory and majesty, both now and forever. Amen.

INTRODUCTION

IN TERMS OF NUMBERS, Hinduism is the third largest religion of the world. The following table gives the comparative strength of all major world religions. From it we see that there are nine hundred million Hindus in the world, of which about 850 million live in India.

Since the government of India does not allow foreign missionaries to enter India, it has become increasingly important to witness to the Hindu Diaspora to win them for Christ so that the Hindus in India will be able to come to Christ. This is not to deny that native missionaries and indigenous churches are playing an important role in witnessing to their Hindu neighbors within India, in spite of opposition and persecution by Hindu revivalist organizations. This may be the reason the omniscient Lord, in His wisdom, has brought about fifty million Hindus to the outside world. If the missionaries cannot go to the Hindus, the Hindus can come to the missionary because of this recent phenomenon.

Table 1: Comparative strength of World Religions[1]

Religion	Number of Adherents	Percentage
Christianity	2.1 billion	33.00
Islam	1.5 billion	21.00
Hinduism	900 million	14.00
Buddhism	376 million	6.00
Sikhism	23 million	0.36
Judaism	14 million	0.22
World Population	6.4 billion	100.00

---

1 Adherents.com. For the purpose of this study, other smaller religions are not taken into consideration.

The Hindu Diaspora[2] is spread from Hong Kong, Indonesia, and Australia in the East to Canada, the United States, Surinam, Guyana, and other countries in South America in the West. This study is an attempt to know the attitudes, preferences, and prejudices of the Hindu Diaspora and to identify ways and means to witness effectively to them.

An overseas Hindu is very different from a Hindu in his native locality in India. He is more broadminded and is not inhibited by local customs and prejudices of his caste fellows. Therefore, he is more open to hear the gospel.

However, this is not the prevalent condition in India today. Just as narrow Islamic fundamentalism is on the rise in the Middle East, Iran, and Pakistan, narrow Hindu fundamentalism is on the rise in several states in India, particularly in the Cow Belt states.[3] Hindu revivalist organizations, such as the Rashtriya Swayamsevak Sangh (RSS), the Hindu Mahasabha, the Akhila Bharatiya Hindu Parishad, the Bajrang Dal, and political parties like the Bharatiya Janata Party (BJP) and the Siva Sena are breathing fire and brimstone on any attempt at witnessing by foreign missionaries or native evangelists. Many states where Hindu fundamentalists are influential have passed laws against "forceful conversion"; many evangelists have been persecuted and murdered, and their churches and homes have been burnt to the ground. Many female evangelists and Catholic nuns have been gang-raped. The execution of Graham Staines, the Australian missionary, and his two little children in Orissa is a permanent black mark on the good name of India and its reputed tolerance of all faiths.

All these incidents make it very important to witness to the Hindus in the Diaspora. If they hear the living gospel of our Lord Jesus Christ, they in turn will be able to witness to their extended family, clan, tribe, and caste in India. The Lord is opening up new avenues to witness to Hindus. It is necessary for evangelical Christians in the new lands, to which Hindus have migrated to come forward and witness the love of Christ, who has given the Great Commission to make disciples of all nations and ethnic groups throughout the world.

---

2   For the purpose of this study, all Hindus residing outside the borders of India are considered Diaspora Hindus. This includes the Hindus living in Nepal, Pakistan, and Bangladesh.

3   For a definition of the Cow Belt, see Paul Pathickal, *The Cross and the Cow Belt of India,* (Enumclaw, Wash.: Winepress Publishing, 2011).

Chapter 1

THE HINDU DIASPORA

THE WORD *DIASPORA* MEANS "dispersion" and initially referred to the dispersion of the Jews among the Gentiles after the Babylonian captivity around 587 BC when Nebuchadnezzar, the king of Babylon, carried many Jewish young men to Babylon after defeating and ransacking Judea and Jerusalem.[4] Dispersion generally, and Jewish dispersion specifically, "were associated with forced displacement, victimization, alienation, loss."[5] In the case of the Hindu Diaspora, some of the above traits may be absent because Hindus were not coerced to leave their homeland.

In fact, Hindus were reluctant to leave their homeland. To them, India, or Hindustan or Bharat,[6] is the holy land. Hindus, especially Brahmin priests, did not look favorably upon foreign travel. The ancient *Code of Manu*[7] prescribes elaborate purification rites if a Hindu ever set foot on foreign soil and came into contact with a *mlecha* (uncivilized person). Different castes must go through different periods of fasting and penance as part of their purification rites to remove pollution from coming into contact with a foreigner, and all must go through ceremonial washing and cleansing. The length of fasting and purification rites depended on the length of the stay abroad. In certain cases, purification could be

4   Leon Wood, *A Survey of Israel's History*, (Grand Rapids, MI Zondervan, 1970), 377.

5   Steven Vertovec, *The Hindu Diaspora*, (London: Routledge, 2000), 142.

6   Bharat is another name given to India through Bharata, the half brother of Rama. Bharata ruled the kingdom on behalf of his exiled brother Rama and returned the kingdom to its rightful king on his return.

7   The *Code of Manu*, the law book of Hindus, prescribes various rules and regulations regarding every aspect of Hindu life.

accomplished only by washing all the clothes used while staying abroad and by bathing three times in the holy Ganges River.[8] No wonder Hindus dreaded foreign travel.

There are other factors that also restricted Hindus' interest in the universe beyond the borders of India. Only the very rich or the very poor would dare to go even to Benares or other holy places on a pilgrimage once in his lifetime. Quite often, there was no guarantee of safe return, but death on the road to the holy place like Benares or the Badrinath Temple in the Himalayas was looked upon as a blessing.

Social factors also contributed to this lack of interest in the outside world. Most often marriages were arranged within the geographic are of the couple. The twin factors of caste endogamy and village exogamy combined to restrict marriage to the same geographic area. Difference in language, food habits, clothing, climate, occupation, and topographical divisions made it very difficult for a Hindu to travel outside his region.

However, the coming of the British changed the situation drastically and dramatically in spite of these religious and social restrictions. Through various combinations of civil and military services, economic needs, educational opportunities, and the availability of national and international transport systems, the world of the Hindus was significantly expanded through exposure to countries outside the borders of their beloved Hindustan.

Abolition of slavery throughout the British Empire in 1834 gave impetus to the migration of Hindus to other parts of the Empire. Most of the Hindus left India as indentured or bonded laborers, while others left as freemen or passengers who could return at any time. The bonded laborer had to stay and work for a period of time, as his travel expenses were paid by the sponsoring agency. However, there was not much difference between the two categories of laborers. The so-called freeman had to sell his property to collect the passenger fare to reach his destination. Unless he worked there for a number of years, he had no economic means to get back to his native place. Major immigration from India began in 1835 to Mauritius, 1838 to Guyana, 1845 to Trinidad, 1860 to South Africa, 1873 to Surinam, 1879 to Fiji, 1896 to East Africa, and subsequently to the Caribbean Island, British Columbia, and California.[9]

---

8   James Forbes Seunarine, *Reconversion to Hinduism through Suddhi,* (Ann Arbor, MI.: University Microfilm, Inc., 1975), 166–167.

9   Bruce W. LaBrack, *The Sikhs of Northern California: A Socio-Historical Study* (Ann Arbor: University Microfilms Inc., 1980) p. 7.

Initially, they did not come to secure a place of permanent residence in the new country. They came for a period, maintaining their ties with the old country, caring for the religious and social values of their caste, upholding traditional kinship obligations, and remitting a major portion of their income to their family back home. Those who came were younger men without wives, and those who were married left their wives and children home. However, as time passed, they brought their families along and settled in the lands to which they had migrated. In due time, they adapted quite well to their new lands and were not interested in returning, even to a newly independent India. They necessarily became an integral part, at least politically if not socially, of their new society.

When a number of countries in Asia, Africa, and Latin America became independent after the Second World War, immigrants from India were faced with hostilities from the natives, which explained the sudden expulsion of all Indians from Uganda by Idi Amin. The hostilities still continue today between the blacks and Indians in South Africa and between the natives and Indians in Fiji and other places.

Large numbers of migrations began to Europe and America after the Second World War. Since India continued to be a member of the British Commonwealth (later renamed The Commonwealth, an association of former colonies of Great Britain), Indians could easily move from one Commonwealth country to another. As a result, many Indians migrated to Great Britain, Canada, Australia, and other Commonwealth countries in search of higher education and employment opportunities.

Many Hindus came to the United States also in search of higher education and employment opportunities. However, this was very limited, as the US government had strict restrictions on visas given to third-world countries. However, in 1965, the US government removed various immigration restrictions, and one of the new ethnic groups that benefited was the Hindu immigrants.[10]

The 1980 census report recognized Asian Indians as a new minority ethnic group. Since this is a recent phenomenon, many Christians in the West do not know much about Hinduism. They may have heard of Transcendental Mediation, the Hare Krishna movement, yoga practices, some guru or holy man from India, or Bollywood actors but have no real knowledge about popular Hinduism. To many Westerners, India is still a distant, enchanted land occupied by an exotic people who follow a strange

---

10   Raymond Williams, "Hinduism in America", *The Christian Century*, March 11, 1987, p. 247.

religion called Hinduism, which stands somewhere between the sublime and the ridiculous. Some of them may have come to the West now, but it is better to ignore them because of their smelly, spicy food and the strange clothes their women wear. This is not to deny that many sincere Christians have tried to communicate the gospel of the living Lord. However, this attempt has been made with a superior cultural attitude and paternalistic mind-set. No wonder it has not been successful.

Hindus in the Diaspora are different from the native Hindus in India. However, Hindus in all its Diaspora cannot be put together in one group. For example, Hindus in Nepal and Bhutan are very similar to those in India. In fact, Nepal is the only Hindu country in the world as even India is not a Hindu country but a secular state. Similarly, Hindus in Pakistan, Bangladesh, and Sri Lanka cannot be put together with Hindus in many other countries of the Diaspora. In Pakistan and Bangladesh, they are native minorities, as they refused to flee to India in spite of persecution during the partition of the country in 1947 when British Raj quit India and divided the country into India and Pakistan.

In most of the rest of the Diaspora, Hindus reside in urban centers. In the US and Canada, they flock to the larger metropolitan areas like New York, Los Angeles, Chicago, Philadelphia, Houston, Dallas, Atlanta, and Toronto. When the immigration restrictions were eased in 1965 by the US government, the first category of Indians admitted were the highly professional people. Officials in India condemned this migration as "brain drain" from India. But the government of India was powerless to stop it, as doctors, engineers, scientists, and nurses sought greener pastures for themselves and their children. In the foreign lands, they soon established themselves as upper-middle-class professionals. Commenting on this group of immigrants, Fred W. Clothey remarks:

> Indian immigrants, perhaps more than any other immigrant group before them, are highly educated, professional people. In a study of 200 Indian families in Pittsburgh, for example, 75.2 % of the entire adult population sampled had graduate degrees, including 86.3 % of the men and 54.9 % of the women. Another 23.3 % were studying, 87.2 % at the graduate level.[11]

---

11   Fred W. Clothey, *Rhythm and Intent: Ritual Studies from South Africa* (London: Blackie and Son Publishers, Ltd., n.d.) p. 164.

The highly professional character of this immigrant population belies some of the stereotypes Westerners have perpetuated of India as a poor, illiterate, economically backward nation. The United States is the largest absorber of Indian talent in science, medicine, engineering, and technology. India's government and private sector industries have tried to raise the salaries of the above categories of people, but the brain drain continues because of the better working conditions, research facilities, and recognition in the United States. According to former Indian Ambassador to the United States, R. K. Narayanan, Indians constitute about ten percent of US physicians.

The Hindu community on the whole is an upwardly mobile group wherever they have gone. According to surveys, they are better than the white community in terms of per capita income, as the average family income is much higher than any other group. After five years of mandatory immigrant status, most of these professionals became citizens of the United States so that they and their children could get educational grants and loans. After they became citizens, they sponsored their immediate family members to come to the United States under the family reunification provisions of the Immigration Act.

The second group of immigrants who came as a result of the family reunification provisions was less educated and found work in factories, hotels, transportation, and nursing homes. Encouraged by their relatives, they enrolled in community colleges and technical schools to better their status. Many of them also started small businesses, such as grocery stores and motels, and employed their relatives to man these establishments.

RELIGIOUS FERVOR OF HINDUS

The Hindu immigrants as a rule are young, well educated, prosperous, enthusiastic, energetic, and are active in establishing Hindu organizations and temples on US soil. There are several Hindu religious organizations in America, and even the secular ones celebrate Hindu festivals besides important national holidays. Some new immigrants go through what Mahatma Gandhi, referring to his experience in England, described as the "Sahara of atheism."[12] Some immigrants have complained in letters to Indian newspapers that the "temple builders" are communalists who are trying to create 'little Indias' in the United States. However, many of them after the initial reaction become more religious in their adopted lands

---

12   M.K. Gandhi, *An Autobiography or The Story of My Experiments with Truth,* (Ahmedabad, India: Navajivan Publishing House, 1927, 1991) p. 59

than they were in India, as they try to preserve their cultural traditions and transmit those values to their increasingly westernized children.

Three factors seem to contribute to this upsurge of religious fervor.[13] The first is the need for societal support. Many Hindus become more active in religion as a way of maintaining their cultural heritage, as the temple and religious gatherings provide a point of identification. They offer a context for meeting social, religious, and national gatherings. They also provide a network of connections across the new country, which in turn provides personal security, better job opportunities, upward mobility, and social gatherings.

The second reason for the new religious fervor is the need to preserve ethnic identity. Hindus want to be active in religious matters in the new lands to transmit their religious traditions to their children. In the native land, grandparents took the grandchildren to temples and bhajens even though their children were not active in religious matters. However, in the new land, there are no grandparents to inculcate religious fervor, and therefore parents, though busy, must do these things to help children be in touch with their religious and cultural roots. If there is a vacuum, children might wander away from the faith of their fathers and get into false cults and religions, which are contrary to Hindu dharma.

The third reason why Diaspora Hindus show more religious fervor is to get recognition and exalted status in their communities. In the new societies to which they have migrated, it is not easy to get recognition. Therefore, Hindu professionals, who have wealth, education, and management skills, are ready to spend their money to establish religious, social, and cultural organizations.

These three factors have contributed to the establishment of Hindu temples and religious and cultural organizations in North America. The following news items should convey the dynamic that is involved:

> The first Hindu temple of its kind in the Western world was built in Flushing, New York in 1977 … The next one was built for Vishnu on a hilltop in Pittsburgh. In May 1978, a five-acre property was purchased in Houston, Texas, to build a temple for the goddess Meenakshi.[14]

---

13   Peter Perira and Mary Lou C. Wilson, *Responding to the Presence of Asian Indians in North America*, Houston 1985, Evangelizing Ethnic America, April 1985, Unpublished, p. 7.

14   *India Tribune*, August 4, 1984, p.13

The first Hindu temple in Ohio has just opened in Dayton. It will serve 300 families in Dayton and 2,000 families in the tri-sate area of Ohio, Indiana and Kentucky.[15]

In May (1984), a new Hindu temple opened in Los Angeles, in Malibu. Three thousand people were present for the ceremonies. 1.5 million dollars was spent on that date. $700,000 was contributed that day. The State Bank of India provided the financing. Another million dollars will be solicited.[16]

Hindu religious and cultural organizations are springing up in all urban centers in America and millions of dollars are spent for building temples across the land. Hindu summer camps and conferences are organized for Hindu children and families along the lines of Christian camps and conferences. Many of these camps are filled in advance.

Dr. Raymond Williams argues that Hinduism in the US may be plotted on two related axes.[17] If it is true of Hinduism in the US, it must be applicable to the entire Hindu Diaspora. The first axis relates to the size of the community. Where only a few Hindus are present in a locality, they will meet together for worship and rituals that are identified with ecumenical Hinduism. The common language in these meetings is English, and the religious texts and rituals are those of orthodox Hinduism, recited in Hindi or the regional language of the worshippers. But when there is a larger community, its tendency is to splinter into regional, linguistic, caste, and sectarian groups. The second axis is length of residence. When immigrants are new to an area, their primary concern is to achieve economic and social security. Religious activity takes place within the family or among friends. Once the family is established, attention then turns to providing a more permanent and structured religious life.[18]

Since every religious family has a corner of the living room or family room for idols and other religious symbols, Hindus can participate in religious activity without going to a temple. This family ritual is the most important element in transmitting religious beliefs and practices to the

---

15   ibid, June 9, 1984, 10

16   ibid, June 1984, p. 10

17   Raymond B. Williams, *The Christian Century*, op. cit. p. 247

18   ibid, p. 248

children. Family worship need not be elaborate or time consuming; all it takes is lighting a candle or bowing before the family idol in the morning or evening. However, special occasions warrant the presence of Brahmin priests, who are available in almost all the urban centers where Hindus have migrated in large numbers.

Wherever there are more than one hundred Hindu families, they discuss the possibility of building a temple. If there are appreciable numbers of specific sectarian groups, they are allowed to have their own idols placed in prominent places, and worship may be conducted in front of them even if the main temple is dedicated to another deity. Hindus have already built many temples in the foreign lands to which they have migrated. Most of them are built on sectarian lines, and Brahmin priests are brought from India, if not for permanent residence, at least on temporary visas for a season.

Diaspora Hindus face many problems in adapting to their new homes. When a Hindu priest recently performed a ritual for an immigrant family in a new temple in Chicago, he chanted a portion of ancient Sanskrit text, naming the sacred rivers of India but including the Mississippi, the Ohio, and the Rio Grande rivers. The children of the family, who understood little of the ceremony, roused themselves at this startling introduction of familiar American rivers.[19] Hindu children born and raised in the United States have little knowledge of the Ganges, the Indus, and the Brahmaputra Rivers or the significance their parents attribute to them. However, by way of contextualization, when the priests include the Mississippi, the Ohio, the Susquehanna or the Delaware rivers in ritualistic ceremonies, they are roused to attention.

PROBLEMS FACING DIASPORA HINDUS

Securing proper leadership to conduct worship and rituals is a problem for Diaspora Hindus. Many of the leaders are Brahmins, and they are reluctant to migrate to foreign lands. But even when they become ready, securing visas is a problem, as they are well educated only in the Vedas. There was some talk about starting a Hindu university in America to train Hindu priests for Diaspora Hindus everywhere.

Another difficult problem is the uncertainty about whether or not they can transmit their religion to the next generation. They are frightened by peer pressure on their children regarding dating, marriage, alcohol, drugs, and family relationships. Divorce is unheard of among Hindus in India

19   ibid, p. 247

for many reasons. Lack of freedom for women may be one. According to Hindu dharma (duty), a woman is never free of the men in her life. Until marriage, they are protected by their parents, after marriage by their husbands, and if they become widows, they are to be protected by their sons. In the lands to which they have migrated, divorce is not uncommon among the majority of communities, and women are free to pursue their lives without depending on a male. Hindu children living in such an environment most likely will copy such lifestyles, they are afraid.

Mass media, such as newspapers, magazines, and television, do not portray India and Hinduism in a positive light. India is considered to be a third-world country steeped in poverty, illiteracy, and superstition, and Hinduism as a religion for the unsophisticated and uneducated masses. In the new country, the attitude of most of the second- and third-generation Hindus is, "Let our parents hold onto their superstitious beliefs, but we who are educated and sophisticated should not have to do anything with their beliefs." It was reported recently that a Hindu couple in Chicago, who were both physicians, took their children to India, never to return, when their oldest daughter, who was a high school junior, told her parents that she was going to Los Angeles on the back of a motorcycle with a white male classmate during spring vacation.

Another problem Hindus face is the scandal of the "high-flying gurus" like Bhagawan Shree Rajneesh, Kirtananda Swami Bhaktipada, and others like them. Rajaneesh was known as the "sex guru" for advocating "free love" among his devotees. In 1981, he established a commune called Rajneeshpuram in Oregon and was embroiled in conflict with the local residents. He was arrested and deported for immigration violations and died in 1990 in Pune, India.[20]

Bhaktipada was once a major figure in the Hare Krishna movement and established a commune called New Vrindaban in West Virginia. He was expelled from the Hare Krishna movement in 1987 and was convicted in US federal courts for racketeering. He had difficulty obtaining land in New Jersey and Pennsylvania for establishing a walled commune to be named City of God.[21]

Hindu leaders are thus faced with the task of presenting a more positive picture of their religion and culture in the lands of the Diaspora. One of the ways in which they try to do this is by helping the poor, the elderly, and the homeless. They maintain that these things are done not necessarily

---

20   *New York Times,* July 11, 2004.

21   *The Philadelphia Inquirer,* November 19, 1987.

for publicity but in keeping with the goals and philosophy of their religion. However, in spite of these pious proclamations and token humanitarian works, their neighbors are still suspicious of the various Hindu sects in their midst. People of Oregon still remember that the devotees of Shree Rajaneesh tried to take over a township government by bringing homeless people from all over the United States, promising them a good life. Now the people are scared whenever a Hindu sect tries to establish a commune in their neighborhood.

There is also the likelihood of tensions and conflicts creeping into the Diaspora Hindus on sectarian and caste lines as they are aligned in India, and as the number of new immigrants increase, these tensions are likely to become more pronounced. The fact that the new immigrants do not have the same educational and professional skills as the earlier ones also increases tension and disruption amongst themselves. All these differences must be taken into consideration when Christians try to witness to the Hindu Diaspora.

In the following chapters, I will attempt to discuss the phenomena of the Hindu Diaspora and how Hindus abroad are different from the native Hindus, the basic tenets of orthodox Hinduism, and how a biblical approach to witnessing to the Hindu Diaspora is important in Christian missionary endeavors.

Chapter 2

ORIGIN AND DEVELOPMENT OF HINDUISM

THE ORIGIN OF HINDUISM is steeped in mystery, as no one knows when or how it began. There is no record of its precise origin or its founder, like Jesus Christ of Christianity or the prophet Mohammed of Islam. There is also no world-shattering event to mark its beginning.

The first problem faced by the student who wishes to study the origin and development of Hinduism is the absence of dates for events in Indian history. The second is the problem of affixing periods of development.[22] The tendency to divide history into ancient, medieval, and modern seems hard to resist. However, it is better to divide Hinduism into four periods for various reasons:

1. The Period of the Vedas and the Upanishads: 2000 BC to 600 BC
2. The Period of Epics and Puranas: 600 BC to 300 AD
3. The Reformation Period: 300 AD to 1800 AD
4. The Modern Period: 1800 AD to the present

This division into the four periods is by no means arbitrary, as these periods correspond to the development of Hindu scriptures and other important events in Indian history. The first two are clear, as they correspond to the great religious books of Hinduism. The third period corresponds to various attempts at reformation and speculative philosophy.

---

22   Troy Wilson Organ, *Hinduism, its Historical Development*, Woodbury, New York: Barron's Educational Series Inc. 1974) p. 7

The beginning of the fourth period starts with the Battle of Plassey in 1757 followed by the Sepoy Mutiny, or the First War of Independence, a century later when the British Raj began to establish colonial rule in India.[23]

The word *Hindu* is derived from the word *Hind*, which was the name of the region through which River Indus flowed from the Hindu Kush and Himalayan mountains in the north to the Arabian Sea in the south. This river was called Sindhu by Indo-Europeans, Hindu by the Iranians, Indos by the Greeks, and Indus by the English[24]. The present states of East Punjab and Haryana in northwest India, West Punjab, and Sind provinces in Pakistan originally constituted the region of Hind, as this river flowed through these areas.

No one is sure about the original inhabitants of this land. Two sites on the banks of River Indus claim two ancient civilizations of the world. Harappa in Punjab lies to the north along the Ravi River, a tributary of River Indus, and Mohanjo-daro in Sind lies further south on the banks of River Indus itself. These two sites were discovered along River Indus by archeologists when a railway line was built between Karachi and Lahore.[25]

No one knows how this civilization was destroyed. Many hypotheses have been advanced, but all of them have holes in them. The first is that the nomadic Aryans, who came from the central Eurasian plateau, could not tolerate the more civilized and settled civilization on the banks of the Indus River. The later Vedas, the sacred texts of the Aryan invaders, speak of the conquest of the dark-skinned people of the walled cities whose success was attributed to the might of the Aryan war god, Indra.[26] Armed with bows and poisoned arrows, they conquered the original settlers. This is supported by the findings from the upper level of the more recent archeological period at Mohanjo-daro: "At these and recent upper layers of the ancient city, human skeletons were discovered sprawled about in grotesque attitudes of violent death."[27] These findings seem to support the

---

23   The rebellion of the Indian soldiers in 1857 is referred to as the Sepoy Mutiny by British historians and as the First War of Independence by Indian historians. See Ramachandra Guha, Makers of Modern India, (Cambridge, Massachusetts and London, England: The Belknap Press of Harvard University Press, 2011) p. 47.

24   Troy Wilson Organ, op. cit., p. 1

25   ibid, 39

26   A.L Herman, op. cit p. 16

27   ibid, p. 18

conclusion that the more cunning and fierce invaders indeed violently and unexpectedly slew a number of people.

The second hypothesis is that the Harappan culture collapsed when disastrous natural forces, such as an earthquake, flood, or fire, destroyed it. The third hypotheses is that internal human forces, such as urban pollution, overpopulation, or a contagious disease (such as a plague or cholera) annihilated a majority of the population as the rest escaped these cities, leaving everything behind them, never to return.

Whatever the reasons, it is unfortunate that the Indus Valley civilization with its art and crafts, language and government, and technology and collective wisdom passed suddenly and terribly from the pages of history.[28] However, its religious heritage lived on in the traditions of the culture that replaced it. The people of the succeeding culture copied many of their beliefs and incorporated them into their religion, resulting in Hinduism.

No one is sure of the date of the Aryan invasion of India. All we can say is that sometime during the period from 1800 to 1500 BC, a series of invasions occurred through the mountain paths of northwestern Hindu Kush Mountains, where almost all the invaders came to India throughout history. The invaders could see the lush, fertile fields of the Indus Valley from the mountaintops and rushed in. The early trickle of the Aryans in the 1800s turned into a torrent by the middle of the second millennium,[29] sweeping before them what remained of the Indus Valley Civilization as they moved into the fertile plains.

Aryans were a group of nomadic people who migrated from the central Eurasian plateau around the shores of the Caspian Sea in search of fertile land. The reason for the massive migration is unknown. It might have been the result of severe drought and famine, an earthquake, or some internal war between the various groups. This migration to the Himalayas and the subcontinent of India occurred almost at the same time as a vast movement of the same people into northern Europe, Iran, the Middle East, and the Greek Peninsula.[30] They settled in the migrated lands and consequently became the ancestors of the Celts and the Teutons in northern Europe, the Greeks and the Latins in the south, and the Hittites and the Kassites in the eastern Mediterranean. All these groups of people are similar not

---

28   ibid, p.20

29   ibid, p.20

30   ibid, p. 20

only in physical appearance but also in their religion, philosophy, social and political structure, and language.[31]

Sanskrit is the language of the Aryans and is the mother of all Indo-European languages. The word *Aryan* is a Sanskrit word meaning "noble one" and the word *Sanskrit* means "elegant" or "well- formed." While the Harappans were short, dark, thick-lipped, flat-nosed, and short-headed, the Aryans were tall, light-skinned, straight-nosed, and long-headed. They brought with them superior weapons, such as the bow and arrow and the two-wheeled, two-horse chariots. They did not like the cities; hence, they destroyed the cities of Harappa and Mohanjo-daro.

The Aryans settled first on the upper tributaries of the Indus River. They had been a nomadic people, but as they began living in simple villages or clan groups, tending their flocks and herds, their lives became less pastoral and more agricultural. Their men were fully occupied with agriculture when they were not fighting, and their women carried on homemaking and gardening. The animals they brought into India were those of a pastoral people, such as cows, horses, sheep, goats, and dogs. They clung to their ancient diet of milk and meat and an intoxicating drink made out of some plants and/or grain called soma, which they offered to their gods as libations to please them.[32]

As they continued their march toward the south of the subcontinent, they encountered the powerful Dravidians, who had settled in India earlier after defeating the aborigines who had escaped to the warm southern mountains. When the Aryans and Dravidians fought each other and lived apart, if not harmoniously, at least with fear and grudging admiration, Hinduism was born as a way of life. It may be defined as civilized Aryanism grafted on primitive Dravidianism.[33] The common tendency to regard noble virtues, such as subtle, intellectual, and highly developed areas, as Aryan and base virtues, such as magic, superstition, and animism, as Dravidian are unfounded. When two civilizations collide by way of war or peace, they influence and borrow from each other. So today no one can say for sure what aspect of Hinduism is Aryan and what aspect is Dravidian.

The Dravidians were no match for the successive waves of invaders that came from the north and subjugated them. Those Dravidians who resisted had to flee further south to the Deccan Plateau beyond the Vindhya

---

31   ibid. p. 20

32   John B. Noss, *Man's Religions*, (The Macmillan Company, New York,1963) p.125.

33   Troy Wilson Organ, op. cit. p. 41

Mountains. As the struggle with the Dravidians subsided, there were intertribal clashes between various Aryan groups, which were immortalized in the two great epics, the *Ramayana* and the *Mahabharata*. In addition, once they settled down in the northern regions of India, the first distinct social classes among the formerly unidentified nomadic people came into existence. These classes were divided based on their occupation, from which the castes of later Hindu society arose.

Each tribe had a presiding king or chieftain, called a raja, whose office was generally hereditary.[34] As his chiefdom became larger, his power and position also increased. Toward the end of the Vedic period, the raja was distinguished from other citizens by a large retinue of attendants, a palace, and ceremonial dress and was expected to have a large army of soldiers to protect him, his subjects, and his territory. He also had a number of priests gathered around to help him get blessings from his clan gods and goddesses. Outnumbering the priests and the warriors were the farmers and herdsmen whose home life was not much better than that of his ancestors. This is the rudiment of the caste system in later Hinduism.

As they settled in the North and had comparative peace, they began to develop an extensive oral tradition of paying homage to their favorite gods and goddesses in hymns and prayers. Folk tales and epic stories came to be sung in groups. Slowly, religious conceptions were developed, out of which came the earliest religious writings called the four Vedas from which all our knowledge of the time is drawn: the Rig Veda, the Sama Veda, the Yajur Veda, and the Atharva Veda. We shall look at them in a later chapter on Hindu scriptures.

India is one of the 127 provinces ruled by Emperor Xerxes mentioned in the Old Testament book of Esther and is an ancient land full of natural resources. Therefore, army after army of great kings and emperors came to India one after another. In 327 BC, Alexander, the great Macedonian king, conquered the northwest provinces. However, his campaign lasted only about two years, and he had to retreat immediately. His conquest made no impression historically or politically in India.[35]

The Persians, the Moguls, the Portuguese, the Dutch, the French, and finally the British came to India for trade and conquest during the course of history but could not penetrate the heartland of India successfully. Even

---

34   John B. Noss, p. 125

35   Romila Thapar, *A History of India* (Baltimore, MD: Penguin Books, 1966) p. 59

great religions like native Buddhism, Jainism, Sikhism, foreign Islam, and Christianity have had only minimal impact upon Hinduism.

HINDUISM IS A WAY OF LIFE

If we do not know much about the origin of Hinduism, we cannot point out a single founder of the religion either. In fact, it has no single founder and cannot be defined easily in positive terms. Broadly, it can be said that all those Indians who have not embraced an alien religion are Hindus. There is no general council that lays down doctrine, no pope or Episcopal bench or assembly that determines policy, and no central place that exerts authority or enforces discipline.[36] It is not a religion in the usual Western sense of the word.

Hinduism is impossible to define in a terse and neat statement, for it comprehends a way of life rather than a narrow churchgoing creed and affects a man's social status, his marriage, the very food he eats, the friends among whom he can mingle, and the occupation he performs.[37] Hinduism may be regarded as a body of customs and ideas that has such pervasive power and defensive force as to absorb or resist any system upon which it comes into contact.[38]

There are certain rules and ceremonies a Hindu is expected to perform. However, even if he does not perform them, he will not be brought before a tribunal or a court of discipline. Hinduism rests essentially on the opinion of his caste fellows, who will excommunicate him only for the greatest offenses, such as embracing an alien religion.

However, Hinduism is not exclusively a matter of customs, as they would not hold together unless they represented certain values. There is no one set of values or doctrines 'delivered unto the saints' once for all. What we have then is a body of ideas, beliefs, and values that together make up the amorphous mixture called Hinduism. Any one of these ideas, beliefs, or values can be dispensed without forfeiting the title of Hinduism, as no one part is absolutely essential. A person born in a Hindu family is a Hindu whether that person believes in any of the Hindu gods, doctrines, or ideas, performs any of the rites, or practices any of the customs. As long

---

36   Percival Spear, *India, Pakistan and the West* (London: Oxford University Press, 1967) p. 33

37   T. Walter Wallbank, *A Short History of India and Pakistan* (New York: Mentor Books, 1958) p. 25

38   Percival Spear, op. cit. p. 35

as he does not claim that he has embraced another religion, he continues to be a Hindu.

Today there are numerous sects and divisions in Hinduism, which worship entirely different gods and goddesses, unknown to one another. A deity worshipped in south India may not be recognized in north India. Hinduism is an amorphous mixture of various religious concepts that have evolved throughout the centuries. Many of the religious concepts of the south, the northeast, and the west may not be recognized as part of orthodox Hinduism. Christianity could get a foothold in the south and the northeast, Buddhism in the northeast, and Islam and Sikhism in the west, but none of them could attract major segments of the population.

Hinduism of the south, the northeast, and the west are very tolerant of other faiths and creeds, but this cannot be said of orthodox Hinduism of central India, which is militant. Hindu militant organizations, such as the Akhila Bharatiya Hindu Mahasabha (All India Hindu Organization), Vishwa Hindu Parishad (World Hindu Council), Rashtriya Swayamsevak Sangh (National Voluntary Organization), Bajrang Dal (Youth Wing), Shiva Sena (Army of Shiva), and the political party Bharatiya Janata Party (BJP) have a strong following. This is the essential Hindustan, the land of the Hindus wherein lies the main line of orthodox Hinduism.

The present form of Hinduism is the result of centuries of development starting with the Vedas and the Upanishads, which are the basic religious texts of Hinduism. Interpretation of these texts is the prerogative of the Brahmin priests. The average Hindu may not know much about the system or the ideas contained in them, and he is not even concerned. He goes about being religious in the manner that has been traditional in his locality, practicing all sorts of beliefs. Animism, fetishism, shamanism, demonolatry, animal worship, and devotion to village gods, goddesses, spirits, and demons are all part of the system with or without the more respected and higher worship of the great deities of the Hindu pantheon.

The ordinary villager is content to worship the village spirits to whom he looks for rain, bountiful harvests, and escape from plague, cholera, small pox, and other contagious diseases. And there are as many spirits and demons as there are villages in India. Since gods and goddesses could easily cohabit and produce children not only among themselves but also with ordinary mortals, there is no scarcity of minor gods and spirits in the villages. Hindu mythological stories are as numerous, if not more, than the stories we come across in Greek mythology. Among the untouchables, or Harijans (people of God) as they are called by Mahatma Gandhi, the founder of modern India, a kind of sub-Hinduism exists, which is little better than primitive animism found in sub-Saharan Africa.

A majority of Hindus practice orthodox Hinduism along with the primitive forms of animism common in their locality even though they may not set foot in the dwellings or the temples of the Harijans. In the same village, one may see majestic temples with high arches for the worship of the great gods of orthodox Hinduism with learned Brahmin priests in attendance, chanting Sanskrit mantras and performing vivid ceremonial rites, along with small shrines or wayside stones or trees for the worship of village spirits and demons. The average villager pays homage at both the majestic temples and the small shrines without any twinge of conscience. The Brahmin priests tolerate the practice as long as the villager comes to his temple and pays respects to them.

All these sects, castes, and divisions in orthodox Hinduism can be seen in Diaspora Hinduism as well. However, the divisions in the foreign land to which they have migrated are less pronounced than in India. For example, images of several deities may be in one temple here in the US while such a thing would not be tolerated in India, where each deity has its own temple or shrine, however small it may be. Various sects and castes are more tolerant of each other in the US.

Let us now see some of the basic tenets of Diaspora Hinduism and how they differ from the orthodox Hinduism seen in India.

Chapter 3

SCRIPTURES AND GODS
OF THE DIASPORA

DIASPORA HINDUS ACCEPT ALL the basic scriptures of orthodox Hinduism, which can be classified under five categories and were written over a period of twenty-five hundred years. Unlike the Bible, there is no organic unity in them. It is not the story of one God coming to Earth to save mankind. There is no foretelling of future events and no fulfillment of earlier prophecy. In addition, Hindus do not believe that their scripture is complete; it is not something that is delivered unto the saints once for all. A holy man may come in the future and add to the existing collection. The five categories are: the Vedas, the Upanishads, the Epics, the Puranas and the *Brahmanas*, *Agamas*, *Darsanas*, and the *Code of Manu*.

The Vedas are considered the best and foremost religious books of Hinduism, as they are the earliest written authority of Hinduism. The word *Veda* is derived from the root *vid*, which means, "to know," and comes from the same root word in Greek, *oida* (to know). Hence, *Veda* means wisdom or revealed knowledge.[39] The Vedas contain the transmitted wisdom of the Aryan invaders who poured in from central Asia about the middle of the second millennium BC[40] and contain a great variety of hymns and prayers, direction for the performance of sacrifices, primitive mythology, and the beginnings of philosophic speculation.

There are four Vedas. The Rig Veda is the most important and original scripture of the Hindus and contains 1017 *suktas*, or hymns, in praise of

---

39   Jack C. Winslow, *The Christian Approach to the Hindu*, (London: Edinburgh House Press, 1958) p. 11.

40   ibid, p. 11

various nature gods. To these hymns, eleven apocryphal hymns are added. To a superficial reader, these hymns may look like songs of praise to gods. However, closer inspection reveals that some of them are magical chants, riddles, and legends. They are not the folklore of primitive and animistic minds, but the work of sophisticated priests seeking long life, material blessings, power, and success. The formula is to praise the god first and then petition him for blessings.

The Sama Veda is basically the Rig Veda rearranged with musical notations for chanting during sacrificial ceremonies, which are to be sung to fixed melodies.

The Yajur Veda is a rearrangement of hymns contained in the Rig Veda for use by priests in orderly worship. It also contains some additional prose material, which are detailed directions for ritualistic service.

The Atharva Veda is late in the development of Vedic literature and contains prose and poetry dealing with magical spells and incantations designed to meet the demands of people who wish to escape from magical spells and evil spirits. The significance of this Veda is that it is the basis for the branch of medicine known as the Ayurveda, which is very popular not only in India but all over the world today. It consists of treatment with roots and plants and is devoid of magic spells. Today there are Ayurveda colleges of medicines and hospitals all over India. Therefore, sometimes the last part of Atharva Veda, dealing with Ayurveda, is called the Fifth Veda.[41]

The authors of these Vedas are unknown. They are attributed to Rishis, or holy men, who have led ascetic lives in continuous meditation for years at a stretch:

The Rishis were saints or patriarchs, human beings highly exalted and unique in nature, who in their abode in the mountain heights of the Himalayas received and passed to men the *sruti* or inspired literature, which remains to this day the infallible standard of perfect knowledge or truth.[42]

The Vedas were written probably between 2000 and 600 BC, during which time a caste of priests emerged in Hinduism called the Brahmins who were the custodians of temples and sacrifices. They held absolute sway over the people. Through the sacrifices and rituals they performed, they claimed they could change the very course of cosmic events. In fact, even

---

41   ibid, p. 60

42   Edmund David Soper, *The Inevitable Choice: Vedanta Philosophy or Christian Gospel*, (New York: Abington Press, 1957) p. 43

the gods described in the Vedas became frightened of these rituals, as the Brahmins could create trouble and fights between various gods through their rituals, pitting one god against another. Thus, the gods themselves became insignificant, and rituals became more important. These rituals, if performed in the manner described in certain treatises, would accomplish the desired result. These treatises are known as the Brahmanas and are appended to the Vedas.

The word *Upanishad* means to sit down beside. Therefore, they are philosophic and ritualistic treatises seated by the side of the Vedas. They were written from around 900 BC to 300 BC. The more important of the treatises written by Brahmin priests gave practical directions for the conduct of all manner of sacrifices in very elaborate detail. They also contain ideas leading to a monotheistic supreme power, which was already evident in the later hymns of the Vedas. The more speculative of the Brahmin priests started thinking in terms of a supreme deity who worked through the ritualistic prayer in changing the course of cosmic events, demanding obedience not only from men but also from gods. If such a supreme deity existed, could he be called the Ultimate Reality of the universe? Thus, the Brahmin priests began to probe behind the forces of nature into the Ultimate Reality. This probing generated new ideas. The Upanishads are the result of their speculation.

There are about one hundred Upanishads. There is no consensus in them as to the correct view of the universe. The dualistic *Sankhya* philosophy, which maintains that matter and soul are two eternal categories of being and that there exists nothing called a Universal Spirit, finds its first voice in the Upanishads. However, the predominant view expressed in the Upanishads is the *Advaida* metaphysic, or monism. This later crystallized into the *Vedanta* philosophy, which maintains that, the ground of all being, whether material or spiritual is the Ultimate Reality called Brahman or Bhagawan. The true self of a man and the world soul are one, identical. This identity is expressed in the *Chandogya Upanishad* in the following way; "*tat tvam asi*," meaning, "That are thou."[43] In other words, the All-soul or the Universal Spirit is the very stuff of which the individual human soul and its consciousness are made. There is no real distinction between the two. Therefore, the objective Brahman and the subjective Self can be equated. When the individual soul "knows" its complete identity with the

---

43   R.E. Hume, *The Thirteen Principal Upanishads* (London: Oxford University Press, 1934) p. 246

Brahman, it celebrates this knowledge with a feeling of unity approaching ecstasy. This unity is called "*nirvana*" or liberation.

The two great epics of Hinduism are the *Ramayana* and the *Mahabharata*, written somewhere between 600 BC and 300 AD. The *Ramayana* is a long epic poem consisting of twenty-four hundred couplets and deals with the story of Rama, an avatar, or descent, of Vishnu, one of the triad of great gods of Hinduism, who came into the world to annihilate Ravana, the demon king. The demon king had stolen Sita, the wife of Rama. In an epic battle, Rama defeated Ravana with the help of Hanuman, the monkey god. However, even after Sita was recovered, Rama was not willing to take her back as his wife for fear of the people, in spite of the fact that Sita went through ritualistic fire to prove her chastity. Finally, when her innocence was fully established, Sita, unwilling to go back to her husband, was taken back by her mother, Earth, by swallowing her into its bosom. Rama was a great warrior-king who sacrificed everything, even his own wife, for the welfare of his people.

The *Mahabharata* is the story of Krishna, another descent of Vishnu and depicts the battle between the good Pandavas and their cousins, the wicked Kauravas. Arjuna, the leader of the Pandavas, was reluctant to fight with his cousins. In the thick of the battle at a place called Kurukshetra, which lies somewhere north of the present Delhi, Krishna, the driver of the chariot of Arjuna, encourages him by telling him that dharma, or duty, is more important than love for his brothers. This advice of Krishna, consisting of seven hundred verses, is called the *Bhagavad-Gita* or *The Song of God*, which is probably the most revered and widely read scripture of the Hindus.

The more important Puranas or ancient tales are eighteen in number. They describe the activities of legendary heroes of the ancient past, including those of Rama and Krishna. They were written somewhere between 300 AD and 1200 AD and rank next to the epics in their influence on the masses as they seek to evoke religious devotion through myths, stories, and legends. Stories about Rama and Krishna belong to this category and have become plots for popular films in almost all Indian languages. The most popular Purana is the *Bhagavata-Purana*, which relates the stories of the ten incarnations of Vishnu. "These stories, in which heroes display virtues and such as honesty, chastity, and self-sacrifice, has played a significant part in the formation of the Hindu moral code."[44]

---

44   Sir Norman Anderson, op. cit. p. 140

The *Brahmanas, Agamas, Darsanas*, and *Code of Manu* are commentaries, laws, and regulations for various purposes to regulate society. There are also ancient law codes, especially that of Manu, the ancient lawgiver. *Brahmanas* are commentaries on the Vedas and Upanishads. The *Agamas* are theological treatises and manuals, and the *Darsanas* are scholarly treatises of different schools of philosophy. However, all Hindus do not universally accept these. They are accepted by different sects within Hinduism and are mostly authoritative commentaries for the followers of individual sects. The Hindu scriptures were written in Sanskrit, the ancient language of the scholar. To write them in any other language was considered sacrilegious. However, in due course of time, in order to break the stranglehold of the Brahmins, hymns and devotional songs were written by devotees of various gods in regional languages.

Finally, it must be remembered that the Hindu scripture is by no means complete. It is not something that is delivered unto the saints once for all. Future collections may be added to it whenever a holy man appears on the horizon. But Diaspora Hindus accept most of these as authentic scripture, with each sect giving more importance to their particular god or goddess and the Purana, or legend, describing their hero-god. Wherever they have a group of their own sect or caste, they establish a temple in honor of that hero-god and install his or her idol in that temple. If there is not a large enough group, they will request an image of their clan or caste god to be placed in a nearby temple of other Hindus and worship their clan god.

GODS OF THE DIASPORA

The consensus among Hindus is that there are 330 million gods in Hinduism.[45] The Aryans of the Vedic age worshipped the powerful objects of nature: the all-encompassing sky, the radiant sun, the gigantic thundercloud, the beautiful dawn, the roaring storm, the all-devouring fire, etc. were among many gods of the Aryans. At this time, there were no temples nor were there any images. And yet they were so personalized that they not only received sacrifice and listened to prayer and praise, but also they were believed to have had their own high home of unapproachable light beyond the sun and the stars where they lived in immortal joy. This indicates the kinship of these Aryans with the other members of the Indo-European family who were also nature worshippers.

All this time, the Aryans were still on the move. They were pressing down the Ganges Valley, enslaving or driving the dark-skinned Dravidians

45   John B. Noss, op. cit. p. 290

farther east and south. According to several historians, these Dravidians themselves were outsiders who had driven the original inhabitants of the land to the hills and forests. At any rate, as is the usual custom, whenever two groups of people come into contact with each other, there is much exchange in terms of customs, habits, and culture, and the Aryans and Dravidians were no exception. Eventually, they intermingled and copied the very habits of those whom they subjected.

As time went by, belief in nature gods decayed. Those Brahmins who had a philosophic bend of mind began to probe into the ultimate reality, while others of less intellect started worshipping all kinds of gods, goddesses, devils, spirits, and heroes. The present system of Hindu gods is the result of centuries of development. The average villager worshipped all gods in his locality. Since gods and goddesses could easily cohabit not only among themselves but also with ordinary mortals, there is no scarcity of gods. Hindu mythological stories are more numerous than the stories found in Greek mythology. Among the lower castes and the untouchables, or the Dalits (oppressed classes) as they prefer to call themselves, a kind of sub-Hinduism exists. Since they are out of the four castes of Hinduism, their religion may be aptly called primitive animism. Their gods are said to be less potent than the majestic gods of orthodox Hinduism.

Who are these great majestic gods of Hinduism to whom the Brahmin priests pay homage in their great temples? Is there any system in the myriad of 330 million gods? Is there a hierarchy among them? Who is more powerful among them? The answers to these questions will vary according to the region and caste of the Hindu who answers them, but a consensus may be found among a majority of Hindus.

At the apex of the system is the Brahman or Para-Brahman, or Bhagawan or the Ultimate Reality or the Universal Spirit. The idea of this Ultimate Reality developed for the first time during the period of the Upanishads. However, no Hindu will ascribe personality to the Brahman, as he is impersonal in nature and does not concern himself with the mundane affairs of this universe. When a Hindu is finally able to liberate himself from the cycle of births and deaths, his *atman* (soul) will merge with this Universal Spirit and achieve *moksha* or *nirvana*, or liberation. His soul will become one with the Paramatman (Supreme Soul or Universal Spirit). Since the *Parmatman* has no personality, character, or attributes, he is indescribable.

It must be noted here that the average Hindu is only vaguely aware of this Ultimate Reality and is not concerned with the speculative philosophy of the Brahmin scholar. Further, his vague idea of a Supreme Spirit pervading all nature is obscured by fear of demons and evil spirits. He regards the Universal Spirit as too great, remote, and impersonal to intervene on his behalf against demons and evil spirits. Since the Universal Spirit is impersonal and quiescent, he has no concern with current human affairs, and therefore, divine intervention, if possible, is the prerogative of lesser gods.

Under the Universal Spirit is the great triad of gods. All orthodox Hindus accept them and pay homage to them. These are three different and distinct gods and are not to be confused with the Trinity of Christianity. In the Christian doctrine of Trinity, God the Father, God the Son, and God the Holy Spirit exist as three in one in the Godhead and are not at loggerheads with one another. When we speak of the Trinity of God in Christianity, we refer to a trinity in unity and to a unity that is trinal.[46]

In the Hindu pantheon, Brahma, Shiva, and Vishnu are three distinct and separate gods created by Brahman, the impersonal supreme deity. To the Hindu philosophers, they stand for the divine functions of creation, preservation, and destruction. Of these three great gods, Brahma is the creator of all things, visible and invisible. He created this world on the model of the heavenly world. In every age, the creation of the various orders is the same. In the present age, he created first the vegetable kingdom, then the animal kingdom, then human beings, and finally, the supernatural beings, consisting of gods, goddesses, devils, demons, spirits, demigods, and lesser spiritual beings. Brahma is the least worshipped of the three gods since he has finished his work of creation and is no longer active in this world. He is not to be feared, as he has left everything to the natural laws of the world.

Shiva is the fiercest of the three gods and is very difficult to be placated. He is said to have a third eye, and if he opens it, anyone on whom his gaze falls will be destroyed instantly. However, he can be made auspicious, as he destroys only the bad to make room for new creation. He is thus identified with life itself as pure energy, including sexual energy. He is also the patron of ascetics and holy men, as they destroy their lower self to seek after the higher self in meditation and prayer.

However, Vishnu is the most popular god of the Hindus, as he is the perfect and patient god of divine love. Whenever he sees values threatened or the good in peril, he exerts all his influence to save the good from the

---

46   Louis Berkhof, *Systematic Theology* (Grand Rapids, Michigan: William Eerdmans Publishing Company, 1974) p. 84

wicked. At times, he even comes to earth in avatars, or descents, to save the good from the bad. Traditionally, he is said to have come down nine times so far, and the last descent is expected in the future at the end of this age.[47]

Let us now see the ten incarnations of Vishnu. First, Vishnu descended into this world as the enormous fish (Matsya) to rescue Manu, the first man, from a general deluge. Second, he came down as the tortoise (Kurma), which swarmed under Mount Mandara and assisted the gods in churning the nectar of immortality, ambrosia (Amrith), from the ocean of milk. Then he came as the boar (Varaha) to lift the sunken earth with its tusks from the bottom of the sea where a demon had carried it. After that, he came as the man-lion (Narasimha) to tear to pieces a demon-father who tried to kill his son for worshipping Vishnu. The fifth descent was as the dwarf (Vamana) to recover the three worlds from a powerful demon-king by means of diplomacy. The sixth descent was as Parasurama (Rama with the axe), who utterly defeated the Kshatriya caste twenty-one times to establish Brahmin supremacy in the land.

The seventh was as Buddha, the founder of Buddhism, who deceived the world with his ill-conceived philosophy of *ahimsa*, or non-violence, so that men may not go away from the path of righteousness as set forth in the Vedas. With this cunning stroke, they absorbed Buddhism into its fold. It is no surprise that Buddhism could not get a foothold in the land of its birth, even though it is quite popular in other South and East Asian countries.

The eighth and ninth descents are the most important, and these are as Rama and Krishna, heroes of the two epics, *Ramayana* and *Mahabharata*. Rama was the king of Ayodhya, whose wife, Sita, was kidnapped by the demon king, Ravana of Lanka, the present day Ceylon or Sri Lanka. In an epic battle, Ravana was defeated by Rama, with the help of Hanuman, the monkey god, and rescued his wife, Sita. Even though Rama was willing to accept Sita as his wife, he forsook her for the sake of his subjects, as they doubted her chastity since she spent time in Ravana's harem. The moral of the story is, he was such a great king that he sacrificed everything for the welfare of his people. Sita proved her chastity through an ordeal of fire and delivered twins for her husband, but instead of going back to his palace, she asked her mother, Earth, to swallow her.

---

47   Geoffrey Parrinder, *Avatar and Incarnation* (London: Faber and Faber Limited, 1970) p. 21. All Hindu Scholars do not agree on the number or the names of the avatars.

Today, Rama is widely revered and worshipped as an avatar that came down from heaven to annihilate the demon king, Ravana, and save his people, and the agitation for restoring the temple at Ayodhya is a very contentious issue throughout India. The Muslim Mogul king, Babar, was alleged to have built a mosque where the Rama temple once stood.

The ninth descent of Vishnu as Krishna is the most remarkable of all, whose story has at least some superficial similarities to the incarnation of Jesus Christ. In the earlier avatars, Vishnu is said to have emitted only a portion of his godhead, but Krishna reflected the most glorious image of the god of preservation. In him, god was really incarnate as he descended as a real man upon the theater of human activity while claiming at the same time the attributes of the Supreme Being with whom he is identified. In the epic battle at Kurukshetra between the good Pandavas and their wicked cousins, the Kauravas, Krishna sided with the good Pandavas. Addressing their leader, Arjuna, Krishna says in Chapter IV, verses 6–8 of the *Bhagavat Gita*:

> Even though I am unborn because of my changeless essence and even though I am the Lord of all created things, in presiding over nature, which is mine, I do incarnate myself by my own mystical power. For whenever there is decline of duty and increase of irreligion, O son of Bharata, at that time I manifest myself. In order to protect the pious and to destroy the wicked and also for the purpose of establishing duty, I incarnate myself in every age.[48]

Krishna thus gives the sum and substance of the purpose of his descent. Whenever the pious are threatened, he comes down to protect them and destroy the wicked.

Rama and Krishna are the most important and latest descents of Vishnu and therefore are worshipped by all orthodox Hindus. Even if there is a local deity in a particular village, the villagers accept these two as superior to their own local deity.

The tenth and final descent of Vishnu, Kalki, will come at the end of time in human form on a white horse to extinguish the visible universe. He is a messianic figure analogous to the messianic ideas in Judaism and Christianity. Since no Hindu scholar gives any chronological dates for

---

48   A.C. Bhaktivedanta Swami Prabhupada, *Bhagavat Gita As It Is* (New York: Collier Books, 1972) pp. 222-227

these ten descents, we are not sure whether this idea of a messiah precedes the spread of Christianity in India.

SHAIVISM AND VAISHNAVISM

Diaspora Hindus pay lip service to all the gods of orthodox Hinduism, but a majority of them belong to the two categories of Shaivism and Vaishnavism. Earlier we saw that Brahma, Shiva, and Vishnu are the three great gods of Hinduism. Brahma is the creator and has left everything to the natural order of things, as he does not interfere in the mundane affairs of the world.

However, Shiva and Vishnu, the destroyer and preserver respectively, are active in the affairs of the world. Followers of Shiva are called Shaivites or Saivites. Sacred ash came to be used as a sign of Shaivism, and devotees use it as a sectarian mark on their foreheads in a u-shaped form and on other parts of their bodies with three parallel short lines. Shaivism has many different schools, reflecting both regional and linguistic variations and differences in philosophy and has a vast literature that includes texts representing various philosophic schools. Shiva temples are spread all over India, especially in Gujarat, Uttar Pradesh, Bihar, West Bengal, Karnataka, Tamil Nadu, and Andhra Pradesh. Parvati, Shiva's consort, and his sons Ganesha and Murugan are popular gods of the Shaivites. The Nataraja Temple in Tamil Nadu, the Pashupatinath Temple in Nepal, and the Mahadeva Temple in Karnataka are very famous.

The holy book of the Shaivites is the *Agamas*, a set of twenty-eight books written in Sanskrit. Each temple follows its own *Agama*. The architecture and layout, the locations of the images, and directions for methods of worship are all prescribed, and no deviation is allowed. Only the Shivacharyas, or Great Teachers, of Shaivism may enter the sanctum sanctorum, and worshippers gather around to witness the rituals of ablution, decoration, and offerings, to pray, sing, and receive ceremonial blessings.[49]

Shaivism has spread to other countries and has left a major imprint on the intellectual life of Cambodia, Vietnam, Java, Indonesia, Nepal, Singapore, Malaysia, and many other South Asian countries. Shaivism stresses the importance of outward and visible signs through ascetic practices, pilgrimages, and temple worship. Therefore, it is sometimes described as the highest form of Hinduism. "Shavism is by far the best that

---

49   http://en.wikipedia.org/wiki/Shaivism

India possesses; judged by its intrinsic merits Shaivism represents the high water mark of India's deeply religious intuition and life."[50]

Shaivism had to retreat to South India, as it came into conflict with Buddhism, Jainism, and Vaishnavism in the North. Shankara advanced the cause of Shaivism, as he chose Shiva as his chosen deity, but his *Advaita*, or non-dualistic philosophy, was too intellectual for the masses to digest. Therefore, Shaivites developed its devotional and intellectual sides through hymns composed in Tamil rather than Sanskrit.[51]

Shaivism is strongly monotheistic. Shiva is portrayed as having three eyes to denote his insight into past, present, and future, with a crescent moon in his hair to denote time and serpents on his neck and arms to denote that he controls the endless cycle of ages (Kalpas)[52] and a necklace of skulls to symbolize the destruction and regeneration of mankind.[53]

The active side of Shiva is represented as Shakti (power), and since he has various activities, his consorts are many. More accurately, his power is represented in a single consort who appears in different forms. The more important consorts are Parvati (mountaineer), Kali (destruction), Durga (blood sucker), Yoni (reproduction), Uma (beauty), Jaganmatri (mother of the universe), and Yogini (asceticism). Kali and Durga form two of the fiercest of his consorts and are worshipped all over India, especially in Bengal.

Vishnu is the god of the Vaishnavites. The conflict between the two main sects resulted in developing rival legends, which enhanced the strength and the number of followers of each sect. When rival kings supported each sect, their strength increased in the local kingdoms. While Buddhism took deep root in isolated pockets of India with the support of the ruling monarchs and in other Asian countries, Jainism lost ground, as it adopted many Hindu ideas and practices and became another Hindu sect.

During the fourth to the eighth centuries after Christ, avatars, or descents or incarnations, became an important aspect of Vaishnavism. The number of *avatars* of Vishnu varied according to the time and locality. By the eighth century, the number came to be stabilized at ten. The first four are as animals and are mythological, while the next five are heroic

---

50   M. Dhavamony in *Religious Hinduism. A Presentation and Appraisal.* Third Edition. Edited by R. De Smet. pp. 265-266, quoted by Troy Wilson Organ, op. cit. p. 289.

51   Troy Wilson Organ, op. cit. p. 276

52   A Kalpa consists of 4,320,000 years, and each Kalpa is divided into four yugas, or ages.

53   Troy Wilson Organ, op. cit. p. 24

humans. Some scholars consider the Buddha as the seventh *avatar,* while some others consider him to be the ninth *avatar.* Incorporating the Buddha as an avatar of Hinduism was a cunning attempt to assimilate militant Buddhism into Vaishnavism.

The tenth avatar is eschatological and has some similarities to the idea of messiah in Judaism, Christianity, and Islam. Did Vaishnavism copy the idea from these religions? No one can say with any certainty. All that can be said is that the origin of the concept of avatar in Hinduism is unknown, although the aboriginal peoples of India had tales of gods appearing *incognito* in animal and human forms.

The concept of *avatars* transformed Vaishnavism to loftier heights, and it became the most important sect in Hinduism. The common man could not understand the speculative philosophy of the Upanishads and received comfort and consolation from Vishnu, the god who saves, by demonstrating his love and comfort in taking on human form to redeem mankind. The avatars of Vishnu as Rama and Krishna lifted the spirit of the common man as legendary stories of the heroes of *Ramayana* and *Mahabharata* were spread in local languages and dialects as Puranas. These Puranas are called the Vedas of the common man, as they recite Vedic material in the form of legends and stories.

There are eighteen major Puranas and an indefinite number of secondary Puranas. The most important of them is the *Bhagavata Purana*, and the tenth book of this Purana recounts the birth of Krishna, his mischievous boyhood, his amorous triumphs over the milkmaids, the destruction of his wicked uncle Kamsa, his marriages, his miracles, and his heroic exploits in helping the good Pandavas over their wicked cousins, the Kauravas, during the epic battle of Kurukshetra. This book, with its emphasis on the amorous exploits of Krishna, turned Vaishnava *dharma* (duty) to *bhakti* (devotion) and from there to *prema* (desire) and *kama* (lust). However, no reference is made in the *Bhagavata Purana* to the erotic love of Krishna for his favorite milkmaid, Radha. This erotic love affair, consummated outside of marriage, opened the floodgates to extreme forms of eroticism, and the gain for romantic literature was tremendous. One of the first literary products was the *Gita Govinda* of Jayadeva (twelfth century), a series of monologues on the love of Radha and Krishna, and is strikingly similar to the Song of Songs of the Old Testament.[54]

In the seventh and tenth centuries after Christ, twelve wandering minstrels called Alvares appeared who drove out Buddhism from India

---

54   Troy Wilson Organ, op. cit. p. 276

and Jainism from South India. Their songs, which number about four thousand, became the prayer book of Tamil Vaishnavism. This collection of hymns is sometimes called *The Tamil Veda*.[55] These simple hymns became very popular and were able to do what the intellectual Advaita philosophy of Shankara could not do in driving out Buddhism and Jainism from South India, particularly from the soil of Tamil Nadu.

Hindu Diaspora reflects both of these two sectarian trends depending upon the allegiance of their caste, clan, or family roots in India. Vaishnavism is more sophisticated, urbane, and moderate in its core values, while Shaivism is more primitive, rural, and extreme. While Vaishnava priests are usually learned Brahmins who bring to their priestly function the dignity of a noble tradition, Shaiva priests are seldom Brahmins but bring to their office the zeal and enthusiasm of personal experience and dedication.[56] The mendicants one sees in India today are mostly Shaivites, who leave their kith and kin in search of liberation from the wretched life in this world.

It is interesting to note here that the two main branches of Hinduism reflect the nature of their gods. Vishnu is an orderly god who relishes the higher aspects of life like love and redemption and is worshipped by his devotees out of love. Shiva, on the other hand, is worshipped by his devotees out of fear and awe; they dread his actions and pray for mercy. He became the god of cremation grounds, while Vishnu became the god of romance and all things beautiful in life.

Some scholars think that the worship of Shiva may have originated in non-Vedic India during the pre-Aryan days. Worship of Shiva most often includes some form of sexual pattern, and the Aryans spoke contemptuously of the phallus-worshippers. Was Shiva a Dravidian god who was incorporated into the Hindu pantheon to please the lower castes? No one is sure. However, it is clear that while Shaivism stresses the importance of outward and visible signs of their sect, which results in ascetic practices, pilgrimages, and temple worship, Vaishnavism stresses the importance of inward and internal signs of emotional life, which results in house worship and reciting passages from the *Ramayana* and *Bhagavat Gita*. If Vishnu is the god of Prema (romantic love), Shiva is the embodiment of Kama (sexual love).

Then there are some gods and temples that are the Diaspora Hindus' favorite places of pilgrimage. Whenever they get a chance to visit their parents or close family, they make it a point to visit their favorite temple

---

55   ibid, p. 276

56   ibid, p. 288

to get blessings from their clan god or goddess. One of these places is the Sabarimala Temple on the banks of River Pampa on the Western Ghats of Kerala State. This hill shrine and its deity Lord Ayyappan are matchless in Hinduism, as he is the symbol of communal harmony. His mother is reported to be Mohini, the female incarnation of Vishnu and Shiva. Therefore, both the Shaivites and the Vaishnavites worship him. During the festival days of Sabarimala, one can see the devotees of Ayyappan traveling from all parts of South India to this temple mount. Those who want to see the image must lead a life of austerity and penance for forty-one days. Entrance into the temple is restricted to males, postmenopausal women, and little girls below ten years of age.

Another god of some importance to the Diaspora Hindus is Ganesha, son of Shiva and Parvati, whose elephant head makes him distinct from all other gods in the Hindu pantheon. He is worshipped all over India and considered to be the patron of arts, literature, and science, and the god of the intellect and wisdom.

Swaminarayan is another god of importance to a prominent sect in Gujarat. Since there are a number of Gujaratees all over the world, they go to this favorite temple whenever they visit their homeland. Even though Swaminarayan was born in Uttar Pradesh, he settled down in Gujarat after visiting all the holy places in India. He has over five million devotees all over the world.

Kali or Mahakali (Great Kali), and sometimes her twin, Durga, are the favorite goddess of the Bengalis. She is said to have three eyes and wears a garland of skulls. She is the power of Shiva and is said to stand on the body of Shiva. During her festival days, a lot of animal and sometimes human blood is shed in her temples.

There are a number of other important gods and goddesses among the Hindu Diaspora. If they cannot go to their favorite place of pilgrimage, they bring an image of their god to the local temple and are allowed to install that image at least during their particular festival days. The same priest may officiate to pay homage to the favorite deity of all the immigrants if they cannot bring their own priest from India.

Chapter 4

KARMA, CASTE, AND LIBERATION
IN DIASPORA HINDUISM

THE MORAL ORDER OF orthodox Hinduism may be explained by the *Doctrine of Karma*. The word *karma* means literally "action" or "deed," and the Doctrine of Karma deals with the inevitable working out of action in new life. A man's body, character, temperament, wealth, health, birth, experience, position, happiness, sorrow, and everything else in this life are the rewards of his past deeds.[57] Every act necessarily works itself out in another birth. The soul alone is indestructible; however, it carries with it the burden of the past. Every good action ennobles it to some degree and helps loosen the grip of the sense-world, while every bad action degrades it and gives the world a greater hold so that a man who persists in right action makes steady progress toward perfection and ultimate liberation.

Continued vice plunges the soul in corruption and degradation in life, but since souls are emanations of the divine spirit, they do not cease to exist until the final liberation when they are submerged with the divine spirit. Therefore, when a man dies, his soul migrates into another existence, the result of his karma in previous lives. The same soul may be in one life a god, in another a man, in a third an animal or even a plant. The series of births and deaths continue in never-ending cycles until it achieves liberation.

The Doctrine of Karma and rebirth does not appear in the Vedic literature of the Aryans. They make their first appearance only in the Upanishads, which we have seen were written after the Aryan invaders had settled down in India. The doctrine of rebirth or transmigration

---

57   J. N. Farquhar, *The Crown of Hinduism* (New Delhi: Oriental Books, 1971) p. 139

of the soul was probably Aryan in origin, as we see it in other people of Aryan origin, such as the Greeks. But the Doctrine of Karma is distinctly Indian, as we see it in no other place. Therefore, it is reasonable to conclude that the Doctrine of Karma was prevalent in some crude form among the vanquished Dravidians and that the victorious Aryan invaders borrowed it from the defeated Dravidians.[58] The Dravidians were a very proud and cultured race, and even in defeat, they exerted some influence over their victors just as they were enslaved and intimidated by the Aryans.

However, it is the Aryan mind that coordinated these two theories of karma and rebirth and made them into a single theory of morality. Today, every saint and philosopher, every guru and holy man in Hinduism subscribes to this important doctrine. Seth Govinda Das, an eminent professor of Benares Hindu University, writes in his book, *Hinduism*:

> The law of *Karma* is the keystone of the arch over which has been built, through the course of ages, the vast edifice of Hinduism. Knock this out and the splendid structure crumbles to the ground. It is no wonder that we strenuously pin our faith to it and defend this vital position against all attacks. We are prepared under the various modern stresses—economic, social, etc.—to loosen our hold on many other practices and beliefs regarded as fundamental in the earlier days, but not on this.[59]

M. Hiriyana, another noted Hindu philosopher, puts it differently:

> The doctrine extends the principle of causation to the sphere of human conduct and teaches that as every event in the physical world is determined by its antecedents, so everything that happens in the moral realm is pre-ordained.[60]

Swami Vivekananda, founder of the Ramakrishna Mission, puts it more succinctly:

---

58   ibid, p. 134

59   Seth Govinda Das, *Hinduism,* cited by Edmund Soper in *The Inevitable Choice* (New York: Abington Press, 1957) p. 99

60   M. Hiriyana, *The Essential of Indian Philosophy* (London: George Allen and Unwin Ltd., 1932) p. 46

Any word, any action, any thought that produces an effect is called Karma. The law of Karma means the law of causation of inevitable cause and effect ... Each one of us is the effect of an infinite past. The child is ushered into the world not as something flashing from the hands of nature ... but he has the burden of the infinite past; for good or evil he comes to work out his own past deeds. This makes the differentiation. This is the law of *Karma*. Each one of us is the maker of his own fate.[61]

Dr. S. Radhakrishnan, probably the most renowned philosopher of Hinduism and a former president of India, writes:

Until we negate, we are bound to the endless procession of events called s*amsara*. The principle, which governs this world of becoming, is called *karma*. There are moral and spiritual laws as well as physical laws. If we neglect the laws of health, we injure our health; if we neglect the laws of morality, we wreck our higher life. Any rational conception of the universe, any spiritual conception of God requires us to recognize the utter and unquestionable supremacy of law in shaping our conduct and character.[62]

Explaining the mode of rebirth, Dr. Radhakrishnan continues:

The soul finds out its future body before it leaves the present one. The soul is creative in the sense that it creates a body. At every change of body, the soul takes a newer form. The state of each existence of the soul is conditioned and determined by its knowledge (*vidya*), its conduct (*karma*) in the previous existence ... The results of learning and conduct cling to the soul ... The ignorant, the unenlightened go after death to sunless demonic regions. The good are said to go up to regions which are sorrowless, through the air, sun and moon ... Beautiful characters attain covetable births and ugly ones

---

61   Swami Nikhilananda, *Vivekananda, A Biography*, pp.199-200, cited by Edmund D. Soper, op. cit. pp. 100-101

62   S. Radhakrishnan, *The Principal Upanishads* (London: George Allen and Unwin, Ltd., 1953) pp. 113-114

miserable births. Heaven and hell belong to the world of time. Rebirth is the lot of man until he attains true knowledge.[63]

These passages are quoted extensively from Hindu philosophers in order to show the lasting influence of the law of karma and rebirth. If a good man suffers or a bad man flourishes, it must be because of their bad or good actions in their previous lives. Here is an attempt to explain away the problem of unmerited suffering. The law of karma and rebirth offers an excellent way of escape by attributing the cause of unmerited suffering to the demerits of earlier lives. Thus, it provides a very plausible reconciliation of the facts of life with the claims of abstract justice. There is no easy escape from the law of karma. One has to endure it completely. The process of birth, death, rebirth, and re-death is an endless cycle until one obtains liberation. The inevitability of this uncertain succession of lives is an increasingly unbearable burden to every Hindu.

The *Doctrine of Karma* and rebirth has been subject to scathing criticism by many skeptical and religious scholars. The skeptics argue that it is an unverifiable law. But then, most of the doctrines relative to the non-physical world are unverifiable. There have been several crude attempts by parapsychologists and phenomenologists to produce witnesses who are alleged to have memory of past lives. Since these are not taken seriously by Hindu philosophers, we need not attempt to disprove it here. Most if not all Hindu philosophers agree that these laws are empirically unverifiable.

One of the earliest to criticize the law of karma and rebirth was A. G. Hogg, a Scottish educational missionary to India. In his book, *Karma and Redemption*, Hogg attacks the doctrine on several grounds:[64] It is deterministic and fatalistic. It leads to narrow and selfish individualism. It is ethically defective because it substitutes a judicial system for a moral order. It has no place for unmerited suffering, and finally, it fails to allow room for repentance and forgiveness.

In spite of these defects, the Doctrine of Karma still holds almost universal sway over all castes and sects of Hinduism. However, the full implication of the doctrine has never been fully understood by the masses. The average Hindu accepts the doctrine as an explanation of the

---

63   ibid, pp. 116–117

64   For a detailed study see A.G. Hogg, *Karma and Redemption* (Madras: Christian Literature Society, 1970) For a summary of these arguments, see Paul Pathickal, *The Cross and the Cow Belt of India* (Enumclaw, WA: WinePress Publishing, 2011) pp. 47-50.

inequalities of health, wealth, status, and position in life and it informs him why certain calamities befall certain men. He has never realized the full implication of the doctrine, which makes even the gods impotent. In spite of it he goes on praying to his favorite god or goddess for health, wealth, children, deliverance from calamities, and success in life.

One of the three ways to achieve liberation is the Karma Marga, or the Way of Works. By carrying out certain rites, ceremonies, and duties, one can add something to one's merits or favorable karma. They will not cancel the unfavorable karma; one has to endure the consequences of past sins inevitably. However, the good deeds can add to one's merits, and by acquiring enough merits, one may be able to pass at death into a higher caste and finally toward liberation.

The Karma Marga thus offers a practical way of escape. The *Code of Manu* is a celebrated law book that tells each Hindu what to do at certain stages in his life. A man must observe all the rules of his caste. Certain rites must be performed at birth, at the name-giving ceremony, at the first feeding of a child, at the first haircutting, at the time of marriage, and at numerous other times till he passes away from this life. There are also elaborate rites following death toward ministering to the departed spirit. If these are not performed properly, the soul of the departed will be in great trouble.

The Karma Marga for women is to obey and serve their men meekly. The *Code of Manu* stipulates that an unmarried female must be subject to her father, a married one to her husband, and a widow to her sons. A woman must never be independent. She should always occupy herself with household duties, yielding unquestioning obedience to the men in her life. A faithful wife, who aspires to dwell with her husband in the next life, should honor and obey him even if he is unfaithful and cruel to her. If he passes away early, she should remain faithful and chaste until death calls her also. Before Christian missionaries came to India, *sati* was prevalent in many parts of the country. Sati is the practice that when a husband dies, his wife must jump into the funeral pyre and immolate herself so that her spirit can accompany his spirit to the next life. The coming of the missionaries and education of women have stopped the practice altogether.

Ordinary Hindus have never realized the full implications of the law of karma, nor have they realized the fundamental dichotomy present in this system. The Doctrine of Gods and the Doctrine of Karma are opposed to each other. All the gods are subject to the law of Karma, and no god can change it any way, shape, or form. No god can be the lord of the moral order. There is no supreme divine force at the center of the moral order. Karma thus becomes a mechanical system, and the Universal Spirit becomes non-moral. This is the fundamental weakness of the Doctrine of Karma.

Educated Hindus are aware of the flaw of the system. However, they are reluctant to challenge it for fear of being ostracized from their caste. In the Diaspora, it may have only limited influence, as the Diaspora Hindu may not be inhibited by caste rules. In any case, educated Hindus will sooner or later be challenged by the fundamental flaws of the system, and it will not survive in the new dispensation. Therefore, they have to form new concepts about God, man, and the moral order of the universe. Christianity is the only religion that can give satisfactory answers to the moral dilemma forced on Hindus by the defective Doctrine of Karma.

THE CASTE SYSTEM

If the moral order of Hinduism is dependent on the Karma doctrine, the social order of the Hindu society is dependent on the caste system. The caste system is a unique feature of the Hindu society, as it is not found anywhere else in this world. The word *caste* is derived from the Portuguese word *casta*, which means race, breed, or kind.[65] The closest equivalents for *caste* in Sanskrit, the ancient language of India, and modern Indian languages are *varna*, meaning color, and *jati,* meaning tribe, clan, or race.

The most common belief is that caste has to do with the different skin colors of the various racial groups in India. The Aryans are light-colored, almost resembling Caucasians; the Dravidians are oily-brown colored, resembling the people of the Mediterranean; and the aborigines are dark-colored, resembling the Negro people of Africa; and the Mongoloids, who occupied the north and northeastern mountains, are yellow-colored.

It is quite possible that even before the Aryan invasion, India already had a multiracial society with the Dravidians at its apex. The tall and fair Aryans did not have much respect for the short, brown-skinned Dravidians. This was not so much because they felt culturally superior, as the urban Indus Valley civilization, with its scripts, arts, sculpture, town-planning, and other crafts, represented a more developed though less vigorous culture than that of the illiterate, sharp-shooting, nomadic

---

65   Herbert Stroup, *Like a Great River, An Introduction to Hinduism,* (London: Harper and Row, 1972) p. 151

Aryans.[66] However, they were more powerful, and as conquerors, they felt superior to the vanquished natives. Thus, a class distinction arose between the Aryans and the natives. In all probability, some sort of caste divisions already existed when the Aryans arrived, which they exploited to their maximum advantage. This explains the division between the fourth caste and the untouchables who, in reality, constitute a fifth caste. We will come to that later.

The Aryan social organization was roughly divided into three functions, namely, authority, power, and production.[67] This closely resembles the division of the society in ancient Greece, whose inhabitants were close cousins of the Aryans in India. Plato divides the state into three classes, namely philosopher-rulers, warriors, and masses. This is the Hindu equivalent of Brahmins, Kshatriyas, and Vaisyas. Brahmins are priests who are given the duty of interpreting the Vedas and performing various rites, Kshatriyas are rulers and warriors to govern and defend the society, and Vaisyas are traders and farmers. These are the "twice-born" castes and are supposed to be of pure Aryan blood. They are called "twice-born" on account of their erudition and learning. They alone have the privilege of wearing the "sacred thread." [68]

The Dravidians constituted the fourth caste, called *Sudras*, and their duty varied from menial service to artisanship. There is a fifth caste, which is technically outside Hinduism. They are the aborigines who escaped the wrath of the Dravidians and the Aryans and live mainly in unapproachable jungles and hills of the interior. Called outcasts or untouchables, they are not allowed even menial service, as they are alleged "to contaminate or pollute" the upper castes if they ever came near them. They come into the outer fringes of the villages and towns once or twice a year to sell the jungle products like honey and nuts in return for sugar and salt. They have never been part of the orthodox Hindu society, which is why we hear of only four castes and not five.

---

66   K. M. Sen, *Hinduism*, (Harmondsworth, U.K.: Penguins, 1961) p. 27

67   John R. Hinnells & Eric J. Sharpe, *Hinduism*, (New Castle Upon Tyne, U.K.: Oriel Press, 1972) p. 128

68   "The sacred thread" is a white cotton thread worn by the men of the three Aryan castes that hangs from the neck to the shoulder. The thread is given to the boys of the three castes at a certain age after long ceremonial rites conducted by Brahmin priests.

Rig Veda declares that each of the four castes in Hinduism has had a separate origin in god: "The Brahmin was his mouth; the *Rajanya*[69] was made from his arms; the being called *Vaisya* was his thighs; the *Sudra* sprang from his feet."[70]

We have here the religious sanction for caste. The source of this kind of conception was probably the necessity for an exclusive life for the preservation of the purity of race and culture. These kinds of endogamous groups are found among a number of ancient societies, but what makes the Hindu caste system a unique form of social organization is the introduction of the Doctrine of Karma and rebirth into this system. Each man is born into his particular caste because of his past deeds. If he had performed good deeds in his previous lives, he is born into a Brahmin family; if he is a step lower, then he is born a Kshatriya, and so on. Thus, a man's caste is held to be an infallible index of the state of his soul.

> It was this reasoned conviction that laid hold of the Hindu mind and made the observance of all caste rules a matter of conscience and also of deep personal interest. Only by living as a faithful member of his caste could a man retain the spirituality his soul had won. To marry a woman of low caste, or to touch an outcaste, was to contract gross spiritual pollution, the result of which would be not merely some social slight, or even excommunication from his caste-fellows, but frightful punishment in hell, and thus all the misery of an animal or outcaste existence in his next life.[71]

> Hindus sincerely believe that the occupation assigned to the caste was the best discipline for the soul of the man born in that caste. *Bhagavat Gita* states: "According to each man devotes himself to his proper work does he obtain summation ... Better one's own caste-duty ill-done than another's caste-duty well-done."[72]

---

69 Another name for Kshatriya, which means one who rules.

70 J. N. Farquher, *The Crown of Hinduism*, op. cit. p. 159

71 ibid, p. 160

72 *Bhagavat Gita*, XVIII, 45, 47

So if you are born into a barber family, you better cut hair. Even if you become a successful doctor or engineer, it is not going to help your soul achieve liberation. In fact, it will not only retard your progress, it may also throw you back a few hundred cycles of birth, death, and rebirth on your march toward achieving liberation, which is the goal of each soul. No wonder caste rules and duties became so rigid that it became unbearable to the lower castes.

In due course of time, the lower castes realized that the system was devised by the cunning Brahmins to keep others in perpetual degradation. There have been attempts to overthrow the dominant roles of the twice-born castes, especially that of the Brahmins. The religious movements of the sixth and seventh centuries before Christ were to a great extent hostile not only to Brahminic sacrifices and rituals, but also to the exclusive pretensions and demands of the Brahmin priests.[73] Yet the process went on, and the Hindu society came completely under Brahminic rules and rites, as they had power not only over other castes, but also over gods by means of their rituals.

What are the results of the caste system? What has this system done to the social structure? Dr. S. Radhakrishnan maintains:

> The institution of caste illustrated the spirit of comprehensive characteristic of the Hindu mind with its faith in the collaboration of races and the cooperation of cultures. Paradoxical as it may seem, the system of caste is the outcome of tolerance and trust. Though it has degenerated into an instrument of oppression and intolerance, though it tends to perpetuate inequality and develop the spirit of exclusiveness, these unfortunate effects are not the central motives of the system.[74]

Therefore, he is not concerned with the evils of the system, but with the underlying principles. When a system produces such evils and perpetually degrades a majority of the society, what is the use of upholding the central motives of the system?

Dr. Radhakrishnan gives high scores to Hinduism for the method by which it has dealt with the problem of racial conflicts. He maintains that there are only four methods by which one may resolve social conflicts:

73   John B. Noss, *Man's Religions*, op. cit. p. 153

74   S. Radhakrishnan, *The Hindu View of Life*, op. cit. p. 67

extermination, subordination, identification, and harmonization.[75] Many nations and religions have tried the first two, and the third is almost impossible to achieve. Hinduism has adopted the only safe course, which is harmonization, allowing each tribe to develop on its own ethnic and tribal lines. Thus, caste was Hinduism's answer to the outside forces that were pressing on it. The caste was the instrument by which Hinduism civilized the different tribes it took on.[76]

According to Dr Radhakrishnan, caste was an attempt to regulate society with a view to minimize differences and foster harmony. Each caste had its social purpose and function with its own code and tradition. When each fulfilled its function, the society progressed. The castes were not allowed to compete with one another, but rather their function was to supplement one another. The caste idea of vocation as service, with its traditions and spiritual aims, never encouraged the notion of work as a degrading servitude to be done grudgingly and purely from economic motives. However, in due course, some groups became dominant and naturally degraded the other groups.

The system of caste has been largely responsible for preserving the Hindu religion and its civilization. Without it, the Hindu culture might have collapsed centuries ago when it was bombarded from within and without. Thus, the caste system has absorbed almost everybody into its fold by the method of harmonization, which has taken place with almost every invader except the fierce monotheists. It was not that Hinduism was not willing to absorb them and their god into its fold; it was ready, but the fierce monotheists like the Muslims, Jews, and Christians did not want anything to do with the myriads of gods and goddesses in Hinduism.

Dr. Radhakrishnan may not be interested in the evils the system has produced, but we cannot escape by closing our eyes to these evils produced by specific religious sanction. The biggest evil is probably the divisiveness we see in Hindu society. The caste system has divided the society into rigid groups with their own traditions, practices, cultures, and gods. The harmonization Dr. Radhakrishnan is talking about is not seen anywhere except on the surface and in name only. When one Hindu cannot come near another Hindu for fear of pollution, where is the harmonization? The caste system has divided the Hindu society into such tight compartments that it is difficult to speak of Hinduism as just one religion or society. Sir K. G. Gupta, a member of the Indian Council before India achieved

---

75   ibid, p. 69-70

76   ibid, p. 70

independence, writes: "The caste system has served useful purposes in the past, but it has not now a single redeeming feature."[77] Lala Lajpat Rai, a great freedom fighter and social reformer, writes: "Caste ... is a disgrace to our community, our sense of justice, and our feeling of social affinity ... a standing blot on our social organization.[78]

Listen to what Rabindra Nath Tagore, the Nobel laureate and the most eminent poet of modern India, had to say:

> This immutable and all-pervading system of caste has no doubt imposed a mechanical uniformity upon people, but it has at the same time, kept their different sections inflexibly and unalterably separate with the consequent loss of all power of adaptation and readjustment to new conditions and forces. The regeneration of the Indian people, to my mind, directly and perhaps solely depends upon the removal of the condition of caste.[79]

From the statements of these eminent men of India, it is clear that the harmonization talked about by Dr. Radhakrishnan is only superficial, as beneath it lays a society divided and subdivided into endless groups. All agree that this divisiveness must go if social progress is to be achieved. However, no one knows how to get rid of the system, which has exerted a kind of socio-religious hold on the minds of the people for several centuries.

Another evil the system has produced is the perpetual degradation of certain sections of the Hindu society, as the system does not allow them to rise above their caste duties and seek a better life. This perpetual subjection and degradation is the most heinous result of the system. Dr. Radhakrishnan may be unconcerned about the evils of the system, but to millions of low-caste Hindus and outcasts it is a burning question of enormous magnitude. In order to escape from the perpetual degradation of themselves and their future generations, many have embraced other religions like Buddhism, Islam, and Christianity. A distinguished Brahmin official has written the following about the work of the Christian missionaries:

---

77   ibid, p. 175

78   ibid, 175-176

79   ibid, p. 175-176

But for these missionaries, these humble orders of Hindu society will forever remain unraised … To the Christian missionaries belong the credit of having gone to these humble homes and awakened them to a sense of a better earthly existence. This action of the missionary was not a mere improvement upon ancient history, a kind of polishing and refining of an existing model, but an entirely original idea conceived and carried out with commendable zeal, and often times in the teeth of opposition and persecution.[80]

Christianity and education have produced marvelous results among these degraded sections of the Hindu society. The whole theory of caste is here proved by ocular demonstration to be radically false because, according to Hindu doctrine, unclean outcasts could not be raised to the level of the twice-born castes. Christianity has shown that they could not only be raised to the level of twice-born castes but even higher by education and training.

The work of the Christian missions has opened the eyes of progressive Hindus to the necessity of raising the lot of the outcasts. As a result, a number of progressive Hindu organizations, such as the Arya Samaj and the Brahma Samaj, have started missions of their own to win the outcasts so that they may not go over to Christianity. A number of national leaders have also tried to raise the lot of these outcasts. Mahatma Gandhi, the father of modern India, relentlessly tried to uplift them. He even coined a new word to describe them—*Harijans*, meaning "the people of God."

Social justice and freedom of work are accepted facts of the constitution of India. Central and state governments have made a mandatory quota system in educational institution and government jobs for them. In spite of all these efforts, caste is still a major factor in the lives of these people. And there are Hindu revival organizations, such as the Hindu Mahasabha and the Rashtriya Swayamsevak Sang, which are willing to defend the caste system with all its ramifications.

Those Hindus who defend the caste system argue that there is as much caste in Christianity as there is in Hinduism, pointing out as examples the system of apartheid in South Africa, the racial hatred between the Whites and the African-Americans in the United States, the racial tensions between the Whites and Asians in England and other parts of Europe, the religious hatred between the Catholics and Protestants in Northern

---

80   ibid, p. 175

Ireland, and the lack of social relationships between the ancient Christians who had supposedly converted from the high-caste Brahmins and the recently converted Christians from the low-castes in some parts of India itself. This exclusiveness practiced by Christians, they argue, is in fact equivalent to the Hindu caste system.

It must be pointed out here that even though these charges are true to a great extent, this exclusiveness we see in certain sections of Christianity is not tantamount to a kind of caste system because there is no religious sanction behind this practice in Christianity. In fact, every true Christian acknowledges this practice with shame and distress because it is contrary to the teaching and example of Christ. Therefore, if there are "caste feelings" in certain sections of Christianity, it is not because of the teaching from the Bible but in spite of it. On the contrary, caste exists in Hinduism, not in spite of the teachings against such practice but because of it. There is religious sanction behind it. Therefore, while Christianity acknowledges caste practices as un-Christian and unpardonable, Hinduism acknowledges such practice as very much a part of Hinduism and very much acceptable. There is much difference between the two standpoints.

Christianity does not believe that each cast or race had a distinct origin in God but rather firmly believes that all races of people descended from Adam and Eve, the first man and woman, created by God in His own image. Because of the sin of man, God expelled him from the Garden of Eden and scattered the people all over the world. Hence, depending upon the geographic area and climate of the land, people acquired different skin colors and facial contours. However, all men are created equal since they are all descendants from the same lineage; there is no such thing as high-caste man or low-cast man. All are of one race despite differences in color and facial features. Differences are trivial compared to the basic unity of mankind, which makes man unique from all other creatures.

In order to redeem mankind, God sent His only begotten Son into this world. Whosoever believes in him shall have everlasting life. There is no difference to Him in terms of color or caste. His message is to be proclaimed to all men. Hence, He gave the Great Commission to His disciples. He could have no doctrine of a special revelation reserved for a few, as *sruti* is restricted to the three twice-born castes in Hinduism. Since all men are children of God, no one is essentially impure and unfit for social intercourse. When Jesus asked a Samaritan woman for a drink of water, she said to him: "You are a Jew and I am a Samaritan woman. How can you ask me for a drink?' Jesus answered, 'If you knew the gift of God and who it is that asks you for a drink, you would have asked him, and he would have given you living water' " (John 4:10). Apostle Paul emphatically states in Galatians 3:2: "There is neither Jew nor Greek, slave nor free, male nor female: for you are all one in Christ Jesus."

When one becomes a Christian, he becomes a new creation. In this new creation, there is no distinction between color and caste. All are one in Christ Jesus. The second birth in Christ is not a formal initiation ceremony when a sacred thread is put on his body, but a revolution within the soul, a spiritual transformation. Only by repentance and forgiveness of sins can a man become a born-again Christian. One does not become a Christian by being born into a Christian family; he will only be a nominal Christian through his natural birth.

When one does become this new creation in Christ, he enters upon the privileges of the kingdom of heaven. The chance is open to everyone irrespective of his color or facial features. Nevertheless, if in spite of this clear mandate some Christians practice caste, it is not because the system demands it but because of the sinfulness of man.

However, unlike Christianity, Hinduism demands caste and praises those who practice it. And it is precisely because of this religious sanction that caste still exists in India in spite of the best efforts of the federal and state governments and progressive Hindu organizations. If caste is to be removed from the soil of India, a radically different religious orientation is absolutely necessary. It is my firm conviction that Christ alone can provide this religious orientation for a society characterized by equality, freedom, and justice to all men.

Even in the twenty-first century, caste is still a factor, although some of the trade exclusiveness is no longer possible. Since the constitution of modern India gives freedom to practice any trade to all its citizens, educated lower castes do not restrict themselves to the traditional trade of their ancestors. However, endogamy seems to endure even in the Diaspora. Since arranged marriages are still the norm, even educated Diaspora Hindus agree to it, so weddings are conducted strictly on caste lines. To summarize, caste is a fact of life even in the Diaspora.

LIBERATION

THE HINDUS OF THE Diaspora, as all native Hindus, believe in universal liberation. It may take millions of cycles of birth, death, rebirth, and re-death before one achieves liberation, but in the end, every soul will reach the ultimate goal of union with the Universal Spirit. The journey may be long and hard, the ebbs may seem as frequent as the tides, but somewhere, sometime, the spirit will work itself free and escape the last tenement to greet its source in eternal union. There is to be in the end no hopeless straggler, no one who finally misses his way. It is claimed that the doctrine not only gives justice but also hope to everyone.

The idea of universal liberation is the direct result of the Doctrine of Karma and transmigration of the soul. If ultimately everyone will be liberated, how does it matter whether one takes a long route or a short route? If you do good deeds or bad deeds, it can only hasten or retard the progress of the soul, perhaps by a few ages or eons. But sooner or later, the end is completely assured. "The firm soul hastes, the feeble tarries. All will reach the summit snows."[81]

No god in Hinduism has the ability to hasten or retard the progress of the soul. Man is simply the victim of a great cosmic process, and the destined end will come whatever he does or does not do. Hindus have said that the doctrine of eternal punishment in Christianity means the defeat of God. No, it does not. God in His infinite wisdom has decided to save the righteous and punish the wicked before the foundations of the world. How can it then mean the defeat of God? Rather, it shows the triumph of almighty God. On the other hand, the Doctrine of Karma and rebirth and the idea of universal liberation in Hinduism means not merely the defeat of God but even his dismissal. God too becomes a powerless creature, watching helplessly the mechanical working out of the law of Karma, resulting ultimately in universal liberation.

Before we get into the meaning and result of liberation as against salvation, let us review the ways to attain liberation. There are three ways: the Karma Marga (the way of works or good deeds), the Jnana Marga (the way of wisdom or knowledge), and the Bhakti Marga (the way of devotion). We have already discussed the Karma Marga when we looked into the Doctrine of Karma and rebirth, which is the way for the common people. The average Hindu is not able to follow the other two ways. So if he followed the dictates of the *Code of Manu*[82] and did what it prescribes at various stages in his life, he would be able to add enough merits in this life to obtain a better birth in his next life. However, if he did not follow

---

81   Edmund D. Soper, op. cit. p. 136

82   The *Code of Manu* is the law book of Hinduism. Manu was the first man on the earth, and his laws were codified much later by Brahmin scholars around 200 BC. Upper-caste Hindus consider it second only to the Vedas in importance, while the lower castes consider it as the basis for all oppression.

the *Code of Manu* and lived a life of evil, he would lose some merits and would return as a dog, hog, or some insect in his next life.

Therefore, the remedy should be to do well and avoid evil actions. Regarding desire, the remedy is to control and subdue one's passions, aiming at disinterested activity through ascetic practices and purifying and transcending all desires by a single-hearted devotion to God. Regarding ignorance, spiritual knowledge of the true nature of the Self and of God must be acquired.

The three ways of liberation must not be understood as watertight compartments because they are inclusive of one another. Depending upon one's caste and status, one may be able to devote more attention to one of the three ways.

The *Mahabharata* calls the Karma Marga "Yoga" and the Jnana Marga "Samkhya." Yoga simply means "method" or "means," and so Karma Marga means disciplined activity. In opposition to this is the Jnana Marga, which consists of renunciation of action, as all action must involve contact with the sense world, which will result in rebirth. Thus, the two paths are sharply distinguished. The Karma Marga is perishable and leads to bondage and rebirth, while the Jnana Marga is imperishable and leads to freedom and liberation. Yet, the *Mahabharata* asserts that both ways are one and the same as they both lead to liberation. The Yoga-followers rely on immediate perception, while the Samkhya-followers rely on accepted knowledge. Disciplined purity and compassion to fellow creatures are common to both ways.

In Hinduism of the earlier period, the idea of sin is vague and incomplete, although everyone who hopes for liberation is asked to desist from sin. Words used to signify sin are very interesting: *enas* (offense), *agas* (fault), *anrta* (unrighteousness), *drughha* (misdeed), and *adharma* (unrighteousness). Only in the mysticism of later Hinduism do we come across any idea of sin as an offense against the all-just and unique God. Sin is really ignorance (avidya), by which man makes mistakes. When one is blinded by the darkness of lust and ignorance, one fails to perceive the soul residing in the heart as part of the Supreme Energy.[83] This energy is forceful light contrasted with the darkness of passion and ignorance. Therefore, the fully enlightened man cannot be but moral. To become one with God, moral purity is essential.

The Jnana Marga maintains that knowledge and wisdom can remove ignorance, and right knowledge is the knowledge of the Ultimate

---

83   *Mahabharata*, 12:54:12

Reality. This right knowledge cannot be gained by reading books but by apprehending the divine reality and the spiritual self of man through intuition and experience, which is possible only through hearing, learning, and repeated study and meditation of the sacred scriptures. To achieve liberation, concentration and suppression of the senses are necessary, as asceticism is conducive to the knowledge of the Absolute Being. The Jnana Marga and the Bhakti Marga are not very far apart. The ascetic and the mendicant are practitioners of both at the same time. By renouncing worldly pleasures, they suppress their lust for material possessions to concentrate on the Ultimate Reality. The ascetic is more of a follower of the Jnana Marga than that of the Bhakti Marga, although he might appear to be a devotee of a particular god or goddess. True devotion to God is indeed filled with wisdom and knowledge.

The Bhakti Marga is the most difficult of the three ways and is reserved for the three twice-born castes only. Those who lack knowledge and strength and are impatient with time cannot choose this way of liberation. Devotion to God is a specific religious attitude and sentiment, the essential features of which are faith, love, and trust in God. It is a direct experience both within and without of the personal God and a changing of the heart to the Supreme Reality whose greatness the religious soul realizes most keenly. You cannot attain this through the first two ways. It can be experienced only through intense devotion and hence only the twice-born castes, which have the strength and knowledge, are capable of this way of liberation. It involves dedication, surrender, religious observances, prayer, fasting, chanting, and mediation. All three would be useless if love of God is wanting. Man cannot be purified without bhakti. A devotee must fix his mind on God, giving up all other thoughts.

In later Hinduism, the Bhakti cult became very prominent. One theistic school maintained that liberation could be achieved only by the help of God's grace and not by one's own efforts. The followers of Ramanuja, a proponent of the non-dualist Vedanta philosophy, were divided over the doctrine of grace into two schools. The northern school subscribed to the monkey-way and the southern school to the cat-way. When a mother monkey jumps from one branch to another, her young one clings to her body. However, when a mother cat moves from one place to another, she takes her young one by lifting it with her mouth. In the first instance, the mother is the mover, but in the second case, the young one does nothing except yield to the will of the mother. The northern school held that the soul gains liberation by cooperating with God actively, while the southern school held that God does everything in liberating the soul.

Finally, whenever a Hindu is able to escape from the cycles of birth and rebirth by any of these ways, where does he go? What is his new mode of existence? Two words that are commonly used in Hindu scriptures to signify final liberation are *Mukti* and *Moksha*, both of which have the same root word, *muc*, meaning to liberate, release, free, or deliver. *Bhagavat Gita* maintains: "With senses, mind, and soul restrained, the silent sage, on deliverance intent, who has forever banished fear, anger, and desire, is truly liberated."[84]

Bhagavat Gita has another term to denote liberation or release from mortal existence: *nirvana*, which literally means "extinction." Sin, doubt, and attachments are extinguished, not the soul. The liberated soul becomes one with Brahman, who has no attributes. This new state is described as one of joy, bliss, and light; a state of spiritual freedom not subject to space, time, or causation.

Even this is not the final end of man. So far, he has only been liberated from the cycles of birth and death and has realized Brahman. Krishna further maintains that nirvana implies not only the realization of Brahman but also the realization of Brahman's mode of being and acting. Both the liberated Self and Brahman may be said to pervade all things, but the omnipresence of the liberated man depends on the omnipresence of Brahman. By love of Brahman, the liberated man realizes the nature of Brahman, and he merges completely with Brahman, losing his own consciousness. He gets into a state that has no likeness to what is known as individual consciousness or activity. In fact, he becomes nothing, as he completely merges with Brahman. Is this state better than the previous state? During the endless cycles of birth and rebirth, he had at least a conscious individuality, but after this merger with the Universal Spirit, he loses his individual consciousness.

To the question, "Where does the liberated soul go after death?" Swami Nikhilananda replies, "It does not go to any place where it has not been from the very beginning, nor does it become anything other than what is has always been—that is to say, Brahman, pure consciousness."[85] What is pure consciousness? We are told, "pure consciousness or super-

---

84 *Bhagavat_Gita*, 5:28

85 Swami Nikhilananda, *The Upanishads* (New York: Harper & Row, 1949) p. 103 as quoted by Edmund
D. Soper, op. cit. p. 136

consciousness is as different from our waking. Consciousness as is our state when we are in dreamless sleep as contrasted with our state when we are fully awake."[86] So, the condition of a man who has left the cycle of life and death is in a state of dreamless sleep from which he will never awaken. Swami Nikhilananda speaks of "the boredom of heaven" and the prospect of a liberated soul as contentless existence.[87]

To a Hindu then is liberation more desirable than life on this earth? That, I presume, depends on the condition in which he finds himself at present. If he has a happy existence on Earth, why should he prefer liberation to the present happy existence? Unfortunately, life is full of miseries, and hence, he would want liberation at frequent intervals of his life when he is faced with pain and suffering. However, at other times, he would not seek liberation. That is the dilemma a Hindu faces in his life.

The Christian idea of salvation is fundamentally different from the Hindu view of liberation. After this mortal body passes away, the Christian believes he will have a continuous, conscious existence in heaven with God and His people forever. He does not pass into nothingness but escapes forever the troubles and sorrows of this world to live happily ever after with his heavenly Father. It is not a life of boredom, nor is it discontented. He does not lose his individuality or consciousness and will be able to recognize everyone in his or her transformed heavenly body. "When the dead rise, they will neither marry nor be given in marriage; they will be like the angels in heaven" (Mark 12:25). This continuous, conscious existence with God in the company of the redeemed for all ages is the hope of Christian salvation compared to the "contentless consciousnesses" of Hinduism.

The average Hindu lives in despair, as he is not sure of liberation in the near future. Hence, he is not too concerned with it. Even the most educated and affluent Hindu minimizes that which is far away in the future and concentrates on what he can enjoy in the immediate future. However, the idea of karma and rebirth has a stranglehold on Diaspora Hindus, as it is a core doctrine of Hinduism.

---

86   ibid, p. 136

87   ibid, p. 137

Chapter 5

SURVEY OF DIASPORA HINDUS

FOR THE PURPOSE OF this study, the Flushing area of Queens Borough of New York City, where at least ten thousand Hindu families live, was chosen to conduct a survey. There are at least two Hindu temples, one Sikh Gurdwara, several ethnic Indian churches, several Indian grocery, sari, and jewelry stores, and special stores selling electronic items for use in India. There are also several restaurants selling rice, curry, chapatti, samosa, iddli, dosa, and other Indian delicacies. In addition, there are several cultural organizations that celebrate Indian national and religious holidays. In sum, it is one of the most prominent centers of Diaspora Hindus and Indian Christians in the Western world. Two others are probably Toronto, Canada, and London, England.

Four methods of data collection were used:

1. Personal interviews
2. Written questionnaires
3. Participant observation
4. Published and unpublished documents

In order to conduct the survey, the writer joined a six-week summer training program conducted by International Missions Incorporated, a mission agency concentrating on witnessing to Hindus and Muslims around the world. During the six weeks, the writer, sometimes along with other members of the team and at other times alone or with one other member of the team, visited Hindu homes in the area to conduct the survey. A local church that is very active in witnessing to the Hindus and Muslims in that area supplied some of the names and addresses, and the telephone directory was used to obtain names, addresses, and phone numbers of the Hindu households in the area. Names posted in the lobbies of the high-rise apartment complexes were also used to locate Hindu families in the area.

A questionnaire was prepared beforehand, and a sample of 165 Hindu families was drawn at random by using the table of random numbers from Rand Corporation's *A Million Random Numbers,* published by The Free Press, Glencoe, Illinois, 1955. When a family was not present at a number drawn or if they refused to answer questions, another family was chosen to complete the survey.

Several problems were encountered. Because the survey was conducted during the summer months of July and August, several families had gone to visit their parents and other relatives in India. This annual exodus is quite common among Hindus, especially among the first generation immigrants. Most often, the parents of this first generation still live in their ancestral homes in India. They may come to visit their children and grandchildren in the new lands, but they do not feel at home in this alien culture and unfamiliar climate. So when they do visit, they come during the summer months and return before the cold season sets in. Therefore, their children and grandchildren go to India to visit them, as well as their favorite temples. While ordinary Americans take vacation to visit summer resorts or beaches, Hindus go to India to visit their parents once every two or three years. Several Indian travel agencies flourish in the area of Flushing, as discount rates are available to travel to New Delhi, Bombay (Mumbai), Calcutta, and Madras (Chennai) by Air India and other airlines.

Another problem was getting into the house or apartment itself. A large city like New York has problems of theft, burglary, rape, and murder, so these families were reluctant to open their doors to strangers, especially if the man of the house was absent. We were asked to come back later, which we did whenever possible. The fact that the writer was an Indian helped somewhat but not much. Advance telephone calls were not much help either. Usually we got some excuse, and therefore it was better to knock on the door and take our chances.

When I went alone, it was difficult to get entrance into a house. When I went with my teammate, a white American girl from a liberal arts college in Indiana who was interested in Hindu evangelism, entry was easier. When a man answered the bell, the writer introduced himself, and if a woman answered, my teammate introduced herself.

Once we were inside, we were not looked upon very kindly. The question in their mind was, "What is this Indian doing with this American girl?" Unfortunately, Hindus generally have a very low opinion about the morality of Christians. But they have only known Christian morality through the behavior of nominal Christian officers of the British-India government, who ruled India before the Indian independence in 1947. British ladies mingling with men during late-night dance parties and the behavior of "rice" Christians, who imitated Europeans, have left the impression in Hindu minds that Christians are promiscuous. They asked us several questions, such as where we lived, whether we lived together in co-ed dormitories, etc. One Hindu gentleman even told us that he was a better follower of Jesus than we were. We had to explain to them the difference between nominal Christians and born-again Christians.

Later in the evenings, the writer went to those homes where the men were absent earlier. Thus, a total of 152 Hindu households were visited where the writer could talk to its occupants and conduct the survey. This sample may be too small, as it is limited to one small geographic area of one city in the Hindu Diaspora. Nevertheless it gives a glimpse into the habits and views of the Hindu Diaspora.

The writer also visited two temples in the area, where he had the opportunity to talk to the priests about their faith and opinions about Jesus Christ, Christianity, and Christians in general.

A number of books and articles written about Hinduism and Diaspora Hindu communities were also used to conduct this study. Several libraries in the New York and Philadelphia areas were very useful.

The survey gives the following results tabulated and discussed in the following tables.

Table 2
Age and Gender Distribution of the Respondents

Age	Male		Female		Total	
	Number	Percent	Number	Percent	Number	Percent
18-29	13	8.6	16	10.5	29	19.1
30-39	31	20.4	25	16.4	56	36.8
40-49	23	15.1	15	9.9	38	25.0
50-59	16	10.5	7	4.6	23	15.1
60 and above	4	2.6	2	1.3	6	3.9
Total	87	57.2	65	42.8	152	100.0

Table 2 shows the age and gender distribution of the 152 respondents. Because the survey was restricted to those who were 18 and above, 77% are between the ages of 30 and 59. This is in keeping with the general trend of Indians living in urban areas. After their retirement, they either move to suburban areas to live with their children or return to India to spend their waning years with extended family who will take care of them because of their wealth and status in the society.

Table 3
Caste of the Respondents

Upper Caste	Lower Caste / No Caste	Total
126	26	152

Out of the 152 respondents, 126 claimed that they were from one of the three upper castes. Twenty-six did not give their caste, as it was optional, which is significant in two ways:

1. A majority of Hindus who have come to the United Sates are better educated than the average Hindu in India. That the

people of the three upper castes are better educated is a well-known fact. In spite of the availability of seats in professional and technical colleges and lower tuition rates, lower castes Hindus have not made significant advances in education.

2. Those who belong to the lower castes and the untouchables try to forget their caste when they have upward mobility. They usually shed their caste names and surnames.

Table 4
Occupations of the Respondents

Occupation	Male		Female		Total	
	Number	Percent	Number	Percent	Number	Percent
White Collar Professional	32	21.1	26	17.1	58	38.2
White Collar Clerical	5	3.3	13	8.6	18	11.8
Business	14	9.2	3	2.0	17	11.2
Blue Collar	32	21.1	13	8.6	45	29.6
Unemployed	4	2.6	10	6.6	14	9.2
Total	**87**	**57.2**	**65**	**42.8**	**152**	**100.0**

The occupation of the respondents is divided into five categories. Professional includes medical doctors, engineers, pharmacists, nurses, accountants, teachers, etc., and 21.1% of the males and 17.1% of the females together make up 38.2% of the respondents in some professional field or another. White-collar jobs also include secretaries, clerks, typists, sales clerks, etc., of which more women are involved than men.

Blue-collar jobs include manufacturing, factory work, automobile workshops, security guards, cab drivers, etc., of which more men are involved than women. Business category means those who are running their businesses like motels, hotels, catering services, etc., either by themselves or in partnership with others. Unemployed includes housewives, full-time students, and those who are currently unemployed.

Those who had professional degrees and jobs in India or elsewhere had to take courses in American universities in order to get similar jobs here when they came to the US. This is true of all professional jobs, especially in the medical fields. This will become clear in analyzing Table 5 in the following pages.

Table 5
Education

Education	Male		Female		Total	
	Number	**Percent**	**Number**	**Percent**	**Number**	**Percent**
Less than High School	5	3.3	9	5.9	14	9.2
High School	28	18.4	15	9.9	43	28.3
Non-Professional Degree	15	9.9	13	8.6	28	18.4
Professional Degree, Diploma, or Certificate	39	25.7	28	18.4	67	44.1
Total	**87**	**57.2**	**65**	**42.8**	**152**	**100.0**

Table 5 deals with the education of the respondents. Only 9.2% had less than a high school education, and 44.1% had some professional education after high school. It should be remembered that until 1976 visas were given only to people with highly professional skills. But after 1976, when the immigrations laws were modified, visas were given to immediate family members of citizens and some permanent residents. Table 5 tells us that there are 67 Hindus who have some professional skills, and Table 4 tells us that only 58 are working in their professional field. This means that 9 out of 67, or 13.4%, could not get employment in their profession. It is reported that there are many doctors who could not get a license to practice medicine in their field in America because they could not get through the licensing examinations. Despite these problems, it is clear that Hindus in the United States are better educated than their counterparts in India.

Table 6
Immigration Status

Category	Male		Female		Total	
	Number	Percent	Number	Percent	Number	Percent
Born in the US	3	2.0	4	2.6	7	4.6
Came directly from India	63	41.4	48	31.6	111	73.0
After living elsewhere one year or more	21	13.8	13	8.6	34	22.4
Total	**87**	**57.2**	**65**	**42.8**	**152**	**100.0**

Table 6 shows the immigration status of the respondents. Only 7 out of 152, or 4.6%, were born in the US, 73% came directly from India, while 22.4% came to the US after residing elsewhere for at least one year. The countries mentioned are Jamaica, Surinam, Trinidad, Guyana, Uganda, and the Arabian Gulf countries, to which they had gone in search of employment opportunities earlier. Due to political issues or unsatisfactory jobs or living conditions in these countries, they came to the more hospitable United States.

GENERATION IN THE US

Table 7 gives some statistics as to what generations are here in the US. Out of the 152 respondents, 84.9% are first-generation immigrants. Immigration on a small scale started immediately after the Second World War when England ceased to be the main country to which Hindus migrated. These earlier migrants came in search of better education, and after graduation, they got job offers and stayed on. Immigration started on a large scale after the 1960s, especially after the 1970s when the immigration rules were relaxed for immediate families to come with the immigrants. Thus, those who came with their parents are categorized as second generation even though they were born elsewhere.

Table 7
Generation in the US

Generation	Male		Female		Total	
	Number	Percent	Number	Percent	Number	Percent
First	76	50.0	53	34.9	129	84.9
Second	11	7.2	12	7.9	23	15.1
Third	0	0.0	0	0.0	0	0.0
Total	**87**	**57.2**	**65**	**42.8**	**152**	**100.0**

Out of the 152 respondents, none were third generation or subsequent, which shows that even those who came in the sixties moved out of the city after a few years because of crime and lack of facilities for them and their children.

TEMPLE WORSHIP

The following table deals with the habit of the 152 Hindus surveyed of going to their temples. It must be pointed out that there are several factors that limit their worship in a temple. The most important reason mentioned was that the image of their favorite family/clan/caste god is not placed in the nearby temple, and therefore, going to the temple serves no purpose. Because of their busy work schedules and their children's extracurricular activities, it is not possible to go to a temple even on Saturdays or Sundays. And older women who are interested in going cannot because of the lack of transportation, as they themselves do not drive. During the winter months, it becomes more difficult with the snow, cold, and early nightfall.

Table 8
Frequency of Temple Worship

Frequency	Male		Female		Total	
	Number	Percent	Number	Percent	Number	Percent
Daily	0	0.0	0	0.0	0	0.0
Weekly	23	15.1	31	20.4	54	35.5
Frequently	27	17.8	30	19.7	57	37.5
Rarely	18	11.8	4	2.6	22	14.5
Never	19	12.5	0	0.0	19	12.5
Total	**87**	**57.2**	**65**	**42.8**	**152**	**100.0**

Table 8 shows that no one goes to the temples every day, but more women than men go consistently. There are 19 men who never go to temple, while there are no women in that category. Those who go to a temple on a weekly basis go at least once a week, quite often more than once a week, but not daily. Frequently means they do not go on a weekly basis but rather during the month. Rarely means they go on rare occasions, such as a holiday or a festival day, but not consistently.

Table 8 shows that Diaspora Hindus are generally very religious. Seventy-three percent (Weekly plus frequently) of those surveyed show that they go to a temple on a consistent basis, while another 14.5% go on rare occasions. This should make Christians ashamed of themselves. Newspapers report that Christians in some European and Western countries go to church less frequently. This of course consists of liberal Christians. Among the born-again or evangelical Christians, the number must be very high especially in the United States.

FREQUENCY OF PRAYER

Table 9 shows the prayer habits of the Hindus surveyed. Prayer here includes any one of the following: burning a wick or sandalwood incense in front of an image or picture of a god or goddess, bowing in front of an image or picture of one's favorite god or goddess on the way to work or school, reciting a few verses from the *Ramayana* or *Mahabharata*, or paying obeisance in any other way in front of an image. Hindus do not have the habit of praying extemporaneously to their god as Christians do.

This table is remarkable for a variety of reasons. First, it shows that more women than men actively participate in prayer. Out of 87 men, only 50 belong to the first three categories, while 61 of the 65 women surveyed belong to the first three categories.

Table 9
Frequency of Prayer

Frequency	Male		Female		Total	
	Number	Percent	Number	Percent	Number	Percent
Daily	0	0.0	0	0.0	0	0.0
Weekly	23	15.1	31	20.4	54	35.5
Frequently	27	17.8	30	19.7	57	37.5
Rarely	18	11.8	4	2.6	22	14.5
Never	19	12.5	0	0.0	19	12.5
Total	**87**	**57.2**	**65**	**42.8**	**152**	**100.0**

Second, the table shows that 20.4% of all Hindus pray daily and at least 37.5% pray frequently. Many homes have a corner of the room reserved for prayer. An image or picture of their favorite god or goddess is placed on the wall or a raised table, and prayer is offered in front of that image or picture—often before they leave for work or school for a safe return.

Favorite God/Goddess

To the question, "Who is your favorite god or goddess?" 59 or 38.8% said that Shiva or one of his consorts, children, or associates was their favorite god. These are Shaivites, or followers of Shiva. Forty-seven, or 30.9%, said that Vishnu or one of his incarnations, such as Rama or Krishna or one of his consorts, children, or associates, was their favorite god. These are called Vaishnavites, or followers of Vishnu. And thirty-two, or 21.1%, said that someone other than Shiva or Vishnu was their favorite god/goddess.

The respondents could not give any lineage or association to any other gods for their favorite god/goddess. Remember that every town and village in India has its own favorite god or goddess, spirit, or godling. Generally, Shaivites are from South India and Bengal, while Vaishnavites are from North India, especially from the Hindi speaking states of Uttar Pradesh, Madhya Pradesh, Chattisgarh, Jharkhand, and Bihar.

Table 10
Favorite god/goddess

Favorite god / goddess	Number	Percent
Shiva and associates	59	38.8
Vishnu and associates	47	30.9
Other than Shiva or Vishnu	32	21.1
None	14	9.2
Total	**152**	**100.0**

Fourteen out of 152 said they have no favorite god or goddess. These are the same fourteen who said they never pray to any god or goddess. Out of these 152, Other than Shiva or Vishnu went to temples for social purposes, such as to meet friends and relatives and to please family members.

POWER OF GODS IN THE DIASPORA

To the question, "Do you think your god is as powerful in your native locality as he is here?" the following answers were given:

Table 11
Power of Gods in the US

Category	Number	Percent
More powerful in the US	0	0.0
The same as your locality in India	74	48.7
Less powerful in US	27	17.8
Don't know	51	33.6
Total	**152**	**100.0**

It is interesting to note that none considered his or her god or goddess to be more powerful here than in his or her locality in India, and 48.7% thought they have the same power. Seventeen point eight percent thought their gods or goddesses were less powerful here than they were in their native locality in India, and 33.6% said they did not know.

There is some awareness among many Hindus that the local deities are powerful in their locality only, and that once they are outside their geographical area, they cannot exert as much power because they are limited by the power of other deities. This phenomenon is known by the term *henotheism* (*heis Theos*, meaning "one god") to denote one powerful god in a locality while accepting the possibility of the existence of other gods. This one god is powerful only in his/her locality, so when the devotee leaves the geographic area of this god/goddess, the devotee is free to worship any other god/goddess.

Most Hindus are aware of a Supreme Being, or high God, who is above all other gods. However, many would not ascribe personality to this high God and call it the Universal Spirit or Brahman. Often Brahman is confused with Brahma, the Creator, one of the triads of gods in Hinduism. Among the lower castes and the aborigines, there is a hierarchy in which the God of Christians, whom they call Parameshwar (Supreme God), is above all the other gods, and under him are the triads of Hinduism, Brahma, Shiva, Vishnu, and all other gods and goddesses below them in power and influence.

PROBLEM SOLVER

The respondents were asked, "When you have a difficult problem, to whom do you go first?" The astonishing results are given in Table 12. The answers are very important for a number of reasons. Relatives include not merely spouse, child, brother, and sister but even members of the extended family; 67.8% mentioned a relative as the first person they go to when they are confronted with a difficult problem, be it financial, family, or personal. This reveals the closeness of Hindus to their kith and kin.

Many keep in touch with extended family through letters, e-mails, and telephone. Many also send money to India, not only to parents and children, but also to brothers, sisters, uncles, and aunts for their children's education, procuring new property, and paying expenses connected with weddings and other celebrations.

Table 12
Problem Solver

Category	Number	Percent
Relative	103	67.8
Friend	27	17.8
Neighbor	7	4.6
Priest/Guru/Religious leader	6	3.9
Others	9	5.9
Total	**152**	**100.0**

A friend is mentioned by 17.8% and a neighbor by 4.6%. Even in spiritual matters, only 3.9% mentioned priests, gurus, or religious leaders. This may be due to the mistrust Hindus have toward Brahmins in general, who are more interested in filling their pockets than helping poor folks.

Even when gods/goddesses are mentioned, no one listed them as the first choice. This is not surprising, as Hindus do not generally consult gods/goddesses for solving mundane problems affecting an individual. Extemporaneous prayer is not part of the life of a Hindu. When a problem arises that affects the whole community or locality, prayer is then offered. Hence, in times of plague, foreign invaders, or lack of rain, prayers are offered to all the village deities.

Among others mentioned are teachers, lawyers, lenders, and social workers.

PRIORITIES IN LIFE

All those surveyed were asked, "What are your priorities in life?" The following six categories were given: education for you or your children, good employment, finance, good housing, religious life, and social/cultural life. They were to be numbered one as the most important to six, the least important. If anything outside these categories were important, they were asked to list it. Differences are evident between male and female respondents.

Answers are tabulated in Table 13. It is interesting to note that education, employment, and finance are the top priorities for the Hindus of the Diaspora. For both men and women, these concerns are clearly important.

There is a definite drop from priority three to four in the bottom three categories. In the case of housing, the difference between men and women is clearly marked. For men, housing is not a big priority while for women it is quite important. Religious life and social/cultural matters are definitely unimportant to both male and female. Religious life is somewhat more important to female than to male, while social life is unimportant to both genders.

Diaspora Hindus have come to foreign lands in search of employment opportunities, better education for themselves and their children, and for acquiring wealth. Men can live in modest accommodations and save money for the future. Religious, social, and cultural matters are relatively unimportant because they have not come here for such purposes.

Table 13
Priorities in Life

Priority	1			2			3			4			5			6			Total		
Category	M	F	T	M	F	T	M	F	T	M	F	T	M	F	T	M	F	T	M	F	T
Education	29	21	50	28	17	45	25	18	43	2	8	10	2	1	3	1	0	1	87	65	152
Employment	28	10	38	26	17	43	23	17	40	6	11	17	3	7	10	1	3	4	87	65	152
Finance	26	18	44	26	15	41	23	12	35	6	11	17	4	8	12	2	1	3	87	65	152
Housing	4	13	17	4	13	17	9	11	20	23	11	34	23	9	32	24	8	32	87	65	152
Religious Life	0	3	3	2	3	5	6	5	11	26	13	39	25	22	47	28	19	47	87	65	152
Soc / Cult. Life	0	0	0	1	0	1	1	2	3	24	11	35	30	18	48	31	34	65	87	65	152
Total	87	65	152	87	65	152	87	65	152	87	65	152	87	65	152	87	65	152	87	65	152

RELIGIOUS SATISFACTION

Participants were asked, "Does your religion satisfy you?" The answers are tabulated in Table 14.

Table 14
Religious Satisfaction

Category	Number	Percent
Completely	0	0.0
To a great extent	23	15.1
Fairly	59	38.8
Poorly	48	31.6
Not at all	14	9.2
No comment	8	5.3
Total	**152**	**100**

No one claimed that his or her religion is completely satisfactory. Several of them maintained that no religion can be completely satisfactory, as life on this earth is full of suffering and misery. Fifteen point one percent maintained that their religion is satisfactory to a great extent; 38.8% said that it is fairly satisfactory; 31.6% said that it is poorly or a little bit satisfactory; 9.2% that it is not at all satisfactory and 5.3% had no comment.

CHURCH VISITS

Table 15 gives a summary of whether they have been to a church.

Table 15
Church Visits

Category	Number	Percent
Never attended a church	87	57.2
Attended once or twice	27	17.8
Attended more than twice	24	15.8

Attended many times	14	9.2
Total	**152**	**100**

Fifty-seven point two percent have never been to a church, while 17.8 % went once or twice, 15.8% attended more than twice, and 9.2% had been to a church many times when Christian friends invited them. From these tables, it is very clear that Christians are not doing a good job in inviting their Hindu neighbors to their churches.

BIBLE READING

Answers to the question, "Have you read the Bible or any portion of it?" are given in Table 16. While 15.1% have never read any portion of the Bible, 13.2% have read it many times, and about half of them have read it more than once. This is encouraging on the surface. However, when questioned further, many of them said that they read it as part of their study of English language and literature in high school or college. The Sermon on the Mount seems to be the most popular passage of the Bible, followed by the Ten Commandments.

Table 16
Bible Reading

Category	Number	Percent
Never	23	15.1
Once or twice	35	23.0
More than once or twice	74	48.7
Many times	20	13.2
Total	**152**	**100**

JESUS CHRIST

To the question, "Have you heard the name Jesus Christ?" all 152 answers were affirmative. The answers to the question, "What do you think of Jesus Christ?" are tabulated in Table 17.

Table 17
What Hindus Think About Jesus Christ

Category	Number	Percent
An avatar or incarnation	72	47.4
A great teacher	47	30.9
A martyr	18	11.8
Don't know	15	9.9
Total	**152**	**100**

Forty-seven point four percent said Jesus was an incarnation like Rama, Krishna, and Buddha, but while the last three were incarnations of Vishnu, the Hindu god, Jesus was an incarnation of the Christian God. Some identified the God of Christians with Bhagawan, or the Universal Spirit of Hinduism. Several maintained that Jesus could be an incarnation of Vishnu and were ready to give Jesus a place of prominence along with Rama, Krishna, and the Buddha. However, no one wanted to give Him exclusivity. Thirty point nine percent maintained that Jesus was a great teacher, while 11.8% held that he was a great martyr who died for his beliefs. Nine point nine percent said they did not know or would not want to say anything about an alien god. None would identify Jesus with Brahman or the almighty God.

COMPARISON OF JESUS WITH HINDU AVATARS

All were asked to compare Jesus Christ with the Hindu avatars, or descents. The results are tabulated below.

Table 18
Comparison of Jesus with Hindu Avatars

Category	Number	Percent
Same	77	50.7
Better	27	17.8
Worse	11	7.2
Don't know	24	15.8

No comment	13	8.6
Total	**152**	**100**

While 50.7% maintained that Jesus was equal to the avatars in Hinduism, 24.4% did not know or had no comment, and 17.8% percent maintained that he was a better incarnation. Reasons given were His simplicity, erudition, love for the poor and the sick, holy life without blemish, miracle-working power, nonviolence, and self-sacrifice in comparison to the life of Krishna and other Hindu avatars. Seven point two percent held that he was a worse incarnation compared to Krishna and others. Reasons given were the following:

1. He was an illegitimate child.
2. He was immoral. Movies, such as *Jesus Christ, Superstar*, and books about Mary Magdalene being His mistress were mentioned as revealing his true lifestyle.
3. His resurrection and ascension were fraudulent stories perpetrated by his disciples.
4. Western society is promiscuous and immoral, and this is a direct result of the influence of Christianity upon Western society.

HINDU LIKINGS IN CHRISTIANITY

Participants were requested to point out things they like in Christianity, if any, and could give as many answers as he or she preferred. These are tabulated in Table 19.

Table 19
Hindu Likings in Christianity

Category	Number	Percent
Person of Jesus	111	73.0
Education & Scientific Progress	77	50.7
Christian Prayer	67	44.1
Religious Devotion	59	38.8
Christian Hymns	49	32.2
Bible/Christian Literature	38	25.0

The columns will not total one hundred percent because each person could give as many items as he or she preferred. Seventy-three percent mentioned the person of Jesus Christ for His piety, simple lifestyle, sacrifice, and holy life. Fifty point seven percent mentioned the educational and scientific progress Christians have made, while 44.1% mentioned Christian prayer, 38.8% religious devotion of Christians, 32.2% Christian hymns, and 25.0% Bible and Christian literature. Liberation of women, concern for the poor and needy, adventurous spirit, individual freedom, and the spirit of enquiry are some of the other items mentioned. However, these were mentioned by only 5–10% of the people surveyed and are therefore not tabulated.

Many of the things mentioned are the outcome of Western secular humanism and enlightenment rather than the direct result of Christian influence. It is clear that Hindus do not separate the two, which is evident in the next table.

HINDU PREJUDICES AGAINST CHRISTIANITY

Participants were invited to give as many answers as they liked to the question, "What do you dislike about Christianity?" Results given are tabulated below.

Table 20
Hindu Prejudices against Christianity

Category	Number	Percent
Permissiveness	119	78.3
Uniqueness of Christ	97	63.8
Forceful conversion	85	55.9
Materialism	69	45.4
White Man's Religion	68	44.7
Christians are Low-Castes	67	44.1
Superiority Complex	65	42.8

Again total will not come to one hundred percent as each participant in the survey could give many answers. Seventy-eight point three percent mentioned permissiveness, 63.8% uniqueness of Christ, 55.9% forceful conversion, 45.4% materialism, 44.7% white man's religion, 44.1%

Christians are low-castes, and 42.8% superiority complex of Christians. Too much freedom for women, lack of concern for the aged, and lack of family solidarity were mentioned my less than five percent of the participants surveyed. It is clear from these answers that Christianity and Western civilization are identical to the Hindus surveyed.

DEFENSE OF HINDUISM

THE RESPONDENTS WERE PERMITTED to give as many answers as he or she chose to the question, "What arguments can you give in defense of Hinduism?" Answers given are tabulated in Table 21.

Table 21
Defense of Hinduism

Category	Number	Percent
All religions are the same	127	83.6
There is only one God	114	75.0
All religions will take you to heaven	107	70.4
Forsaking one's religion is betrayal of family	94	61.8

Out of the people surveyed, 83.6% maintained that all religions are the same, 75.0% maintained that there is only one God and that this God manifests himself in different forms in different ages, 70.4% held that all religions will ultimately take you to the same place, and 61.8% held that forsaking one's religion is betrayal of family, clan, tribe, caste, and ancestors.

The last three tables call for detailed analysis, which will occur in the following three chapters.

Chapter 6

HINDU LIKINGS IN CHRISTIANITY

OF ALL THE THINGS Hindus like in Christianity, the person of Jesus is the most important. Therefore, he must be introduced as the point of contact to attract Hindus to the religion Jesus established when he came into the world. Remember that Hinduism is a very tolerant religion and is always ready to receive and incorporate new ideas into its fold.

THE PERSON OF JESUS CHRIST

More than anything else, Hindus admire the person of Jesus Christ. This is clear from the survey, as 73.0% of Hindus surveyed held that they admire him more than anything else in Christianity. Forty-seven point four percent thought he was an incarnation, 30.9% thought he was a great teacher, and 11.8% considered him a martyr. Thus, 90.1% admired him in some way. In Table 18, where he was compared to Hindu avatars, 68.5% thought that he was either the same or a better person, whereas only 7.2% thought he was worse. Reasons given are not valid, as they result from misconceptions and lies without any historical accuracy, showing ignorance of history rather than prejudice. Therefore, all these data indicate that Hindus admire the person of Jesus Christ.

This admiration is in keeping with the religious thinking of the Hindus in India and abroad. Mahatma Gandhi, the father of modern India who used nonviolent struggle to achieve freedom for his country from the British Empire in 1947, said he could accept Jesus as a martyr, an embodiment of sacrifice, and a divine teacher.[88] Gandhi was attracted

---

88   M.K. Gandhi, *An Autobiography or The story of My Experiments with Truth* (Ahmedabad, India: The Navajivan Trust, 1927) p. 113.

by Jesus' humility, simplicity, and the saintly qualities as he walked on this earth. The New Testament, especially the Sermon on the Mount detailed in Matthew 5–7, was his favorite reading material.

Gandhi made use of the theme "love your enemies" and nonviolence preached by Christ in the struggle for independence for his country. While he was in South Africa, he fought against the racial policy of apartheid with love and nonviolence. Once, when he was refused permission to enter a church because of the color of his skin, Gandhi was reported to have said that if colored men were not admitted, Jesus, who was a Palestinian Jew, would not have been admitted into that church. And if Jesus was not in that church, why should he (Gandhi) waste his time attending that church?

Hindus in general would have no problem admitting Jesus as one of their gods. He would be put on a high pedestal equal to, if not above, the Buddha, Rama, and Krishna. Remember that the Brahmin scholars accepted the Buddha as one of the avatars of Vishnu by claiming he showed why people should not follow his way, as it was not the way of orthodox Hinduism. Rama, in spite of his victory over Ravana, acted cruelly to his own wife, Sita, by expelling her from his kingdom in order to please his subjects, even though she had demonstrated her chastity by going through the ordeal of fire. And Krishna was a mischievous character who stole and lied to satisfy his lust. Compared to these avatars, Jesus was a godly person of spotless character who knew no sin. The miracle worker from Galilee, with his simplicity, erudition, and holiness, would have been a great avatar of Hinduism and might have been put above the other nine avatars of Hinduism if only he had been born in India. But Jesus had to be born in Bethlehem to fulfill prophecy.

The biggest problem is that Christians will not allow the incorporation of their God into the Hindu pantheon. They want uniqueness and exclusiveness for Jesus. Hindus are not familiar with that kind of exclusiveness, however saintly he may be. Therefore, Jesus has to stand outside the Hindu pantheon of gods, in spite of the attempts of several liberal Christians to see unknown Christs in Hinduism. Nevertheless, the person of Jesus Christ attracts Hindus immensely. They highly regard him despite the fact they cannot have him as one of their gods.

In witnessing to Hindus in general and particularly to Diaspora Hindus, the person and work of Christ must be emphasized. They know him only in his incarnate state, so emphasis must be placed on three other aspects of his life.

1. The Pre-incarnate Christ

Christ as the second person of the Trinity was present in creation. He was the Logos, the Word of God. Apostle John tells us:

> In the beginning was the Word and the Word was with God and the word was God. He was with the God in the beginning. Through him all things was made; without him nothing was made that has been made. In him was life, and that life was the light of men (John 1:1–4).

Christ came into the world for the specific purpose of dying on the cross of Calvary for the sins of the people. Therefore, his death was not that of a mere martyr, however lofty that may be. His death was that of the Son of God, through which he made reconciliation possible between God and men. Thus he became the only mediator, representing both sides between a holy God and sinful people. This idea of self-sacrifice for a cause, even if on a smaller scale, was valid and reasonable to Mahatma Gandhi, Martin Luther King Jr., and Nelson Mandela through their nonviolent disobedience movements.

2. The Resurrected Christ

The life of Christ did not end on the cross at Calvary or in the tomb in which his body was buried. The angels asked the ladies who went to the tomb to see his body, "Why do you look for the living among the dead? He is not here; he has risen" (Luke 24:5–6). He arose on the third day, as he had prophesied, and revealed himself to about five hundred witnesses (1 Corinthians 15:6). His resurrection is not a fraud perpetrated by his disciples but a fact of history. His disciples, their writings, his contemporary witnesses, and the Christian church that spread to all the continents of the world are powerful witnesses of his resurrection. One of the twelve disciples, the apostle Thomas, who was the last to believe in his resurrection, traveled all the way to the land of the Hindus to spread Christ's gospel. The church established by Thomas stands to this day in the midst of Hindus in India.

3. The Soon-coming Christ

This Christ who ascended into heaven and is seated on the right hand of God, the Father, will soon come to judge the world in righteousness. He who is equal with the Father came down to this world as a suffering servant in that faraway manger in Bethlehem almost two thousand years ago. However, when he comes again, it will not be as a suffering servant but as the victorious king (Matthew 24:31–32).

Christ's story is not made up by a poet but revealed by God himself through over forty prophets and apostles. This revelation is contained in the sixty-six books of the Bible that was written over a period of fifteen hundred years by its authors who did not know each other, as they lived in different countries and climates. And yet it has unity throughout because God is the ultimate author of the Bible, who used the particular writing style of each human author. Hence, the Bible is called the inspired, inerrant, and infallible Scripture revealed by the omniscient God.

Hindus know only the incarnate Christ. The aspects of his pre-incarnate state, resurrection, and second coming must be explained to them so that they can see him as God and Savior and not merely as the miracle worker from faraway Galilee.

EDUCATIONAL AND SCIENTIFIC PROGRESS

Table 19 shows that 50.7% of the Hindus surveyed admire the educational and scientific progress of Christians. This is because Hindus generally identify Christianity with Western civilization, which has its benefits as well as drawbacks. The drawbacks will be discussed in the next chapter, but here let us discuss the benefits.

There is no doubt that Western culture and civilization are molded and guided by Christianity, especially by Protestantism since Martin Luther's Reformation in the sixteenth century. Max Weber, an eminent German social scientist maintains:

> That the spirit of hard work, of progress or whatever else it may be called, the awakening of which one is inclined to ascribe to Protestantism must not be understood, as there is a tendency to do, as joy of living nor in any other sense as connected with the Enlightenment.[89]

Christianity, of course, is not responsible for the excesses and the decadence in the Western culture.

Hindus admire the educational, scientific, economic, and social progress made by Europeans and Americans. The progress achieved by the Western nations in technology, physical sciences, social sciences, medicine, art,

89   Max Weber, *The Protestant Ethic and the Spirit of Capitalism*, trans. by Talcott Parsons (New York: Charles Scribner's and Sons, 1958) pp. 44-45.

literature, education, and other fields are viewed with grudging admiration. Once, in ancient times, India could boast of a superior civilization on the banks of the Indus and Ganges rivers, which had two great universities at Nalanda[90] and Takshashila[91] around the time of the Buddha in the sixth and fifth centuries before Christ. However, these ancient civilizations fell apart due to foreign invasion and internal dissensions, while Western nations made tremendous advances in education and science. Why? Has the God of Christians blessed them in an unprecedented way? Is there a connection between the progress of the people and the power of their God?

Hindus see the progress not only of the Western nations but also of the Indian Christians. While the numerical strength of Indian Christians is only about three percent, the influences they exert on India's educational, scientific, social, and economic spheres are enormous. They rightly attribute this progress to Christian influence, as honesty, punctuality, industry, and frugality are particular Christian virtues. Proverbs 22:29 tells us, "Seest thou a man diligent in his business? He shall stand before kings" (KJV).

CHRISTIAN PRAYER

Table 19 shows that 44.1% of the Hindus surveyed like Christian prayer and usually asked Christian friends to pray for them, especially if there was sickness in the family. Extemporaneous prayer is not a common practice for Hindus. Prayer mostly consists of reading from the Vedas or one of the epics.

An intimate relationship with one god, as is the case of the personal relationship of a born-again Christian with Jesus Christ, is not normal in Hinduism. Often the Hindu gods are feared and propitiated rather than adored. Visitations of disease, famine, plague, earthquake, storm, hurricane, and other natural calamities are attributed to the displeasure of one god or another, and a Hindu tries to propitiate that particular god by special prayers, sacrifices, and offerings so that these scourges would be removed.

Since there are millions of gods in Hinduism, one more god, even if the God of the Christians, is not a big problem as long as he does not demand exclusiveness. Hindus do not want to displease any god, so they

---

90   Romila Thapar, *A History of India* (Baltimore, MD: Penguin Books, 1966) p. 154

91   Today it is called by its Greek name, Taxila.

will do everything to please any god as long it does not displease his caste and clan fellows.

In many instances, Hindus are aware of the supreme power of the God of Christians and do not want to displease him in any way, lest he should become angry. So the prayers of Christians to their God are welcome, especially if it will heal someone who is sick in their family.

RELIGIOUS DEVOTION

Table 19 shows that 38.8% the Hindus surveyed admire the religious devotion of Christians. Hindus see Christians of all denominations going to worship services on Sundays, some going to prayer meetings and Bible studies on Saturdays and other days, and Christian children going to Sunday school during the school year and Vacation Bible School during the summer. This is in sharp contrast to their own lifestyle, as they do not have a particular day of the week for religious services. Even on Saturday, which is supposed to be their religious day, Hindu men are not seen going to the temples. Hindu ladies, on the other hand, go to the temples on certain important festival days. Men usually go only when a temple festival is organized, but such occasions are more social occasions rather than time for prayer or meditation. Many temples still do not allow women and lower castes to enter their inner sanctums.

CHRISTIAN MUSIC

IN THE UNITED STATES, when you turn on the radio, you are likely to hear some Christian music, and 32.2% of the Hindus surveyed testified that they like Christian music and hymns.

As noted earlier, the Bhakti movement became prominent in later Hinduism.[92] In the Bhakti Marga (Way of Devotion), devotion to god is a specific religious attitude and sentiment, the essential features of which are faith, love, and trust in god. It is a direct experience, both within and without, of the personal god, a clinging of the heart to the Supreme Reality. Quite often, native Christian songs, hymns, and lyrics express these very same emotions of faith, love, and trust in Jesus Christ. Hindus identify with these emotions, with the difference that the object of their devotion would be Rama, Krishna, or some other god.

Any hymn with religious fervor attracts Hindus. If the music is melodious and meaningful, they would repeat it, even if it is dedicated

92   See page 49

to Jesus Christ. Christian music was very popular during inter-religious services during the freedom struggle for independence from British colonial rule. Mahatma Gandhi, a devout Hindu, and Jawahar Lal Nehru, a secular humanist, were very tolerant of other religions, especially Christianity, in spite of their opposition to conversion from one religion to another.

BIBLE/CHRISTIAN LITERATURE

Table 19 shows that 25.0% of the Hindus surveyed stated that they like the Bible and other Christian literature. During the British colonial rule, portions of the Bible, such as the Sermon on the Mount and the Ten Commandments, were introduced in almost all Indian school textbooks to teach English. This love for English literature, as evidenced by the reading of the Bible and Shakespeare, has continued even after independence, especially in South India.

The Bible has been translated into almost all the Indian languages. From Table 16, we see that 23% of the Hindus surveyed have read portions of the Bible at least once, 48.7% have read it more than once, and 13.2% many times. This love that the Hindus have for the Bible and Christian literature must be utilized further. More modern and accurate versions of the Bible must be produced in their native languages, and more Christian literature and songs must be written in the local languages so that they will be within everyone's grasp.

Almost all of the 152 Hindus participating in the survey could speak at least some English. However, this does not mean that they can read and understand English well. Matters of the heart are best explained and understood in the mother tongue. Relatives of the immigrants may not know English well, as they have come through the Family Reunification Clause in the Immigration Act of 1965, which came into law in 1968. Therefore, it is very important that the Bible and other Christian literature should be printed in Indian languages to be distributed to new immigrants who come to the new countries in order to win them for Christ.

POWER OF GOD

There is a power struggle in all mission fields between the almighty God and the gods of heathenism, and Hinduism is no exception. The average Hindu is aware of this power struggle, even though he may try to ignore or suppress its existence.

There is a general belief that the spirits and godlings of the outcasts and tribals who constitute the fifth caste in Hinduism are at the bottom of the totem pole. Above them are the local gods and goddesses of the Sudras, the fourth caste. And above them are the gods and goddesses of the twice-born castes of the Aryans. The great triads of gods Brahma, Shiva, and Vishnu are at the apex of the totem pole, especially the last two, whose temples have attendant Brahmin priests ever ready to pay homage and sacrifice. There is a feeling that the God of the Christians is more powerful than any of these great gods of Hinduism.

There have been numerous accounts of this power struggle between God and the gods of Hinduism, and in every case, God came out triumphant. Psalm 96:4–6 tells eloquently of this power struggle:

> For the Lord is great, and greatly to be praised; he is to be feared above all gods. For all the gods of the nations are idols, but the Lord made the heavens; honor and majesty are before him, strength and beauty are in his sanctuary.

Aware of this power struggle, Hindus fear and admire the power of God.

Another factor worth remembering is that that there is constant bickering between the various gods of Hinduism. One god is pitted against another, and in this battle, other gods have to take sides. There are numerous stories of battles between various gods in the Puranas. Sometimes one god might win, but at other times, another will win. But Hindus know there is no such problem in Christianity, as there is only one God. Even those Hindus who do not understand the concept of the Trinity and may think that the Father, the Son, and the Holy Spirit are three gods know very well that there is perfect harmony in the Christian Godhead. The Bible reports no incident of animosity or disharmony between the Father, the Son, and the Holy Spirit.

Hindus admire and fear the power of almighty God. In witnessing to Diaspora Hindus, these seven aspects must be emphasized.

Chapter 7

HINDU PREJUDICES AGAINST CHRISTIANITY

HINDUS DISLIKE A NUMBER of things they associate with Christianity. Anyone who wants to witness to a Diaspora Hindu must be aware of these prejudices to intelligently converse with them.

These prejudices are a product of history. Jawaharlal Nehru in his *An Autobiography* mentions that a small Christian community existed in the small southwestern state of Kerala almost from the beginning of Christianity. "Few people realize that Christianity came to India as early as the first century after Christ, long before Europe turned to it and established a firm hold in south India."[93] However, it was such a small group compared to the millions of Hindus that it could not exert any influence upon them. The problem with the small Christian community was one of mere survival rather than expansion or advancement.

Consequently, the larger Hindu community saw Christianity only after the Europeans came to India first for trade and then for establishing colonies and finally for empire building. Hindus generally think that every white person is a Christian, as they do not distinguish between born-again and nominal Christians. This had disastrous consequences in witnessing, as we shall see in the following pages.

Hindu prejudices against Christianity are many and are tabulated in Table 20. We need to look at them carefully to see the reasons behind those prejudices so we can remove misunderstandings.

---

93   Jawaharlal Nehru, *An Autobiography* (New Delhi, Oxford University Press, 1936) p. 273

1. Permissiveness.

Many Hindus, 78.3%, maintain that there is too much permissiveness in Christianity. While Hindus choose marriage partners through horoscope compatibility and arranged marriages between families, Western Christians allow their youngsters to date and choose their own partners. Among Western Christians, dating is not only normal but is almost demanded by the society to get a suitable marriage partner.

Hindus see white men and women mix freely through Hollywood and other Western movies and television serials, and disapprove that Western Christian women do not cover their shoulders and knees. Many of the sexually transmitted diseases have come to India through so-called Christian European sailors. On important occasions, especially Christmas and New Year, they see Western men and women dancing into the early morning hours, drinking without inhibition. At least some of the newly converted "rice" Christians tried to imitate these Western customs and practices with disastrous consequences to the cause of Christ. Hindus saw what was happening and hence believed that becoming a Christian meant loose moral values and licentiousness.

In the Western countries of the twenty-first century things got worse. Living together without marriage, homosexuality, the spread of Aids, HIV, and sexually transmitted diseases are viewed as clear proof of permissiveness, which Hindus believe is the norm in Christianity. They do not know the words of Jesus in the Sermon on the Mount given in Matthew 5:27–28: "You have heard that it was said, 'Do not commit adultery.' But I tell you that anyone who looks at a woman lustfully has already committed adultery in his heart."

It is important to show Hindus that permissive behavior is not normative for believers in Christ, and that movies and television shows do not represent Christian ideals. What they represent is decadent Western civilization in its worst form, and Hindus should not equate them with Christian morality and culture. Those who want to witness to their Hindu neighbors must point out that these are not the outcome of Christianity but the result of secular humanism, romanticism, and decadent Western culture.

All white men and women are not true Christians; they are Christians in name only. The licentiousness and sexual freedom are contrary to the teachings of Christ. Christianity is in fact the most moral of all religions. The seventh commandment in Exodus 20:13 states clearly, "You shall not commit adultery." Punishment for adultery was death by stoning in ancient

Israel, and any sexual contact outside the marriage bond is absolutely and unequivocally forbidden in the New Testament. Our Lord Jesus Christ did not water down the commandment, but made it stricter.

The demands of the new kingdom of Christ are indeed very strict, and it is only by the grace of God that any man or woman will be able to enter into it. So, far from being permissive, Christianity is the most moral of all religions. If some of the white men and women indulge in self-gratification, they are indeed living in sin, and no unclean person shall enter into the kingdom of God. That goes for brown men and women also who have become Christian in name only.

2. Uniqueness of Christ

Hindus generally like the person of Jesus Christ. However, when he is presented as the unique savior of mankind or the only begotten Son of God, they tend to disagree. Table 20 shows that 63.8% of Hindus surveyed object to the concept of the uniqueness of Christ or the only revelation of almighty God given to mankind. They can accept him as *one* of the incarnations of almighty God but not as the *only* incarnation or as the only mediator between God and man.

Paul Clasper, a former missionary to Burma (now called Myanmar), narrates an interesting story.[94] When he was in Rangoon, he used to take Western visitors to a Hindu temple. The priest wanted to put a Christian symbol on a vacant wall in the temple, which he felt would then represent all the major religions. His desire was that a Christian would contribute a Christian symbol as an indication of their desire for tolerance and a better understanding between the two faiths. He was sure that most people in the West came to know God through Jesus Christ as Krishna was the path for many Hindus, and he hoped that prejudice would not keep Christians from contributing a Christian symbol to his temple.

It is not clear whether the priest's wish was fulfilled or not. But Christians would not contribute a symbol because they are intolerant, but because the Bible does not allow them to do so. The first commandment of the Decalogue prohibits them from worshipping other gods and making graven images (Exodus 20:3–4). Further, the Acts of the Apostles says: "Salvation is found in no one else, for there is no other name under heaven given to men by which we must be saved" (Acts 4:12).

---

94   Paul Clasper, *Eastern Paths and the Christian Way* (Maryknoll, NY., Orbis Books, 1982) p. 30

If the uniqueness of Christ as the only Savior of mankind is a stumbling block, the Christian cannot help it. While customs, manners, culture, or any other trapping should not be allowed to stand in the way of Hindus accepting the gospel, the uniqueness of Christ is not negotiable.

There have been attempts by well meaning but misguided Indian Christians to find out "unknown Christs" in Hinduism. One bishop of an Indian church went as far as to say that *Bhagavat Gita* should be read as the first lesson in church worship services instead of the Old Testament, followed by the New Testament lesson as part of the indigenization process. However, he made a hasty retreat when he realized his folly.

All these attempts to make Jesus less than the unique Savior of mankind are bound to fail because it is the biblical truth. As Galatians 4:4 makes clear, he came at the fullness of time once for all as the suffering servant of God for the sake of man to die on the cross of Calvary, and he will come again at the end of time as the victorious king to judge mankind (1 Thessalonians 4:16–17). The uniqueness of Christ is not negotiable. Without it, there is no gospel, or good news, and no Christianity.

3. Forceful Conversion

Another Hindu prejudice is the alleged attempt of Christians to "forcefully" convert Hindus. In Table 20, 55.9% of the participants felt that there was some subtle attempt at forceful conversion. Forceful here does not mean political or physical pressure. Even if that were true during the British Empire days, it is no longer valid in India or anywhere else the Hindus now live. Forceful here means various kinds of economic or social inducements to become Christians.

The Nyogi Commission, appointed by the state government of Madhya Pradesh, produced a bombshell in 1956 in India when it reported that most of the conversions were made forcefully.[95] Some of the charges leveled against the missionaries were that they exercised undue pressure on minors and illiterates and offered economic and social inducements. The National Christian Council and the churches in the region had no difficulty showing that the charges were fabricated to discredit the work of the missionaries and local churches.

The widespread impression among Hindus is that they and their children are offered employment opportunities and scholarship grants in Christian educational institutions as a subtle force to convert them. On

---

95   Report of the Christian Missionary Activity Enquiry Committee, Madhya Pradesh, 1956, (*Nagpur: Government Printing Press, 1956) 2 Volumes.*

the surface, the charge seems valid. However, upon closer examination, it is clear that such charges are not valid. What actually occurred was that once a Hindu became a Christian, he or she was shunned and threatened by the extended family and caste, and the convert naturally came to the missionary or the local pastor for help and support. So if the convert was helped in any way, how can that be interpreted as a bribe or an economic inducement for conversion? The help was given after the fact of conversion, not as an inducement for conversion. This is not to deny that there may be isolated cases where someone came to Christianity not because of his faith but was expecting economic assistance. However, such cases have been rare, and such people would not have lasted as Christians unless there was a change of heart as well.

Those who make such wild, swooping allegations do not understand genuine Christianity. If in fact such inducements are given as a bribe or inducements for conversion, neither the giver nor the taker has any knowledge of the cross of Christ. Christians do not want to make Hindus nominal Christians but strive to make people of other religions real followers of Jesus Christ.

4. Materialism

Of the Hindus surveyed, 45.4% of the Hindus surveyed felt that Christians are materialistic. Hindus as well as other people regard the East as spiritual and the West as materialistic. Arnold Toynbee, the eminent British historian, speaking of the future, held that the insights of the religions of the East would be more deeply influential than the dominant technology of the West.[96] Hindus feel that even now Hinduism is more spirit-oriented than Christianity, while Christianity is more material-oriented than Hinduism. Christians are more prosperous materially because they work hard and save, while Hindus care more for spiritual matters than material things.

There is no question that the West, as well as Christians as a community, is more prosperous than the East and the Hindu community. This is not necessarily because of the difference in their attitude toward material and spiritual things but rather with the concept of the "total man" in Christianity and Hinduism.

Hindus divide the life of a man into four stages. During childhood and youth, for example, from his birth to the age of eighteen, he is supposed to learn. Then comes the age of the householder, between twenty-one and forty-five years of age, when he has to raise a family. From the ages of forty-six to

---

96   Paul Clasper, op. cit. p. 5.

sixty, he is to be a hermit, renouncing all family ties to seek enlightenment. During the tag end of his life, say from the age of sixty-one to his death, he is to be a *sanyasin,* a homeless wanderer, holy and freed from all earthly ties.[97] As a result, at any given time a number of *sanyasins* are seen all over India, wandering aimlessly, searching for spiritual truths that they could not achieve during the last three stages of their lives. These people are not productive members of the society, so ordinary working members of the society are urged to support the so-called spiritual men at all times.

A Christian does not have to go through these various life stages. He has to abide in his "calling" throughout his life, a task set aside by God for him, and he can be as spiritual at twenty-five as when he is fifty-five. He does not have to renounce his calling in order to become spiritually oriented.

> The only way of living acceptable to God was not to suppress worldly morality in monastic asceticism, but solely through the fulfillment of the obligations imposed upon the individual by his position in the world.[98]

Every legitimate calling has the same worth in the sight of God. Working hard legitimately, saving money for the future, and investing in legitimate enterprises will not make a man less spiritual. Therefore, a Christian who works hard and provides things for his family is not materialistic. The injunction of Christ is, "But seek first his kingdom and his righteousness, and all theses things will be given to you as well" (Matthew 6:33). This does not mean that one will become rich and prosperous in life when one becomes a Christian, which is part of the false doctrine of "prosperity gospel." A Christian is to be satisfied with his life and seek after the things of God throughout his life whether he becomes rich or poor. Peace of mind, looking for the appearance of Jesus in the clouds of heaven, and then entrance into the kingdom of God are the hallmarks of his life at all times.

5. White Man's Religion
Christianity as the religion of the white man was mentioned by 44.7% of Hindus surveyed. This view is prevalent in spite of two well-known facts:

97   David G. Bradley, *A Guide to World Religions* (Englewood Cliffs, N.J.: Prentice Hall, Inc. 1963) p. 89

98   Max Weber, op. cit., p. 80

a. Many history books mention that Christianity came to Kerala, the southwest corner of India, almost from the very beginning of Christianity and before white men became Christians. It is a well-known fact that a small Christian community existed in that corner of India continuously from the first century.[99]

b. Western missionaries came to India only after Vasco da Gama came to India in 1498.

In spite of these well-known facts, Hindus think that Christianity is the religion of the white man, and that it came to India as an appendage of colonialism. This is because the small Christian community that existed in Kerala from the middle of the first century was a small, obscure group in a tiny corner of the subcontinent. Differences in language, climate, food habits, dress code, and lack of transportation and communication kept this small community from being noticed by the larger Hindu community.

So for all practical purposes, Hindus believe the Europeans brought Christianity with them when they came to India for trade. However, once they got a foothold in India, they used their superior power in arms, ammunition, and diplomatic skills in pitting one princely ruler against his neighbor to establish their colonial rule over the natives. Imposing their religion over the natives was a natural by-product of this cunning strategy.

K. M. Panikkar, a well-known South Indian diplomat and historian, who ought to know better because he is from Kerala, in his book, *Asia and the Western Dominance*, maintains that Christian missions came into Asia as the handmaid of the domination of Western powers and that these missions have never really touched the hearts of the Asian people.[100] In 1953, immediately after India achieved independence from Great Britain, he predicted that with the withdrawal of colonialism, missions would run into inevitable collapse.[101]

Panikkar is only partly correct in saying that Christian missions came to Asia as the "handmaid" of the domination of Western powers. It is true that the Western missionaries for the most part came after Western powers came to Asia. But more often than not, they came without the help

99 Jawaharlal Nehru, *My Autobiography*, op. cit., p.273

100 K.M. Panikkar, *Asia and Western Dominance*, cited by Stephen Neill, *The story of the Christian Church in India and Pakistan* (Grand Rapids: Wm. B. Eerdmans, 1970) p. 167

101 ibid, p. 167

or support of the commercial and colonial leaders, who at best gave the missionaries only nuisance value, as their work made the natives hostile to all Westerners.

In some cases, missionaries came in spite of active opposition of these commercial and colonial masters. A case in point is the work of the pioneering missionary, William Carey. He was not even allowed to establish his mission or a printing press in the territory held by the British East India Company in Calcutta. Therefore, Carey had to go a few miles up the River Ganges to establish his mission in Serampore, which was held by a Danish company at that time.

Panikkar is absolutely wrong on two other counts. He maintains, "These missions have never really touched the hearts of the Asian people."[102] The fact that millions of people in Korea, China, Indonesia, and his own native India are turning from Confucianism, Taoism, Islam, Hinduism, and Animism to the cross of Christ is living proof that the hearts of the Asian people are not merely touched but turned toward the Lord and Savior, Jesus Christ. Panikkar made his prediction that "with the withdrawal of colonialism missions will run into inevitable collapse" almost sixty years ago. Almost all the Western powers withdrew from their Asian colonies by the middle of the twentieth century, yet their withdrawal only increased the zeal and enthusiasm of native Christians. While some of the independent countries do not give entry permits to Western missionaries now, local Christians have picked up the slack, and independent Christian churches and evangelists are marching triumphantly toward the goal for which the risen Lord has called them to evangelize their lands.

It seems highly unlikely that anyone who has seen the nail prints on the risen body of Christ and experienced the joy of the new life in Christ would ever go back to the gods they have forsaken when they made the decision to accept Christ as their Lord and Savior.

6. Christians are Low-Castes

Among the high-caste Hindus, there is the general perception that Indian Christians are converts from low-castes. It is true that many from the lower castes came to Christianity through mass movements early in the twentieth century, and low-castes usually eat beef, as do the Western Christians. The conclusion is that anyone who eats beef must be of low-caste origin and embrace Christianity not because of their faith but to get out of their

---

102   ibid, p. 167

caste duties. These people are called "rice Christians."[103] These low-castes, Hindus argue, have never understood the richness of the Hindu *dharma* anyway. A good Hindu should have nothing to do with the religion of the Westerners and of the low-castes.

It is true that many low-castes and outcasts have become Christians initially for social and economic reasons. By becoming a Christian, a low-caste person could get out of the rigid caste system and the degradation it entailed for him and his progeny. In any mass movement from one religion to another, a number of people are involved, and sometimes the motives for conversion are mixed. People turn to Christianity initially for a variety of reasons: a desire for self-improvement, education for their children, the conviction that they have been bad and should become good, escape from a degraded lifestyle, freedom from karma and rebirth, and many other reasons.[104]

Nobody wants to deny these initial motivations, but the blame for this must lie with the Hindu society that degraded them for generations. Why blame the missionaries or Christianity for the crimes perpetrated by the high-castes on their unfortunate brethren in the name of their religion?

Hindus call this change "conversion by force" and look upon the converted natives with disdain and contempt. When the converted say they are Christians, Hindus view them as turncoats who have renounced the religion of their ancestors for temporal gains. Hindus forget that these unfortunate low-castes had no reason to be proud of their religion in the first place. Their ancestors suffered enough in the wretched system; why should they continue suffering for a painful, degrading memory? They are happy they finally got out of the system for themselves and their future generations as they enjoy the freedom obtained in Christ.

And the charge that all Christians came from the outcasts and low-castes is erroneous. The ancient Syrian Christian community of Kerala is reported to have been descendants of Brahmin priests who were converted by Apostle Thomas himself, and therefore they are better known as the Thomas Christians of Kerala. "Syrian" as a prefix is a misnomer, as the Thomas Christians came under the influence of the Syrian patriarchs much later when they were called the Syrian Christians.

There have been many conversions from high-castes during the course of history, although there have been no mass movements from high-caste

---

103   J. Waskom Pickett, *Christian Mass Movements in India,* (Lucknow: Lucknow Publishing House, 1969) p. 152.

104   Ibid, p. 155

Hinduism to Christianity in spite of the attempts by missionaries like Robert de Nobili, who claimed he was a "Christian Brahmin" and wanted to convert high-caste Hindus to high-caste Christianity. He forgot there are no high-castes and low-castes in Christianity[105]

In Christianity, there are no castes. There are only two groups of people, nominal Christians and born-again Christians. Nominal Christians are Christians in name only; they do not show they are followers of Jesus by word or action. Born-again Christians are the genuine followers of Jesus, as they show it through their words and actions. Although they sometimes fall short of that ideal shown by their Master and Lord, they consistently try to follow that ideal.

7. Superiority Complex

Forty-two point eight percent of the Hindus surveyed said they dislike the superiority complex of the Christians, especially that of the Western Christians, which they feel is the result of centuries of conflicts and prejudices. Actually, it has to do more with secular humanism and the Enlightenment of Europe than Christianity itself. Hindus quite often do not make these distinctions. Hence, the charge against Christianity.

Western superiority in many areas is taken for granted. In science, technology, military strength, material wealth, social reform, and in many other areas, the superiority of Europe and America is clearly evident. However, quite often Christianity, as the religion of the white man, is associated with the excesses in these areas, which is further accentuated by well-meaning but misguided missionaries and Western Christians. Christianity is presented, if not as the product of superior Western culture, at least as part of the package of civilizing the third-world countries. Often the gospel is preached with a paternalistic attitude in the cultural trappings of the West. Some of the Indian Christians, especially those who are educated in the West, show the same kind of paternalism.

However, this is contrary to the teaching of Christ. He, who was equal with the Father, came to Earth to dwell among men as an ordinary man. Hindus are attracted to His simplicity, humility, and gentle attitude. Therefore, the gospel must be contextualized to make it relevant to the

---

105   C.B. Firth, *An Introduction to Indian Church History*, (Delhi: ISPCK, 1961) pp. 111-113

Hindus and preached without the cultural trappings of the West. It must be made relevant without any paternalistic attitude.

These prejudices of the Hindus, whether real or imaginary, must be clearly understood when the gospel of the living Lord is witnessed to the Diaspora Hindus.

Chapter 8

DEFENSE OF HINDUISM

HINDUS PUT FORTH MANY common arguments to justify Hinduism as one of the great religions of the world. They point out the antiquity of Hinduism, which is called the *sanatana dharma*, or eternal religion.

Quite often when they are witnessed to, Hindus will advance one or more of the following arguments. Therefore, it is necessary to know these arguments in advance in order to counteract them with the Christian faith.

1. All religions are the same
Table 21 shows that 83.6% of Hindus surveyed maintain that all religions are the same, as they all teach how to lead a good, moral life. "Do not steal," "Do not commit adultery," "Do not murder," "Honor your father and mother," etc. are common moral values advocated by all religions, so it does not matter what religion you follow. If you lead a good, moral life, you will be blessed not only in this life but also in the life hereafter.

But are all religions the same? If there is only one true God, can he reveal himself in many ways, some of which are contradictory to one another? The Bible tells us:

> Yet he has not left himself without testimony: He has shown kindness by giving you rain from heaven and crops in their seasons; he provides you with plenty of food and fills your hearts with joy (Acts 14:17).

Natural revelation is given to each and every nation, group, and individual and should lead everyone to the knowledge of the true God, who made heaven and Earth, who is the beginning and the end, and who rules everything. Unfortunately, man does not follow that lead. Hence, there is need for what is called "special revelation." Where do we find this special revelation? All the scriptures of the various religions claim that theirs is this special revelation. Hinduism also claims that the Vedas are revealed knowledge to holy men of the ancient past.

As to who has revealed this knowledge to these holy men, the answer is not specific. The god who revealed these things must be Brahman or the Universal Spirit by implication. However, the very same Brahman would not interfere in the affairs of men. Thus, it is clear that the Vedas are an attempt by the Rishis to know Brahman. But we have already seen that there is no underlying unity in the Hindu scriptures. Quite often, they contradict one another. Hence, this special revelation cannot be from the one true God.

All other religious literature, except the Bible, belongs to this category. Even the Quran, the holy book of Muslims, stands or falls with the testimony of one man, the prophet Muhammad. If the Bible, containing the thirty-nine books of the Old Testament and the twenty-seven books of the New Testament, is the only revealed scripture, the Quran cannot belong to the same category because it contradicts the Bible on several occasions.

The Bible, written by over forty different authors during a period of fifteen hundred years in many different countries and climates, claims to be the only revealed scripture, and its claims are sustained by an examination of its contents. In spite of the diversity in human authors and the circumstances in which they were written, there is an underlying unity in the Bible because, "All scripture is God-breathed and is useful for teaching, rebuking, correcting and training in righteousness, so that the man of God may be thoroughly equipped for every good work" (2 Timothy 3:16).

This true God, who created and sustains the world, revealed himself at various times through his prophets. However, since the world did not listen to these prophets, he intervened in history by sending his only begotten Son to die on the cross of Calvary for the sins of the world: "In the past God spoke to our forefathers through the prophets at many times and in various ways, but in these last days he has spoken to us by his Son, whom he appointed heir of all things, and through whom he made the universe" (Hebrews 1:1–2).

Therefore, all scripture is not the same, and consequently, all religions are not the same. This is not to deny that there are sound moral teachings in other religions. There are, and they exist because they were written by people who were made in the image of God. However, they were attempts by well-meaning people to grasp the mysteries of the invisible God. But authentic revelation is given only in the Bible because God decided to reveal himself to man. Therefore, the Bible is the only inspired, inerrant, and infallible Word of God.

The Christian then cannot subscribe to the thesis that all religions are the same because the Bible, the only revelation made by God, who made heaven and Earth, tells us: "Salvation is found in no one else, for there is no other name under heaven given to men by which we must be saved" (Acts 4:12).

However, this does not give the Christian liberty to speak against, much less ridicule, what other men sincerely even if mistakenly believe to be their scripture and incarnations. He may be forced to speak against certain points in their religion, but even then he will do so with love and compassion rather than in anger or hatred. His friendly criticism will be positive rather than negative, and his message will be to plead with all men to consider the claims of the Bible in which the Savior of mankind is revealed. He will not do so from any superior cultural or paternalistic attitude. In fact, he should admit that he himself was a sinner saved by the grace of God, and that the salvation obtained by him is open to every individual through forgiveness of sins and reconciliation with the true God.

2. One God manifests himself in different forms

Seventy-five point one percent of Hindus surveyed believe there is only one God, but he manifests himself in many forms. This one God is called by different names by different people. Some call him Vishnu, others call him Shiva, while others call him Allah, Christ, or Buddha. But all these are the manifestations of the same God and seek to approach and understand the same Brahman.

The Christian must disagree with his Hindu brethren. He has to maintain that Jesus Christ is the unique revelation of God to mankind and is the only mediator between holy God and sinful man. The only true God intervened in history at the fullness of time to reveal himself, which Hebrews 1:1–2, quoted earlier, makes very clear. The only begotten Son not only came and dwelled among men, but he also died on the cross of Calvary and made atonement for the sins of many.

Hindus who recognize many gods and various religious teachings as authentic and valid find this claim of Christ's uniqueness narrow and abhorrent. They have difficulty accepting Christ alone as the Way, the Truth, and the Life and that without him no one can receive salvation. Raja Ram Mohan Roy, a contemporary of William Carey, admired the person of Christ but nevertheless made fun of the doctrine of atonement:

> Nothing can be a more acceptable homage, or a better tribute to reason, than an attempt to root out the idea that the Omnipotent Deity should be generated in the womb of a female and live in a state of subjugation for several years, and lastly offer his blood to another person of the godhead, whose anger could not be appeased except by the sacrifice of a portion of himself in human form. So no service could be more advantageous to mankind than an endeavor to withdraw them from the belief that an imaginary ritual and observances, or outward marks independently of good works, can cleanse men from the stains of past sins and secure their eternal salvation.[106]

But in spite of his ridicule of the doctrine of atonement, Mohan Roy considered Jesus as "pure light innocent as a lamb, necessary for eternal life as bread for a temporal one and great as the angels of God, or rather greater than they.[107]

Mohan Roy's conclusion is not new. There were some Gnostic philosophers in the late first and early second century who had the same idea. However, the idea that God cannot come to Earth and live among men did not originate in philosophic Hinduism but in secular rationalism. No wonder Mohan Roy appeals to reason rather than Hinduism in belittling the doctrine of incarnation and atonement.

Mohan Roy maintained that while Christians should approach God through Christ, others might approach God through other ways. Mahatma Gandhi, whose admiration for Jesus and fascination of the Sermon on the

---

106   Robin Boyd, *An Introduction to Indian Christian Theology*, quoted by C.A. Lamb, *Jesus Through Other Eyes* (Oxford: Latimer Press, 1982) p. 16

107   ibid, pp. 16-17.

Mount and the crucifixion are well known, once wrote to a Christian lady:

> I came to the conclusion that there was nothing really in your scriptures which we had not in ours, and that to be a good Hindu also meant that I would be a good Christian. There was no need for me to join your creed to be a believer in the beauty of the teachings of Jesus or try to follow his example.[108]

Gandhi seemed to regard Jesus at times as one of the names of God. He wrote that Jesus "expressed, as no other could, the spirit and will of God. It is in this sense that I see him and recognize him as the Son of God."[109]

Gandhi maintained that Jesus Christ did not belong solely to Christianity but to the entire world, all races, and peoples. To him, the cross was a "timeless truth" from which he drew continually for inspiration in his struggle for freedom for his country. Ramakrishna, in whose name the Ramakrishna Mission was founded by his disciple Vivekananda, claimed to have practiced all religions: "Hinduism, Islam, Christianity, and I have followed the paths of different Hindu sects ... I have found that it is the same God towards whom all are directing their steps, though along different paths."[110]

Ramakrishna's outlook does not grasp the real meaning of the incarnation and atonement of Christ, as the true God does not manifest himself in different forms. The only valid manifestation came in the person of Christ:

> The Word became flesh and lived for a while among us. We have seen his glory, the glory of the one and only Son, who came from the Father, full of grace and truth (John 1:14).

> For in Christ all the fullness of the Deity lives in bodily form and you have been given fullness in Christ, who is the head over every power and authority (Colossians 2:9–10).

---

108   Stanley Samartha, *The Hindu Response to the Unbound Christ*, quoted by C.A. Lamb, op. cit., p. 17

109   ibid, p. 17.

110   ibid, p. 20

Christ differs altogether from all the avatars of Hinduism, Krishna being the latest and probably the most celebrated, who is reported to have come down from the abode of Vishnu to annihilate a few wicked people. We are living in an age of ecumenism when liberal Christians are seeing "unknown Christs" in Hinduism, while Hindu scholars are trying to equate Krishna with Christ. Is there any similarity between Christ and Krishna? If not, what is the uniqueness of Christ that must be shown to the Hindus?

In his incarnate state, Jesus was a godly person of spotless character who knew no sin and gave himself up as a ransom for many by his willing sacrifice on the cross. Krishna, on the other hand, was an ungodly character of mischievous behavior, who stole and lied to achieve his selfish ends. Even when he is purged from the lewd and erotic aspects of his character that disfigures and debases him, he comes infinitely short of the glory of Jesus.

Regarded in its brightest aspects, Krishnaism recognizes the idea of God descending to the level of the fallen creature and becoming man. Krishna points out a method of escape from the necessity of repeated births and rebirths so that man can have liberation from the cycles of birth and death. In spite of the flagrant contradictions in the Hindu doctrine of avatar, Krishnaism bears witness to a consciousness of moral guilt that is inherent in man that can be removed only by reconciliation with God. However, this reconciliation with God is not possible through Krishna but only through the cross of Christ.

When measured by biblical standards, Krishnaism is only shadowy and unsatisfactory. Hindus, especially the followers of Krishna, believe that the divine and human natures cannot coexist within one person. The one essentially excludes the other. Gods may be able to come down and exist as humans, but then they must abandon their divine nature. And when they regain their divine form, they have to surrender their human form. Thus, when Krishna goes back to his celestial abode, he completely lays aside the perishable flesh he had assumed while coming down to Earth. Krishna is said to have died at the random shot of a hunter and was thus liberated from his earthly body.

Krishna differs altogether from the God-man of the Bible. In Christ, the only mediator between God and man, the divine and human natures are united to form one person. When he came down to Earth from heaven, he did not abandon his divine nature but rather took upon himself the nature of man without losing any of his moral or non-moral attributes:

> Nothing is mentioned of any abandonment of divine attributes, the divine nature or the form of God, but only a divine paradox is stated here. At his incarnation, he remained in the form of God, and as such he was Lord and Ruler of all, but he also accepted the nature of a servant as part of his humanity … He was not revealing himself on earth in glorious or glorified human form, but in the form of a servant.[111]

Jesus was truly God and truly man in his incarnate state. He did not have to show his majestic divine form like Krishna, as he showed his divine form and nature continuously through his words and deeds in grace and truth. After his resurrection from the dead, he did not abandon his human form completely, as he asked the apostle Thomas to touch the nail prints on his body to confirm that he was the Lord (John 20:27).

When Jesus comes back at the end of the age to judge the earth, we are assured that "this same Jesus, who has been taken from you into heaven, will come back in the same way you have seen him go into heaven" (Acts of the Apostles 1:11). In other words, he did not abandon his human nature completely when he ascended into heaven. The transformed body of the Lord will continue to bear the marks of his suffering when he comes triumphantly as the victorious king at his second coming.

Therefore, there is no similarity between Krishna and Christ. Krishna and the avatars of Vishnu did not do the work of Christ because they were not mediators between God and man. Christ is the only mediator between holy God and sinful man. A mediator has to represent both sides, as he is the bridge that unites both sides of a chasm. Krishna is said to have left his human form when he went back to the abode of Vishnu, and his descent was not to make reconciliation between God and man. Even if he wanted to make that reconciliation, he could not have done so because of the law of karma, which makes such reconciliation impossible even if the mediator is divine.

Therefore, Christ is unique. He came down without shedding his divine qualities but took upon himself the additional nature of man to make reconciliation possible between holy God and sinful man. He accomplished his task by his death and resurrection. The law of Karma is

---

111   Jacobus J. Muller, *The Epistles of Paul to the Philippians and to Philemon, The New International Commentary on the New Testament* (Grand Rapids: Wm. B. Eerdmans Pub. Co., 1955) p. 82

not at work here but the principle of divine grace, which is unparalleled in any religious history.

Hindus in India as well as in the Diaspora must be told of this irresistible grace so that they too can accept the God-man of the Bible as their only mediator in order to be reconciled with the only true God.

3. All religions will take you to the same place

The third argument advocated by Hindus is that all religions will take you to the same place ultimately. Seventy point four percent of Hindus surveyed believe in this universal liberation where, although it may take millions of cycles of birth, death, and rebirth, ultimately everybody will reach the summit of union with the Universal Spirit.

In Hinduism, the idea of hell is not predominant. At its worst, hell is only a temporary place where the soul is kept by Yama, the god of death. There is no permanent place for hell in Hinduism but rather is something you suffer in this life for your misdeeds arising out of ignorance.

Hindus believe that one can achieve liberation through other religions as well if one follows the precepts of one's religion and lives a good, moral life. Therefore, all religions will take you to the same place. If that is so, why change one's religion? Follow what your ancestors have handed down to you, and you will be all right. This is the reason why Hinduism is not a missionary religion.

Do all religions take us to the same place? We have already seen that the Hindu idea of liberation and the Christian idea of salvation are not the same. In the Hindu idea of liberation, one's soul is absorbed into the Universal Spirit where it merges with it and loses all individual consciousness forever. However, the Christian idea of salvation holds that one's soul does not lose consciousness. He will have a continuous consciousness existence in heaven with God and the company of the redeemed forever.

For a Christian, this conscious existence in heaven is far superior to and desirable than the life of the happiest and richest man in this world. Hence, a Christian always seeks after the things of God. Apostle Paul exhorts his readers:

> Since, then, you have been raised with Christ, set your hearts on things above, where Christ is seated at the right hand of God. Set your minds on things above, not on earthly things. For you died, and your life is now hidden with Christ in God.

When Christ, who is your life, appears, then you also will appear with him in glory (Colossians 3:1–4).

This short life on Earth is full of trouble and suffering, and these are to be borne willingly, however painful they may be, for the glory that is to be his in the next life. Hence, the Christian idea of salvation is marked by robust optimism. For a Christian, death is a release from this mortal body when his soul will be ushered into the presence of the Lord. However, for a Hindu, death is a release into an unknown beyond. Thus, liberation from the present mode of existence for him is marked by inertia, apathy, and pessimism.

A true Christian cannot subscribe to any form of universal salvation. Those who prefer darkness, those who die in their sins, and those who reject the claims of Christ will be cast into the lake of fire for all eternity. This does not mean that in our witness we should call hell-fire upon the Hindus or ridicule them if they do not accept Jesus as their Lord. Nevertheless, it must be made clear that reconciliation with God is possible only through Jesus Christ, and that those who reject the claims of Christ are indeed going to die in their sins.

There is a debate still raging in some Protestant circles as to which view Christians should take of non-Christian religions other than Judaism. There are three main viewpoints:

a. The first view, prominent in liberal circles, is there is an element of truth in other religions, which is explained in terms of an original revelation that was never completely lost or forgotten. Others see in them the work of Christ himself hidden to them as the eternal Logos, "the light that lightens every man." In their view:

> (Christ) was present in every age to every race, but he was not known as such. Heathenism is related to Christianity as law to gospel, reason to faith, nature to grace. The heathen is like a blind man, feeling the sun's warmth but not seeing the sun itself. Christ was within heathenism as natural potency but not yet as a personal principle.[112]

---

112   E. L. Allen, *Christianity among Religions*, quoted by Sir Norman Anderson, *Christianity and World Religions*, (Downer's Grove: Intervarsity Press, 1984) p. 170.

It was only, they argued, when the Word was made flesh that he could be known as the personal Savior and Lord. As a corollary, it is held that there are specific values in each religious system, but only in Christianity are these values found in their proper balance and relationship. The gospel alone, therefore, can correct and complete the partial insights found in other religions.

This view generated an influx of new ideas in India. Liberal scholars have started finding "unknown Christs" in Hinduism. At one time, there was a suggestion to read the *Bhagavat Gita* in place of the Old Testament as the first lesson in liturgical worship services. Fortunately, saner minds prevailed, and the suggestion was rejected.

b. The second view is the opposite of the first; namely, that other religions do not emanate from God but from the Devil himself. The darker side of the ethical teachings and sacrificial systems in other religions are highlighted to show that they had indeed originated from the Devil. If there are rays of truth in them, they are explained in that Satan can sometimes appear as an angel of light. Emphasis is put on the fact that these religions inevitably deny, as Islam does, the unique claims of Christ.[113] Leslie Newbigin, an Anglican bishop who served in India for a long period, maintains that there is indeed an element of truth in this claim:

> The sphere of religions is the battlefield par excellence of the demonic. New converts often reject with horror and fear all forms of their old religions while the missionary may think of it as only "folklore."[114]

Newbigin further points out that it is the "noblest" adherents of these religions who oppose the gospel tooth and nail, as it was the Pharisees and the Sadducees who crucified the Son of

---

113   Sir Norman Anderson, op. cit. p. 171

114   Leslie Newbigin, *The Open Secret* (Grand Rapids: Wm. B. Eerdmans, 1978) pp. 192-193

God.[115] The Brahmins oppose the gospel more than any other Hindu caste.

c. The third view sees these religions as neither divine revelation nor as satanic deception but as human aspiration. Those who subscribe to this view can be subdivided into two groups. The first group considers Christianity as the nearest approximation to ultimate truth, the highest attainment of man in the age-long evolution of religion. The other group considers Christianity as the only revealed religion from God, while all the other religious systems are human attempts to find God.[116]

When we analyze these groups a little more carefully, we come to the conclusion that there are only two main groups. The two subgroups in group three belong to the first and second groups respectively. To the liberal Christian who does not believe in the virgin birth of Christ, in the miracles of our Lord, and in the second coming, Christianity is only the highest attainment of the "reason of man." To the subgroup in group three, who consider Christianity as the only revealed religion from God, all other religions at least partly owe their origin to the "father of lies." He may not want to proclaim it as such when he confronts others, as it would not be in "love and charity," but that is his basic assumption because that is what the Bible tells him:

"You shall have no other gods before me" (Exodus 20:3).

"Acknowledge and take to heart this day that the Lord is God in heaven above and on the earth below. There is no other" (Deuteronomy 4:39).

"For all the gods of the nations are idols, but the Lord made the heavens" (Psalm 96:5).

"I am the first and I am the last; apart from me there is no God" (Isaiah 44:6).

---

115   Ibid, p. 193

116   Sir Norman Anderson, op. cit., pp. 171-172

"Is there any God besides me? No there is no other Rock; I know not one" (Isaiah 44:8).

"Salvation is found in no one else, for there is no other name under heaven given to men by which we must be saved" (Acts 4:12).

It is difficult for a Christian to endorse all religious systems as relative and preliminary, which will lead to a deepening of the understanding of the true God. We know that God has given the natural revelation to all mankind: "The heavens declare the glory of God; the skies proclaim the work of his hands" (Psalm 19:1).

The apostle Paul clearly states, "Since what may be known about God is plain to them, because God has made it plain to them" (Romans 1:19) Every man and woman on Earth ought to see the invisible God when they see the beautiful objects of nature He has created:

> For since the creation of the world, God's invisible qualities—his eternal power and divine nature— have been clearly seen, being understood from what has been made, so that men are without excuse. For although they knew God, they neither glorified him as God nor gave thanks to him, but their thinking became futile and their foolish hearts were darkened. Although they claimed to be wise, they became fools and exchanged the glory of the immortal God for images made to look like mortal man and birds and animals and reptiles (Romans 1:20– 23).

If the natural revelation was not enough for man to see the invisible God, He gave him the special revelation (Psalm 19:7–11): "The law of the Lord is perfect, reviving the soul. The statutes of the Lord are trustworthy, making wise the simple" (Psalm 19:1). And if that was not enough, almighty God sent his only begotten son into the world to reveal all that is necessary for man to live a righteous life in this world:

In the past, God spoke to our fathers through the prophets at many times and in various ways, but in these last days, he has spoken to us by his Son, whom he appointed heir of all things, and through whom he made the universe. The Son is the radiance of God's glory and the exact representation of his being, sustaining all things by his powerful word (Hebrews 1:1–3).

Therefore, it is difficult for a Christian to endorse Hinduism as relative or preliminary. From the Aryan scholars, who wrote the Vedas and the Upanishads, to the latest writers of the Puranas and the Vedanta philosophy, there were men who tried to know this invisible God. As Christians, we need not condemn or ridicule any branch of Hinduism as something that lies between "the ridiculous and the sublime." Nevertheless, it is our duty to point to the cross of Christ and call them to repentance and reconciliation with the true God.

All religions will not take us to the same place. Only Jesus Christ will take us to reconciliation with the true God who created the heavens and the earth and gives us eternal salvation.

4. Forsaking Hinduism is betrayal of family, caste, and ancestors

Sixty-one point eight percent of Hindus surveyed felt that forsaking Hinduism and accepting another religion is betrayal of family, clan, caste, and ancestors, living as well as dead. This has been a problem in evangelizing Hindus as well as adherents of other Asian religions. Filial piety and respect for the elders is a hallmark of these religions, such as Hinduism, Buddhism, Confucianism, Taoism, Shintoism, and Animism. Even when adherents of these religions feel that Jesus Christ is the true incarnation of God, a final break with the religion of their ancestors is painful to them, as it will be interpreted as betrayal of family and clan as well as living and dead ancestors.

Ancestor worship is very common among all oriental religions. "Honor your father and your mother" is a basic precept of all religions. However, in all oriental religions, such as Hinduism, Buddhism, Confucianism, Taoism, and Shintoism, it is not merely important but is recognized as an essential component for the stability of society. This filial piety in those religions revere not only the living parents but also the dead ancestors. In Hinduism, children are obligated to spend up to three years in mourning for their departed parents, and there are elaborate rituals for the veneration of the dead. When a parent dies, the funeral pyre is to be lit by the eldest son. The absence of a male child is considered a great shame because then there will be no one to provide for the ancestral spirits. Marriage is a family duty and concubinage is permissible to produce a male offspring.

After the death of a parent, there are elaborate ceremonies involving presentation of gifts to the Brahmin priests and food for the assembled relatives and friends. The ceremonies are repeated almost daily until the twelfth day when the departed soul is dispatched to the *Prithu-loka*, the abode of the ancestors, to enjoy every sort of bliss in the company of other departed souls.[117]

These ceremonies must be repeated on a smaller scale at frequent intervals until the first anniversary of the death and thereafter on every anniversary until the offspring dies. At each new moon, it is the duty of a Hindu to offer a libation of oil and water to his deceased father as well as to his grandfather and great-grandfather. Thus, ceremonies for the departed ancestors constitute a big part in the life of a Hindu.

This ancestral piety in Hinduism is a great barrier for the Hindu in becoming a Christian. When an elder son becomes a Christian, he can no longer perform these ceremonies. Therefore, his caste fellows feel that tradition and family loyalty have been trampled by an alien religion. Relatives of the converted man not only become furious with him, they also lament the sorry state in which his departed ancestors have to suffer in "the abode of the departed ancestors." They do not know what is to be done under the circumstances and are in a helpless and confused state. This is too much for the would-be convert. Why forsake the religion of the ancestors and leave them in a helpless state in the domain of the departed souls to suffer for all eternity?

Another problem very close to this is the thought that of all his long line of venerable family members, the convert alone will be able to enjoy the blessed state in the company of the redeemed with Christ when he becomes a Christian. What about his dear parents and other ancestors and relatives? Why would he want to enter this blessed eternity while his parents suffer eternal damnation? Will he not be considered selfish if he cannot bring his ancestors with him? But they are already dead, and in Christianity, there is no ritual, prayer, or penance with which he can even

---

117   For a detailed study of the Hindu customs regarding ancestral piety and ceremonies, read *Hindu Customs and Ceremonies* by J.A. Dubois and Henry K. Beauchamp, (Oxford, The Clarendon Press, 1947) pp. 489 – 500.

attempt to help them. This has agitated the minds of Hindus as well as others where ancestral piety is a strong component of their religion.

A twofold answer can be given to this vexing question. The first is that we do not have to make a judgment regarding the eternal destiny of any other person: "So then, each of us will give an account of himself to God. Therefore let us stop passing judgment on one another. Instead, make up your mind not to put any stumbling block or obstacle in your brother's way" (Romans 14:12–3). The Lord is a righteous judge. He will judge every one righteously. As the psalmist says: "They will sing before the Lord, for he comes, he comes to judge the earth. He will judge the world in righteousness and the peoples in his truth" (Psalm 96:13).

If he judges us, we will be found wanting in many areas of our lives: "If you Lord, kept a record of sins, O Lord, who could stand? But with you there is forgiveness; therefore you are feared."(Psalm 130: 3-4) But His justice is tinged with mercy and grace. The Bible is very specific that there is no salvation apart from the grace of Christ: "Salvation is found in no one else, for there is no other name under heaven given to men by which we must be saved" (Acts 4:12).

The question is quite often asked, "What about those who lived and died before the atoning death of Christ?" The apostle Paul makes it very clear that even during the Old Testament times Jews and proselytes were saved not by the works of the law but by the grace of God through their faith. Quoting many Old Testament passages through a series of arguments in Romans 3:10–18, Paul maintains that there is no one on Earth who has earned salvation through his own righteousness, knowledge, kindness, reverence, or search for God:

> Where, then, is boasting? It is excluded. On what principle? On that of observing the law? No, but on that of faith. For we maintain that a man is justified by faith apart from observing the law. Is God the God of Jews only? Is he not the God of Gentiles too? Yes, of Gentiles too, since there is only one God, who will justify the circumcised by faith and the uncircumcised through that same faith (Romans 3:27–30).

But what about the Gentiles who lived before and after Christ? Paul maintains that they will be judged by the law that is "written in their hearts, their conscience also bearing witness" (Romans 2:15). On the day of judgment, God will judge the secrets of men through Jesus Christ. But the problem is, if God judged everyone according to his deeds and thoughts, no one would be saved. "All our righteous acts are like filthy rags" (Isaiah 64:6). Therefore, we need the righteousness of our Lord Jesus Christ to stand before the throne of judgment. But the ancestors of the intended Hindu convert never had the opportunity to hear the gospel of salvation. So where will they go? This is what troubles the Hindu convert.

All we can say is that we do not know. And we need not judge any one in advance because it is not our job. The righteous judge alone knows which seats are reserved in heaven for whom. We do not know how many, if any at all, are reserved for pious men of other religions who did not accept the atoning sacrifice of Calvary. Therefore, we need not condemn anyone because they never had the opportunity to hear the gospel of salvation. This should give us the impetus to go into the lanes and by-lanes of every place on Earth with the life-giving gospel of our Lord so that no one in our generation should be denied the chance to hear the good news.

Leslie Newbigin maintains that the emphasis of the New Testament regarding the last judgment is one of surprise:

> It is the sinners who will be welcomed and those who were confident that their place was secure who will find themselves outside. God will shock the righteous by his limitless generosity and his tremendous severity. The ragged beggars from the lanes and ditches will be in the festal hall and the man who thought his clothes were good enough will find himself thrown out (Matt. 22:1–4). The honest, hardworking lad will be out in the dark while the young scoundrel is having a party in his father's house (Luke 15). The branch that was part of the vine will be cut off and burned (John 15). There will be astonishment both among the saved and among the lost (Matt. 25:31–46). And so we are warned to judge nothing before the time (1 Corinthians 4:1–5).[118]

When our Lord was asked, "Lord, are only a few people going to be saved?" he answered that there are many who strive to enter the kingdom, but they will not be successful (Luke 13:23–24). But there will be many, he said:

---

118   Leslie Newbigin, *The Open Secret*, op. cit. p. 196

People will come from the east and west and from north and
south, and will take their places at the feast in the kingdom
of God. Indeed there are those who are last who will be first,
and first who will be last (Luke 13:29–30).

While this lack of knowledge about the eternal destiny of others
should make us reluctant to judge, it should prompt us to witness to them
effectively. It is the duty of the new convert as well as others to witness to
the living Hindus while telling them that the destiny of their ancestors is
not in their hands but in the hands of a righteous and gracious God. We
need to be concerned only with the living and not with the dead.

The second argument may further encourage the new convert. The
affections we have in this life for a father, mother, child, sibling, or spouse is
limited to this world. In the next world, while we will be able to recognize
others, our affections will undergo a revolutionary change. In answer to the
Sadducees' question as to whose wife the woman who had married seven
brothers in succession would be in the resurrection, our Lord answered:
"You are in error because you do not know the Scriptures or the power
of God. At the resurrection, people will neither marry nor be given in
marriage; they will be like the angels in heaven" (Matthew 22:29–30).

There will not be any husbands, wives, fathers, mothers, sons or
daughters in heaven; we will be like the angels in heaven in our transformed
bodies. Our affections will also undergo some revolutionary changes.

During his earthly sojourn, our Lord indeed loved his mother and
brothers. However, he gave us glimpses into the new relationship we will
have with him in the next world. While he was talking to people, his
mother and brothers stood outside, wanting to talk to him. When it was
brought to his attention, he outlined the new relationship: " 'Who is my
mother, and who are my brothers?' Pointing to his disciples, he said, 'Here
are my mother and my brothers. For whoever does the will of my Father
in heaven is my brother and sister and mother' " (Matthew 12:48–50).

Therefore a Hindu need not hesitate to accept the Savior as Lord, as the
present affections he feels toward his ancestors will undergo revolutionary
changes in the next world. His dead ancestors will only be pleased that he
accepted the Lord and Savior of mankind as his own Lord and Savior.

Chapter 9

CHRIST AND DIASPORA HINDUS

HINDUS BELIEVE THAT A local deity is more powerful and influential in that locality than anywhere else. But once a Hindu is outside the area of the local deity, it cannot exert much influence upon him. Therefore, Diaspora Hindus are free from many of the taboos and customs of their native locality. Remember that many Hindu deities are feared and not loved, so Diaspora Hindus are free from the fear of their old gods and goddesses as well. The old ancestral deity cannot do much harm to them in the foreign land, even if they do not fulfill the vows and follow in the footsteps of their forefathers.

However, this does not mean that they are ready to abandon their beliefs handed down to them from ancient times. They have tried to synthesize those beliefs with reason and modern scientific discoveries to the best of their abilities. But quite often that is not possible and hence the helplessness. Many of the religious ideas are empirically unverifiable, as they belong to the realm of the spirit world, so they subscribe to the theory of continued suspense of unbelief.

Before Sir Edmund Hillary of New Zealand and Tensing Norgay of Nepal reached the top of Mount Everest on May 29, 1953, many Hindu pundits maintained that their reaching the peak was impossible, as it was the abode of Shiva. However, after they triumphantly reached the peak, Hindu pundits held that it either was a false claim or Shiva must have vacated his abode before the humans set foot on his mountaintop.

The Diaspora Hindus dismiss such claims as fables that belong to medieval times. For the most part, they are young, educated, and have scientifically inclined minds. What they cannot empirically verify, they relegate to the back of their minds and go along with their aged parents, as they are unwilling to cause any problem in the family, clan, and caste relationship. Therefore, from the survey and discussions, the following characteristics of the Diaspora Hindus must be taken into consideration when witnessing to them.

1. Age of the US Hindu

Only four out of the 152 respondents were sixty years and older. This means that an overwhelming majority of the adult Hindu population, 96.1%, is below sixty years of age. Any effort at witnessing to them must be geared toward this age group. Out of this group, almost 77.0% are between the ages of thirty and fifty-nine, half of them between thirty and thirty-nine.

2. Caste of the US Hindus

In the survey, 126 out of 152, or 82.9%, claimed that they were from one of the three upper castes. A few others might also be from these same castes because it was fashionable during the freedom struggle and afterward to renounce the caste from their last names. So the actual percentage of upper-caste Hindus may be slightly more than the 82.9% indicated. This is again relevant in evolving a strategy for witnessing to US Hindus.

3. Occupation

THE TYPICAL US HINDU is well employed: 38% are professionals, another 12% hold white- collar jobs, 30% hold blue-collar jobs, and 11% have their own businesses. Only 9% are unemployed, which includes housewives and students. The conclusion is that almost 61% hold white-collar jobs. They are hardworking and industrious. According to US census figures, Indian immigrants have a better per capita income than the white people in the US.

4. Education

Out of the 152 Hindus surveyed, only fourteen, or 9.2%, were not high school graduates. Sixty-two point five percent have post-secondary education, and almost 44.0% have professional degrees, diplomas, or certificates. The high level of education is mainly due to the immigration policies of the US government. Despite the efforts of the government of India to stop highly qualified professionals from leaving India, better salaries, research facilities, and living conditions attracted many Hindus to the US. So the average Hindu in the US is a highly qualified professional.

The situation has changed to some extent since the survey was conducted, as relatives of the first immigrants have come to the United States because of the Family Reunions Acts of the Immigration and Naturalization Service. In any evangelistic strategy, this fact must be taken into consideration.

5. Migration Status

Out of the 152 Hindus surveyed, only 4.6% were born in the US. The rest, 95.6%, have come directly from India or were originally born in India but have come through a third country after living there for some time. Eighty-five percent are first generation Hindus in the United States. In short, Tables 7 and 8 show that 95.4% have come directly from India to the US, bringing with them their old Hindu worldview. This must be taken into consideration in any evangelistic strategy.

6. Worship and Prayer Habits

In popular Hinduism, there is nothing known as congregational worship. On rare occasions, *bhajens* (hymn-singing) are held where a priest or guru explains certain passages from the Vedas or one of the Puranas to the assembled people. Among US Hindus, this is rare for reasons already explained in earlier chapters. Absence of a priest or guru only accentuates the problem. Only 35.5% of the Hindus surveyed go to a temple on a weekly basis, while 37.5% go infrequently.

When it comes to domestic worship, 20.4% are involved in some kind of daily act of worship to their favorite deity, while another 50.7% do so infrequently. This shows that US Hindus are very religious in their foreign land. This must be taken into consideration in evolving an evangelistic strategy.

7. Power of Gods in the Foreign Land

Table 11 shows that no Hindu considered his favorite deity to be more powerful in the US than in his locality in India. Forty-eight point seven percent think they are as powerful here as there, 17.8% feel they are less powerful here, and 33.5% did not know. In folk Hinduism, local deities are considered powerful only in their own locality. Each deity has a certain influence in that locality, but once a person is out of that locality, the local deity cannot exert much influence on him or her. Therefore, US Hindus are free from many of the taboos and customs of their native land.

Remember that in folk Hinduism many of the deities are feared, not loved. Therefore, in the US, they are free from this fear. The old ancestral deity cannot do much harm in the foreign land, even if they do not fulfill the vows and follow in the footsteps of their forefathers. This must be noted in any attempt to witness to US Hindus.

8. Gods as Problem-Solvers

TABLE 12 SHOWS THAT Hindus do not look to their deities for solving personal problems. In times of general need for the whole village or a region, prayers are offered to all the deities or to a particular deity. For example, in case of a plague or lack of rain, prayers are offered to placate the deity in command of that particular area. But unlike Christianity, supplications are not made for problems of everyday life. Extemporaneous prayer is not common in popular Hinduism. One must solve one's own personal problems using one's own mind and body. In case advice is needed, one must go to the closest relative or friend before going to the guru or priest.

Active, personal relationship with a particular god is unusual in Hinduism because one god, however powerful he may be, is not able to solve all the problems of an individual. If such a high god exists, he is too distant and unapproachable to interfere in the mundane affairs of an individual. In any evangelistic strategy, this must be stressed. An intimate relationship with Jesus Christ is not merely necessary but essential, for he is the High God, who is not only all-powerful but is also approachable and interested in even the mundane problems of each of his devotees.

9. Felt-Needs

HINDUS IN THE US have generally three felt-needs. Table 13 shows they are education for themselves and their children, good employment opportunities, and financial well-being. Housing, religious matters, and social/cultural matters are less important, especially when they land in the United States, but they seriously consider the last three once they are settled.

In any evangelistic strategy, this must be taken into consideration. Friendship can be established by pointing out better educational opportunities for them. Social contact with them is absolutely necessary before one can witness to them. Nothing is more important to them than their felt-needs, as they are here essentially for the first three things mentioned above. When one contacts them, these are their areas of interest. A point of contact can be made about any of these three felt-needs, which will open up opportunities for friendship. Any tangible help in these areas will enable them to trust us, and friendship can be developed based on this trust.

When an immigrant family moves into a neighborhood, they have several felt-needs, such as transportation, babysitting, schools for themselves and their children, grocery shopping, banking, etc. If the Christian neighbor can offer any help in these areas, that will win their friendship. The first two years after moving into a new locality is the most crucial period for friendship and receptivity.[119] After those years, the immigrant tends to move deeper into his own cultural enclave within the community at large by networking relationships and then loses receptivity to the gospel. This must be taken into consideration in our evangelistic strategy.

10. Religious Satisfaction

No US Hindu claimed he was completely satisfied with his religion. Fifteen point one percent maintained that it was satisfactory to a great extent, and 38.8% said it was fairly satisfactory. This means that 46.1% are not satisfied with their religion at all. No one is entirely satisfied with the religion of his ancestors, and this is important in our strategy. Since the religion of his forefathers is not satisfactory, he is looking for something that can satisfy his innermost needs.

The Old Testament prophets frequently told Israel that the heathen shall come because they have heard that "God is with you" (Zechariah 8:23). The apostle Paul admonished the church in Thessalonica, "Make it your ambition to lead a quiet life, to mind your own business and to work with your own hands, just as we told you, so that your daily life may win the respect of outsiders and so that you will not be dependent on anybody" (1 Thessalonians 4:11–12). Through its genuine life in Christ, the church ought to attract those without the Savior, as this Savior alone can satisfy the innermost needs of the Hindu who has come to the foreign land.

11. Knowledge of Christianity

US Hindus are at least superficially aware of Christianity. Almost 43% of Hindus surveyed have attended one or more church services (Table 15), and almost 85% have read at least some portion of the Bible as part of their English language study (Table 16). But these statistics may be deceptive because, like the Ethiopian eunuch in Acts 8:27, they were reading the

---

119   Peter Pereira and Mary Lou C. Wilson, op. cit., P. 10

Bible and attending the church service without someone explaining the meaning to them. Just as Philip explained the Bible to the eunuch, someone needs to explain the meaning of the Bible to open the eyes of the Hindus so they can really see the Savior who died for them also.

12. Knowledge of Jesus Christ

All the Hindus surveyed have heard the name of Jesus Christ. Forty-seven point nine percent thought he was an incarnation of almighty God but not God himself, 30.9% maintained that he was a great teacher, and 11.8% held that he was a martyr who died for his principles. Only 9.9% had no comment.

Hindus generally appreciate Jesus' lifestyle and message to the poor. They can identify with his asceticism and his miracles. Table 18 shows that he is a better incarnation than their own incarnation of Krishna. Generally, US Hindus are at least superficially aware of Jesus Christ, but they have not really understood him or the claims he makes as the Messiah, the Son of God, the second person of the Trinity. So, however vague and superficial this awareness may be, it should be further emphasized and deepened in any evangelistic strategy.

13. Hindu Likings in Christianity

HINDU LIKINGS IN CHRISTIANITY have already been documented and discussed in Chapter 19. But how do we make use of these likings in our quest for evangelism? As has been mentioned before, Diaspora Hindus know only about the incarnate Christ, the miracle worker from Galilee who led a simple, austere, and ascetic life, and can easily identify with him. However, they do not know much about the pre-incarnate Christ or the resurrected, living, soon-coming Christ who will judge the world in righteousness. Their philosophy and worldview do not allow them to understand the claims of Christ as Savior and judge of the world. This must be emphasized after friendship and trust have been established.

Hindus often grudgingly admire the educational, scientific, and technological advances of the West. They rightly believe that there is a correlation between the progress of a people and the power of their God. This too must be exploited in any evangelistic strategy.

Hindus also admire the prayer habits, religious devotion, music, and religious literature of Christians. All these things must be emphasized after the initial contact has been made.

14. Hindu Prejudices against Christianity

Most of the Hindus' prejudices against Christianity are not against Christianity per se but against Western secularism. The permissiveness, materialism, and superiority complex of the Western culture are not really products of Christianity but the by-product of Western secularism and humanism, but Hindus do not understand the difference between nominal Christians and born-again Christians; hence, this equivocation. Differences between Western culture and real Christianity must be made clear. We must emphasize that permissiveness, materialism, and superiority complex are not based upon the Bible but exist in spite of it.

Christianity does not believe in forceful conversion, and all castes are equally welcome in Christianity. The uniqueness of Christ is fundamental to Christianity, and there can be no compromise on that issue. However, that is not to be thrust upon anyone. It will necessarily come up after the initial contact is made. Paul E. Little, in his popular book, *How To Give Away Your Faith*, maintains that eventually we must cross the bridge of friendship and bring the nonbeliever into direct confrontation with the Lord Jesus Christ so he realizes his personal responsibility for or against him.[120] Up to this time, he lacked the necessary information about Jesus Christ. At best, he knew him only as a martyr, an incarnation, or a miracle worker who lived an austere life. The nonbeliever had a lot of misunderstandings and gaps in his knowledge of Jesus Christ. After spending a lot of time with him and giving him time to digest and reflect on the claims of Jesus, it is time to confront him. The uniqueness of Jesus is fundamental to Christianity because he is the only mediator between God and sinful man. This uniqueness of Christ is not negotiable because without it there is no gospel or Christianity.

HATRED AGAINST US HINDUS

CHRISTIANS IN THE US, whether they are white, black, Hispanic, or Indian, must respond to the Hindus in their midst with friendship and tolerance. These Hindus are aliens in this land and are looking for acceptance and

---

120   Paul E. Little, *How To Give Away Your Faith* (Downer's Grove, IL: Intervarsity Press, 1966) p. 44.

friendship from their neighbors. However, quite often what they receive is hatred and prejudicial treatment. A few years ago, Jersey City, New Jersey, saw the phenomenon of Dotbusters, a gang of young white youths that has been terrorizing Hindus living in Jersey City and its surrounding areas.[121] The name Dotbusters was derived from the movie *Ghostbusters*, with *dot* referring to the adornment found on the foreheads of Hindu women. This particular gang was said to go through the telephone directory, looking for Hindu families and businesses to terrorize. Quite often, the Dotbusters spray-painted their homes and businesses are spray-painted with "You dirty Hindu" or "Go back to India. You are not wanted here." This behavior was due to jealousy of the Hindus taking good jobs in industry and technology.

No wonder Hindus think that the white community is prejudiced against them, and that they equate the white community with Christianity. If born-again Christians can befriend them without any ulterior motives, it will go a long way in attracting them to their Lord Jesus Christ.

A TYPICAL U.S. HINDU

BEFORE DEVELOPING A STRATEGY for ministering to Hindus in the US, it is important to know who a typical US Hindu is. From the survey, it is evident that among the adult population of the Hindus in the Flushing area, 97.4% are below the age of 60, and about 35% are between the ages of 30 and 39. About 82.9% are from the three upper castes. Only about 9% are unemployed, and almost 61% have white-collar jobs. About 62.5% have postsecondary education, and about 44% have a professional degree, diploma, or certificate. About 95% are first-generation immigrants here. Almost 73% go to a temple at least infrequently. They have come to this country mainly for education for themselves and their children, employment, and finances. They do not go to their deities for finding solutions to the day-to-day problems of life but prefer to go to a relative or a trusted friend instead. No one is completely satisfied with his religion, and they have a superficial knowledge of Christianity and its founder, Jesus Christ.

From the above information, we can conclude that a typical US Hindu is a young, upper-caste male professional, aged 35, not very religious but still wants to do what his forefathers have done before him, even though he is in a foreign land. He does not go to the temple daily, as he has neither the time nor the need to do so. He lives in a comfortable house or apartment,

---

121   *Aswametham*, Vol. 9, No. 10, October 1987, P. 19.

where a corner of his living room or family room is reserved for his favorite deity. However, he does not particularly spend much time in front of the deity except to bow before it on his way to work to please the deity as well as the women in his household. His wife does most of the things to please the deity, such as lighting a lamp each evening and offering a prayer and a flower each morning. He has many questions regarding his religion but prefers to keep quiet so he does not offend his wife, parents, or relatives. He has a superficial knowledge of Christianity. He likes Jesus but not his so-called followers, as he has found only professional jealousy and hatred from his white colleagues. In spite of his superior skills and knowledge in his profession, he is not receiving the recognition or salary he deserves from his company.

Although he is not completely satisfied with his own religion, he has not found anything better. Some simpleminded and well-meaning Christians have tried to befriend him and talk to him and his wife about Christianity, but he has not found anything meaningful in their religion. In order to maintain the friendship, he has gone to their church a couple of times, but he is not interested in forsaking his religion for Christianity, as he does not like Christians' way of life and Christianity's morals. He does not want his children to date anyone, and after they have received their education and have found good jobs, he will arrange marriages and thus choose his children's life-partners. If suitable matches cannot be found here, he can get one from his caste and clan in his native land.

A typical US Hindu is attracted by the simplicity, erudition, and the miracle-working power of Jesus Christ, but he does not find any of those things in Jesus' so-called followers. Rather, they quite often exhibit the opposite of what Jesus stood for. Rampant materialism, permissiveness, and licentiousness are the order of the day among the whites and blacks in this so-called Christian land. Even the Indian Christians, who have come to this country in search of education and employment like the Hindus, exhibit the same tendencies, at least to a certain extent. He is an upper-caste man who does not want to do much with this kind of people.

STRATEGY FOR MINISTERING TO US HINDUS

IN THIS ENVIRONMENT OF mistrust, prejudice, and hatred, how do we minister to the Hindus in our midst? We cannot ignore them, because they *are* in our midst. If we want to communicate the gospel to them, we must respond to them by crossing the bridge in love and caring. They will not come to us unless we take the initiative to meet them socially. Only by consistent effort will we be able to gain their trust and confidence by going over in Christian love, which is credible and incarnational.

First of all, we must meet them socially. More Christians need to be welcoming when a Hindu family moves into their area, as not knowing them socially results in fear. They are ordinary people, and just like any other ethnic group, they have the same hopes and aspirations for a better life. When a new family moves into a residential area, it is the secular "welcome wagon" and others who meet them. However, if a Christian church group or family would welcome them, it would be an important first step.

After the initial first step, friendship can be established through caring about and helping them. A new family needs information and help in a number of areas, such as schools, doctors, hospitals, banks, township offices, local markets, and other establishments where they have come to live. Orienting them to the pitfalls in business transactions, such as buying kitchen appliances, motor vehicles, or engaging plumbers and electricians, will be a great help to them. If a Christian neighbor can help in these areas, it will go a long way in building bridges of friendship. It requires time and effort, but it is worthwhile in showing Christ's love through these efforts. In doing these ordinary things, we are showing them that we care for them and love them as a neighbor without any ulterior motives. T. Watson Street, in his book, *On the Growing Edge of the Church,* describes this as being "profoundly available":

> To be there on the sport in a life long commitment and a continued, sympathetic crossing into other people's ways, language and customs … in love to break through geographic and cultural barriers, the barriers of language and race and economic conditions and political viewpoint, to identify with another person and to become profoundly available for him.[122]

Very few Christians take the time and make the effort to become profoundly available to a Hindu. However, wherever someone has taken

---

122   T. Watson Street, *On the Growing Edge of the Church* (Richmond: John Knox Press, 1965) p. 93

the time and effort, the results have been astonishing. This is the core of friendship evangelism.

An outgrowth of friendship evangelism is needed to address community needs. We have seen that there are many Diaspora Hindus in the US. On the one hand, they want to cling to the old values of family, caste, and clan relationships practiced in India. In a typical household in India, the father is the head of the family, and his wife and children obey him absolutely. He is a despot who runs the household at his will, and his caste fellows support him, come what may. However, in the new land, things are different; he cannot rule with the iron hand. His wife and children will listen to him only if he is reasonable. If he tries to rule like the despot he was in India, there will be conflict between him and his wife and between him and his grown children. His wife is most likely a professional woman who is in touch with other women and has absorbed some of the North American value system through her friends, newspapers, and television. There is generation gap between him and his children. Drugs, alcohol, divorce, juvenile delinquency, permissiveness, and many other maladies that plague the American landscape are now slowly creeping into the Hindu community as well.

Christians, especially born-again Indian Christians, can do a lot in these areas by counseling individually and as a family unit. However, these sessions should not be preaching sessions. A biblical understanding of husband-wife and parent-child relationships as described in Ephesians 5:21–6:4 and Colossians 3:18–21 will provide valuable insights in resolving conflict in such situations. Christians must find ways to include their new Hindu neighbors in neighborhood meetings and picnics to help them whenever and wherever needed.

Chapter 10

A BIBLICAL APPROACH
TO WITNESSING

A WITNESS IS ONE who has seen something with his own eyes. A Christian witness is one who has seen the risen Lord with his inner eyes and has experienced the forgiveness of his sins. His Hindu neighbors should be able to see the transforming effect on the quality of his surrendered life so that even before the Christian has contacted him, the Hindu neighbor is already aware of his separated life. The Christian will have already earned the trust of his Hindu neighbor by the quality of life he leads. J. H. Bavinck in his book, *An Introduction to the Science of Missions,* maintains:

> Our approach ought to be of such a nature that those who bear the gospel do not stand in its way but appear rather as living introductions to the message. Only then may it be hoped that when the gospel is subsequently preached, it will fall on fertile soil.[123]

The Christian's life must be an introduction and an invitation to his Hindu neighbor, who is groping in the dark, to a personal encounter with the living Lord. With this as introduction, the Christian will be able to talk to his Hindu neighbor and earn his trust. Secondly, it is essential that the meeting be filled with *agape* love. The Christian is not going to his Hindu neighbor out of humanitarian love for him, to throw him a piece of his Christian pie mixed with superior cultural trappings, but out of genuine

---

123   J.H. Bavinck, *An Introduction to the Science of Missions* (Philadelphia: Presbyterian & Reformed Publishing Co., 1960) p. 89.

sacrificial love for him because the love of Jesus compels him to reveal the Savior. As long as he thinks of his Hindu neighbor as an alien with a lot of superstitious beliefs from which he should be saved, the path to a genuine encounter in love will be blocked. Meeting-in-love includes the recognition of himself in his Hindu neighbor, a sympathetic feeling of guilt, and a sincere desire in Christ to do for his Hindu neighbor what Christ has done for him, as the apostle Peter says: "You may declare the praises of him who called you out of darkness into his wonderful light. Once you were not a people, but now you are the people of God; once you had not received mercy, but now you have received mercy" (Peter 2:9–10). A Christian cannot look another person in the eye with Christian love without being reminded of the darkness out of which Christ has called him. Bavinck continues: "In the proper approach, there is always an awareness of being on the same level with a person, and there is a real consciousness of our common guilt in the eyes of God. It is this which gives the approach a warm undertone."[124]

Finally, the approach must be an encounter where two people permit the light of God's Word to shine over and into their lives. In such moments, all consciousness of race and color, class and rank disappear, and the Christian and his Hindu neighbor remain standing together before God.[125]

The point of contact may be anything the Christian has observed in his conversation with his Hindu neighbor. There are many things in Hinduism that are superficially akin to something in Christianity, so incarnation; sacrifice, prayer, devotion, death, heaven, liberation, or any other belief can be a good point of contact. The old belief must be examined carefully with love and understanding without offending the neighbor, while at the same time, it is to be compared and contrasted with what is revealed in the Bible.

A real confrontation may develop when Hindu's age-old belief and its relevance is questioned. However, as the Christian has already earned his neighbor's trust, this confrontation should take place in an atmosphere of love, and he should never ridicule or mock the age-old belief, however illogical it may seem. As long as the discussion is centered in love and not in animosity or hatred, the friendship should continue. Even if the Hindu neighbor is not convinced of the message, he can always go to the Christian another time, for the seed has been planted in his mind and will work

---

124   ibid. p. 127.

125   Ibid. p. 128

slowly, as the Holy Spirit is the convicting agent not the wisdom of man. In this approach, one must note the following:

1. Universality of Sin

MAN IS BORN A sinner. He does not become a sinner by committing sin, but rather he commits sin because he is a sinner. There are several direct statements throughout the Bible that point out the universality of sin in every human being:

> "When they sin against you—for there is no one who does not sin …" (1 Kings 4:46).

> "Who can say, 'I have kept my heart pure, I am clean and without sin'?" (Proverbs 20:9).

> "There is not a righteous man on earth who does what is right and never sins" (Ecclesiastes 7:20).

> "What shall we then conclude then? Are we any better? Not at all! We have already made the charge that Jews and Gentiles alike are all under sin. As it is written: 'There is no one righteous, not even one' " (Romans 3:9–10).

> "For all have sinned and fall short of the glory of God" (Romans 3:23).

> "If we claim to be without sin, we deceive ourselves and the truth is not in us" (1 John 1:8).

In addition to this universality of sin, the Bible informs us that sin is the heritage of man from the time of his birth, present in human nature so early that it cannot be considered as the result of imitation:

> "Surely I was sinful at birth, sinful from the time my mother conceived me" (Psalm 51:5).

> "Who can bring what is pure from the impure? No one!" (Job 14:4).

In Ephesians 2:1–3 (KJV), the apostle Paul tells the Ephesians that they were "dead in trespasses and sins," that they were "by nature the children of wrath, even as others." The term "by nature" points to something inborn and original as distinguished from what is subsequently acquired. Therefore, sin is something original in which all men participate and which makes them guilty before God. Further, the Bible tells us that death is visited upon those who have never exercised a personal and conscious choice to accept Jesus Christ as personal Lord and Savior:

> "For the wages of sin is death, but the gift of God is eternal life in Christ Jesus our Lord" (Romans 6:23).

> "Therefore, just as sin entered the world through one man, and death through sin, and in this way death come to all men, because all sinned" (Romans 5:12).

> "For just as through the disobedience of the one man, the many were made sinners, so also through the obedience of the one man the many will be made righteous" (Romans 5:19).

So sin is universal. The sinful state and condition in which men are born is designated as "original sin," but it does not mean that God created man as a sinner, because God created man in His own image. However, because of the fall of Adam, his sin is imputed to all his posterity and is called "original sin" because it is derived from the original root of the human race and is present in the life of every individual from the time of birth. Therefore, it cannot be regarded as the result of imitation. Furthermore, it is the inward root of all the actual sins we commit by thought, word, and deed.

2. Total Depravity of Man

The Bible teaches not only the universality of sin as present in every human being but also that man is totally depraved. Man who is made in the image of God lost that image when he disobeyed God's commandment. After the fall, man became not only corrupt by nature but also acquired a natural bias toward evil. Left to himself, man cannot please God. However, total depravity is a much-misunderstood doctrine and therefore needs further elucidation.

First of all, total depravity does *not* imply following:[126]

1. Every man is as thoroughly depraved as he can possibly become.
2. The sinner has no innate knowledge of the will of God or a conscience that discriminates between good and evil.
3. Sinful man does not often admire virtuous character and action in others or is incapable of disinterested affections and actions in his relations with his fellow man.
4. Every unregenerate man will, in virtue of his inherited sinfulness, indulge in every form of sin; it often happens that one form excludes the other.

However, total depravity *does* mean the following:

1. The inherent corruption extends to every part of man's nature, to all the faculties and powers of both soul and body.
2. There is no spiritual good in the sinner at all in relation to God, only perversion.

The following Bible passages prove the above statements:

> The Lord saw how great man's wickedness on the earth had become, and that every inclination of the thoughts of his heart was only evil all the time (Genesis 6:5).

> They are darkened in their understanding and separated from the life of God because of their ignorance that is in them due to the hardening of their hearts. Having lost all sensitivity, they have given themselves over to sensuality so as to indulge in every kind of impurity, with a continual lust for more (Ephesians 4:18–19).

> There is no one righteous, not even one; there is no one who understands, no one who seeks God. All have turned away,

---

126   Louis Berkhof, *Systematic Theology* (Grand Rapids: William B. Eerdmans Pub. Co., 1941) p. 246

they have together become worthless; there is no one who does good, not even one (Romans 3:10–12).

For in my inner being I delight in God's law; but I see another law at work in the members of my body, waging war against the law of my mind and making me a prisoner of the law of sin at work within my members. What a wretched man I am! Who will rescue me from this body of death? (Romans 7:22–24).

Every man is polluted by sin, and every faculty of every man is corrupt. Man cannot come to the living God by his own efforts. The image of God that was bestowed upon man when God created him has become corrupt by the sin of Adam, and that man cannot correct himself. Good works cannot save man. The righteousness of man is a filthy rag in the sight of the holy God.

This is quite contrary to the Hindu teaching on sin, as the Hindu understanding of sin varies from group to group and even from individual to individual. Some Hindus believe that sin involves committing wicked deeds, to others it is disobeying one's conscience, and to still others it is mere selfishness. And to some Hindus, sin is merely ignorance. Swami Vivekananda once said: "It is sin to call anyone a sinner."[127]

3. MAN NEEDS FORGIVENESS

The totally depraved man cannot find God on his own efforts. Despite the Doctrine of Karma maintains that forgiveness is immoral, Hindus have been seeking forgiveness for their sins from various gods by a variety of ways, but to no avail. Brother Bhakt Singh, a well-known evangelist of India who has established many small house churches in North India as well as in Andhra Pradesh and Tamil Nadu, and who is a convert from Sikhism, emphasizes the importance of forgiveness in his preaching ministry. In a conversation he had with George W. Peters, he was asked:[128]

---

127 *Lausanne Occasional Papers. Christian Witness to Hindus, No. 14, Thailand Report* (Wheaton: Lausanne Committee for World Evangelization, 1980) p. 10.

128 George W. Peters, "Issues Confronting Evangelical Missions", in *Evangelical Missions Tomorrow*, Wade T. Coggins and E.L. Frizen, eds. (South Pasadena: William Carey Library, 1977) p. 167.

"When you preach in India, what do you emphasize? Do you preach to them the love of God?"

"No," he said, "not particularly. The Indian mind is so polluted that if you talk to them about love, they think mainly of sex life. You do not talk to them much about the love of God."

"Well," I said, "do you talk to them about the wrath of God and the judgment of God?'

"No, this is not my emphasis," he remarked. "They are used to that. All the gods are mad anyway. It makes no difference to them if there is one more who is angry!"

"What do you talk to them about? Do you preach Christ and him crucified?" I guessed.

"No," he replied. "They would think of him as a poor martyr who helplessly died."

"What then is your emphasis? Do you talk to them about eternal life?"

"Not so" he said. "If you talk about eternal life, the Indian thinks of transmigration. He wants to get away from it. Don't emphasize eternal life."

"What then is your message?"

"I have never yet failed to get a hearing if I talk to them about forgiveness of sins and peace and rest in your heart. That's the product that sells well. Soon they ask me how they can get it. Having won their hearing, I lead them to the Savior who alone can meet their deepest needs."

The words of Brother Bhakt Singh reveal at once the difficulty and the immensity of speaking to Hindu audiences. The words and terms we use are interpreted with many Hindu ideas and conceptions, and without them we cannot communicate. One has to be very patient. In due course of time, understanding will gradually increase, and the new meaning of the words and concepts will become clear.

So forgiveness of sins is very important in the life of a Hindu. He might have gone to Benares and made several oblations, sacrifices, and prayers, and given to the poor to add to his karma for forgiveness from his favorite god. But he has not found peace, rest, and forgiveness of sins. Hence, as Brother Bhakt Singh reveals, it is time to lead them to the Savior who alone can forgive sins and give peace and rest.

4. Man Needs a Mediator

There have been many gods, avatars, and mediators in Hinduism, but they all came to destroy one wicked man or another. None of them came to save sinners or to destroy sin. In fact, it would have been impossible for anyone to do so, as none of them claimed to be the Absolute God and all of them died natural deaths.

It has already been mentioned that Krishna, the ninth avatar of Vishnu, the god who saves, is the most glorious image of the god of preservation. In him, it was stated, god was really incarnate, as he descended as a real man upon the theater of human activity. He reveals the purpose of his incarnation thus: "In order to protect the pious and to destroy the wicked and also for the purpose of establishing duty, I incarnate myself in every age."[129] The purpose of Krishna's incarnation was to protect the pious and to destroy the wicked so as to establish duty on Earth, but the need to save sinners, forgive sins, or destroy sin itself is not mentioned.

The incarnation of Christ, on the other hand, was not to destroy the wicked or to rescue the pious from wicked men but to minister to sinners so they would be free from their sins. He thus came to rescue sinners by sacrificing himself on the cross of Calvary. Christ loved the sinners but hated sin, so he came to separate the sinners from their sins by giving his life as a ransom for many. "But now he has appeared once for all at the end of the ages to do away with sin by the sacrifice of himself" (Hebrew 9:26).

"Even though he was God, he did not consider equality with God something to be grasped, but made himself nothing and took upon himself the form of a servant" (Philippians 2:6–10), "that he by the grace of God should taste death for every man" (Hebrews 2:9).

---

129   A.C. Bhaktivedanta Swami Prabhupada, op. cit. pp. 225 -227.

"In bringing many sons to glory, it was fitting that God, for whom and through whom everything exists, should make the author of their salvation perfect through suffering" (Hebrews 2:10).

"Since the children have flesh and blood, he too shared in their humanity so that by his death he might destroy him who holds the power of death—that is, the devil—and free those who all their lives were held in slavery by their fear of death" (Hebrews 2:15).

Hindus have been living in bondage all these centuries. Even those who have left India and claim to be enlightened still hold onto the age-old beliefs that cannot save them because of the Doctrine of Karma. Jesus Christ, the only mediator between God and man, came to become a faithful high priest and to make reconciliation for the sins of those who would accept him as their personal Lord and Savior.

Christ is the only one who came to take away the sins of the people, and he is the only one who claimed to do so out of all the so-called avatars and emanations of God. He alone represented both sides, God and man, because he was the only God-man who could bridge the gap between holy God and sinful man.

The prophet Isaiah saw Christ almost seven hundred years before his incarnation: "We all, like sheep, have gone astray, each of us has turned to his own way; and the Lord has laid on him the iniquity of us all" (Isaiah 53:6), and John the Baptist, who was the precursor of Jesus, saw him "as the Lamb of God, who takes away the sin of the world" (John 1:29). He tasted death for every man and in the place of every man, and those who believe this truth are saved from tasting it themselves. The apostle Paul states, "God made him who had so sin to be sin for us so that in him he might become righteousness of God" (2 Corinthians 5:21). Christ came to this world and died on the cross of Calvary to accomplish many things, but above all, to die for the sins of man. His death is the foundational requirement of every blessing that the redeemed enjoy today and will be enjoying in the life hereafter.

Sinful man who has alienated himself from holy God cannot find salvation on his own. All the good works and all the pilgrimages to every place, including Bethlehem or Jerusalem, cannot avail anything to man.

Therefore, God was merciful, and in keeping with the promises he made to Adam and Eve and to Abraham and his descendants, he sent his only begotten Son into this world. By his willing death and sacrifice, he has become our mediator, without whom no one may approach the throne of grace.

Just as Adam's sin is imputed to his posterity, God will impute the righteousness of Jesus Christ, the second Adam, to all those who believe in him. "For as by one man's disobedience many were made sinners, so by the obedience of one shall many be made righteous" (Romans 5:19). There is only one way to righteousness, salvation, and eternal life, and that way is through Jesus Christ.

Chapter 11

WITNESSING TO DIASPORA HINDUS: FRIENDSHIP EVANGELISM

FRIENDSHIP EVANGELISM IS THE most effective way to witness to Diaspora Hindus. There are other methods, such as street evangelism or pamphlet evangelism. However, they are less successful than friendship evangelism. As the name suggests, the method of friendship evangelism is simply to make friends with your Hindu neighbors and acquaintances without any ulterior motive but to befriend him because of your genuine love for your brother. The mere fact the Hindu is your neighbor or acquaintance is reason enough to become better acquainted with him, as he is a stranger in a new land and has many felt-needs. He will be very glad to talk to you. But first of all, you must earn his trust before you venture to tell him about Jesus.

The following factors are important in any effort at witnessing, but they are very important in friendship evangelism.

1. The Character of the Witness

The character of the witness is very important to the one who is to receive the message. A true witness is one who has seen something with his own eyes, not someone who has overheard something from someone else. If you have not seen Jesus Christ with your inner eyes and have not experienced him, you cannot be an effective witness to anybody, least of all to a Hindu. This is not to say you have to become a super-saint before you can begin witnessing. If that were the case, no one would be able to witness because we are all sinners. The crucial question is, even though you may not be perfect, have you seen the resurrected Lord and enjoy him? Have you seen Jesus with your inner eyes of faith? Have you experienced him in your life? If you can testify to the saving grace of Christ in your life, you can be a witness.

Your Hindu neighbors should be able to see the transforming quality of your surrendered life. Our Lord said, "All men will know that you are my disciples if you love another" (John 13:35). The apostle Paul wanted to live "so that the life also of Jesus may be manifested in his mortal body" (2 Corinthians 4:11 KJV). He followed Jesus to the extent that he could ask his followers, "Follow my example as I follow the example of Christ" (1 Corinthians 11:1). What makes us true followers of Christ is neither our intellectual acceptance of certain ideas nor conformity to rules and regulations but possession of the Holy Spirit and a certain way of life acceptable to our Lord. A Hindu lady is reported to have said to a missionary, "If your Jesus is like you, I want to know him."[130]

Do our lives make Hindus want to know Jesus? The Lord's challenge still compels men to follow him. All we need to do is to become willing instruments in his mighty hands. But before we can do so and witness effectively to the transforming power of Jesus, something revolutionizing must have happened to us, and others should be able to see the new creation in us. Our words, deeds, behavior, and dealings must witness to the One who revealed himself in grace and truth while he was still on this earth. This will compel your Hindu neighbor to take note of you and, through you, the Savior, whom you want to proclaim. The apostle Paul told his young protégé, Timothy, "Don't let anyone look down on you because you are young, but set an example for the believers in speech, in life, in faith, and in purity" (1 Timothy 4:12).

Timothy, along with all the other messengers of the gospel, must live in such a way that would show the Savior they proclaimed, which must come first through deeds and then through words. In Hindi, which is derived from Sanskrit of which all the Hindu scriptures are written, there is a proverb that says, "*Karo pahale, kaho peache,*" meaning "Do first, speak later."

Deeds are silent words. Even before you open your mouth to tell about Jesus, your Hindu neighbor has already heard your silent words through your deeds, such as your facial expressions, gestures, and manner

130   Donald W. Carruthers, *How to Share your Faith,* (Atlanta: Lay Revival Publications, 1968) p. 9

of movement, which have already made an impression upon him. The reception you receive when you begin to tell him about Jesus depends upon your deeds. If you and your wife are not loving and caring toward one another, your children are not obedient, or your family life is not exemplary, your Hindu neighbor does not want to have anything to do with either you or your God.

Stephen Neill, who worked in India as a missionary bishop for many years, concludes in his book, *Christian Faiths and Other Faiths*:

> Primarily the Christian task is to live out the life of Jesus Christ before the eyes of men. They cannot see him. They will not see him, unless they can see him in the lives of his followers. If Christians are as different from others as they ought to be, questions may arise in the minds of those who watch them. This may give the Christian the opportunity to sharpen up these questions in the enquiring mind, to suggest that perhaps the answers to such questions as are given in the Hindu system are not entirely satisfactory and lovingly to point those who are willing to listen to the one in whom all human questions can receive their all-sufficient answer, the Lord Jesus Christ.[131]

2. Be a Good Listener

When we see our Hindu neighbor, we must greet him cheerfully without any prejudice. Hindus are generally a very friendly people. Although a Hindu may not take the initiative in greeting us, he will reciprocate our greetings. We must remember that we have been here first.

Out of the 152 participants in the survey, 84.9% are first-generation immigrants (see Table 7). Hence, we must take the initiative in greeting him. He will consider it a great privilege to be greeted by you and wants to be accepted and appreciated in the new land. If you are his neighbor, he will ask you to come into his house. Hindus are a very trusting people, quite often to the detriment of losing their valuables, limbs, and life itself. The story of a Hindu female graduate student in one of the universities in Philadelphia a few years ago comes to mind as an illustration. When someone knocked on her dorm room door and asked for permission to use her telephone, she gladly let him in. The intruder not only robbed her but also raped and killed her.

---

131   Stephen Neill, *Christian Faith and Other Faiths*, op. cit. p. 124.

Still, Hindus will invite you into their homes and, no matter what time of day it is, will offer you a drink. It is absolutely essential that you accept his offer, as it is a symbol that you have accepted his friendship. The moment you accept his drink, even if it is only a glass of water, you are no longer a stranger but a friend. By not accepting it, you are not endearing yourself to him and have already lost half the battle by declining his offer of friendship.

Once you are inside, ask a lot of questions about him, his family, parents, religion, and the geographic area of his birthplace. Let him talk, as he is prone to talk about his family and clan, and be a good listener. Quite often, we hear, 'Nobody really listens. People are too busy to listen to others. Everyone is preoccupied with his own thoughts, needs, necessities, worries, problems, hopes, and aspirations,' and 'Don't tell me about your problems; I have got plenty of my own' is frequently heard among friends and acquaintances. That is our story, the story of modern man in the twenty-first century. We are too busy talking to listen to others. And not only are we too busy to listen, we also don't know how to listen. Many books are written in many languages and many seminars are held throughout the world on the art of listening. It is a tragedy that listening is considered an art. But if one wishes to be a good witness for Jesus, he or she must first know how to listen.

Quite often we employ "emotional filters," hearing only what we want to hear and shutting out what we do not want to hear. Psychologists maintain that we cripple our critical faculties by our emotional involvement, so when the speaker hits one of our pet peeves or prejudices, we stop listening and begin rehearsing our objections, without hearing the speaker out completely. Before he completes his sentence, we want to jump in and offer our opinion worth two cents.

A witness must be a good listener, and God wants us to be. You may not want to act upon them, but at least you owe others a hearing. Otherwise, you will be wasting your time as well as theirs. Richard S. Armstrong, pastor of Second Presbyterian Church in Indianapolis, Indiana, in his remarkable book, *Service Evangelism*, offers what is called the "C" rules of good listening from the PROOF Seminar (Probing Responsibly Our Own Faith). The six Cs are the following:[132]

---

132   Richard S. Armstrong, *Service Evangelism* (Philadelphia: Westminster Press, 1979), pp. 93-94.

1. **Compassion:** The word *compassion* literally means, "to suffer with," from the Latin *com* (with) and *pati* (suffer). To listen well, I must love sincerely; to love sincerely, I must have a genuine compassion for others. I must be able to feel what the other feels, to share his or her agony, to empathize. That means relating to the other person as an individual, a unique person, not a "type" to be classified and labeled.

2. **Concentration:** The other person must feel that I am really "hearing" him or her, really listening. This means focusing my attention, my eyes as well as my ears on the person, concentrating on what is being said and not what I want to say next. It means learning to read expressions and "body language" so that I can discern the feelings behind the words. It also means that my own facial expressions and body language must convey to the other person that my complete attention is assured. Face language, like other forms of communication, is a two-way process.

3. **Control:** I must learn when to speak and when not to speak. I must control my urge to answer every question asked or to say more than I need to say. I must not be threatened by silence, realizing that I need not fill every gap with my own words. That takes patience, sensitivity, and self-control.

4. **Comprehension:** I must try to understand where the other person is "coming from." My responsibility as a listener is not to agree but to comprehend. I must remember that how we relate to each other is always affected by our previous experiences. I need not be threatened, therefore, by the other person's negative reaction to me, nor should I stop listening when my own reaction is negative. I must comprehend "what is going on" as well as what's being said.

5. **Clarification:** Clarification is an essential part of good listening. It assumes and depends upon comprehension. If I know what's going on, I can help the other person to discover it as well by raising questions that help to clarify the issues or decision being faced. A good listener helps the other person to understand the situation being described.

6. **Commitment:** Good listening presupposes a relationship, and as a Christian, I am committed to do what love demands. If I am genuinely concerned with the other person, I must make

myself available. I give the lie to my listening if I don't follow through in whatever way is called for. In other words, good listening must issue an appropriate action.

To sum it up, then, if you are not a good listener, you cannot be a good ambassador of Christ, as good listening is an indispensable ingredient of witnessing. When the Hindu speaks about his religion, his heritage, and his traditions, do not belittle them, but encourage him by asking pointed questions. There are hundreds of traditions and gods in Hinduism. In spite of all you have read and studied, you may not know anything about the particular god of your friend. So listen carefully in order to ask him intelligent questions.

3. Be A Good Speaker

WHEN YOU WITNESS, YOU are sharing your faith with your neighbor. Tell him what the Lord has done in your life lately not what he has done twenty years ago. You should be able to speak with conviction, sincerity, and authority. There is little secret here.

There are millions of gods and goddesses in Hinduism, and every locality and sub-caste has its own favorite god or goddess. However, the astonishing thing is that the local deity has little power outside his locality. But the Hindu who is away from his native region may still worship his favorite god, mainly out of fear for the extended family he has left behind.

Table 11 shows that no Diaspora Hindu believes that his favorite god is more powerful in the foreign land than he is in his native place. Forty-eight point seven percent holds that his favorite god has the same power here, 17.8% less powerful here, and 33.5% do not know. From this, we see that the local deities are less powerful in a foreign land. So when you tell a Diaspora Hindu the blessings you have received from your God recently, he may not be able to tell you what his god has done lately for him. When you press him as to why he does certain things, he may say that he does so because his family always did it that way. He may not have a logical explanation for the many things he does or believes in.

You should not monopolize the conversation. You don't have to tell it all at once. He may not understand the mysteries of your faith, as it will take time for him to comprehend the person and work of Christ and his uniqueness. The Hindu is coming from a polytheistic religious background, so you must wait for the right moment to speak in humility from your heart and not your head. You should not try to show off your knowledge, especially the defects and shortcomings of his religion. Let him speak of his religion and his understanding of it, and let him discover for himself the inconsistencies and contradictions in his system. Let the name of Jesus Christ be magnified, not your name, your church, or your denomination.

4. Do Not Condemn His Religion

AT NO POINT IN your conversation should you condemn or belittle the Hindu religion. Although you may find it illogical and contradictory on several points, you must remember that he was brought up in it and his parents have greatly influenced his religious understanding, so he may not be able to see the contradictions. And even when he is able to see these contradictions, he will try to cover them up or rationalize them.

If you belittle his gods or other elements in his religion, especially at your first meeting, he will feel insulted, and you will lose him, and it will not be easy to befriend him again. After you have gained his trust and friendship, if you point out the contradictions in his system, he may laugh at you. So it is better to wait and allow him to see for himself the contradictions in his religious system. Remember, you are only an instrument in the hands of the Holy Spirit.

There are certain barriers standing in the Hindu's way, blocking his view of the true God. He has so far seen only false gods and goddesses through the manmade system of Hinduism. When you present the claims of Christ as the only mediator between the one true God and sinful man, he has a lot of catching up to do because he comes from a system where there are many gods and mediators. He may be ready to accept one more god and mediator. However, that will not do for Christ. You may want to talk about the exclusive claims of Christ, but the Hindu will have difficulty understanding such a God and concept.

Conversion and regeneration are works of the Holy Spirit, and you are simply witnessing to the resurrection of Christ. When you share your faith with a Hindu, you are giving the reason for the hope within you. You don't have to condemn the Hindu religion or ridicule his gods to establish the supremacy or uniqueness of Christ, as he is already supreme and unique. What you are to do is to help the Hindu see it for himself at his own pace and in his own time.

5. Do Not Argue

When you witness, you should not get into an argument for the sake of argument, meaning you should not argue with a Hindu to win a point. Although you may win the point, you will lose him, as he is a very intelligent person and you may not be able to match him point for point in your argument. Reason and logic have been strong points of Brahmins from ancient times.

When the non-scholarly William Carey, the father of the modern missionary movement, wanted to go to India as a missionary, several objections were raised. Many said that this half-baked village cobbler-schoolmaster will not be able to argue with the learned Brahmin scholars? Of course, his critics did not know that Carey was not going to engage in religious debates but to point out the resurrection power of the risen Lord through the anointing of the Holy Spirit. Carey did not win any debates, as he did not engage in any. However, he was able to translate the Bible into several Indian languages and win many souls for Christ as he yielded his life to the Lord.

Our duty is not to engage in religious debates and arguments but to point out the Master who died for mankind. After all, our only goal in witnessing is to glorify God. Some people have the wrong notion that the object of evangelism is to convert people and establish churches. Those are noble, important goals, but they are secondary to the central objective, which is glorifying God. And the only power that can do this work is the Holy Spirit. The problem with most debates and arguments is that the goal is often the success of the winner and the defeat of the loser. Our God is a jealous God, and He does not want to share His glory with the winner of a debate.

Debates and arguments are self-defeating. Even if you win an argument, your Hindu opponent is going to feel dejected and defeated. And quite often, religious debates are non-conclusive, as they cannot be substantiated empirically. So you are going to lose even when you think you have won an argument. Therefore, it is better not to get into arguments and debates.

The only medium through which the Holy Spirit works is the Word of God. Therefore, we are to use the Word of God as revealed in the Bible when we witness to our Hindu neighbors. Even when Jesus was tempted by the Devil, he used it, so we can do no less.

You may point out that Hindus do not accept the Bible as the Word of God, and this will give you another great opportunity to present the uniqueness of the Bible and the Savior it proclaims. Even though the Bible was written over fifteen hundred years by almost forty different authors in different countries and climates, there is an underlying unity and cohesiveness in it and reveals only one God. The Hindu scriptures cannot make any such claim. There is no underlying unity in them, and often they are contradictory. This will enable our Hindu neighbor to see the contradictions and the inconsistencies in his religious system.

6. Love Your Hindu Neighbor

Above all, we must love our Hindu neighbor and make him our friend. Earn his trust and confidence. Reassure him that you have no ulterior motive in befriending him, and that all your concerns for him are actuated solely by the love of Christ. Without this love and concern for him, your witness is of no avail. With this love and concern for his well-being, you have every chance in the world. We cannot help anyone until we care for that person. D. L. Moody, one of the greatest evangelists who ever lived, said in his last formal address: "If I convince a man that I love him, it will break down every barrier, and I can reach him; there is a time coming in his life when I can reach him if I only bide my time, if I am filled with love."[133]

D. L. Moody knew how to convince any man that he really loved him and cared for him. But the love we show must be sincere; if we fake it, our Hindu neighbor will sense it immediately and start questioning in his mind, "What is the catch? What does he really want?" Our love must be sincere, without any ulterior motives, reflecting the redemptive love of God in sending His only begotten son to the cross of Calvary. This is agape love, which means sacrificial love. The apostle Paul phrases it beautifully in 1 Corinthians 13:1–3:

> If I speak in the tongues of men and angels, but have not love, I am only a resounding gong or a clanging cymbal. If I have the gift of prophecy and can fathom all mysteries and all knowledge, and if I have a faith that can move mountains, but have not love, I am nothing. If I give all I possess to the poor and surrender my body to the flames, but have not love, I gain nothing.

---

133   Donald W. Carruthers, op. cit. p. 37

When you go to your Hindu neighbor, if you do not have sincere love and a caring attitude, your words will sound like noisy gongs and clanging cymbals without conveying the music of love.

Dr. Howard Hendricks, in his book, *Say It With Love*, discussed this need for love in his inimitable style:

Do you remember the fairy tale of the ugly toad who was really a handsome prince? All he needed to break the spell of the wicked witch was a kiss from a beautiful maiden. But what beautiful maiden would stop to kiss an ugly toad? Obviously, only one who stooped first to talk to him and get to know him. We who wear the beauty of Jesus Christ through his grace pass by many frightened, lost, ugly souls. A hurried, superficial touch of courtesy cannot convey a message of love. It can only begin. Love moves into the realm of need, flows into a life to share remedies.[134]

Sacrificial love has a price. God did not send his Son into the world to condemn it but to redeem it by shedding his own blood. We must show at least a little bit of that sacrificial love for His sake when we witness to our Hindu neighbor. If he senses your love and concern, he will open up. However, if you go to him with a superior attitude and tell him in effect, "There it is. Take it or leave it," he is likely to leave it, without ever wanting to see you again. God said it with love, and we who are his ambassadors must also say it with love if we want to earn our Hindu neighbor's trust and confidence.

7. Pray with Him and for Him

Prayer is very important in witnessing. Pray before you go to meet your Hindu neighbor. After all, you are only an instrument in the mighty hands of the Holy Spirit. This is his work, and we are to be guided and directed by his leading. Our Lord promised us that the Comforter would bring all things to our remembrance (John 14:26), so when we yield ourselves humbly to the leading of the Spirit, he will take over our thoughts, words, and deeds.

This attitude of prayer and humility must be evident in our conversation with our Hindu neighbor. We are not lawyers but ambassadors and witnesses for our Lord. An ambassador must present his case in all humility and respect and make clarifications when asked. We need not enter into arguments or debates but present convincingly our case in humility and respect.

---

134   Howard G. Hendricks, *Say It With Love* (Wheaton: Victor Books, 1974), p. 9

If our Hindu neighbor allows, we should pray with him and for him. Table 19 shows that 44.1% of Hindus surveyed like our prayers. Therefore, with his permission, we should pray for him and his family before we leave his home. And it is important that we pray for him after we retreat to our own homes, as this will give us a burden for his salvation, which should continue until he accepts the Lord. There is no time limit as to how long we should pray for him. We must pray and continue to interact with him until he realizes our love and concern for him and accepts us and our Savior, which he will in time. Prayer is absolutely important in our task of witnessing to our Hindu neighbors.

Chapter 12

A POSITIVE PRESENTATION OF THE GOSPEL

A POSITIVE PRESENTATION OF the gospel is the result of my actual experience in witnessing to the US Hindus and my discussions with those who have had vast experience in working with Hindus in the US. Anyone interested in witnessing to US Hindus may choose his own point of contact and take it from there, always remembering that the Holy Spirit is your guide in presenting the Son of God to the Hindus.

I am indebted to Dr. James Kennedy and his excellent book, *Evangelism Explosion*, for basic ideas for this presentation.[135] However, while Dr. Kennedy's presentation is targeted toward all people, this presentation is contextualized for the Hindus of the Diaspora, especially the US Hindus. A summary of the presentation is given below, followed by a detailed presentation of the gospel to a Hindu.

A SUMMARY OF THE PRESENTATION

I. Introduction
a. Greetings
b. Religious Background
c. Our Fellowship
d. Testimony

II. The Good News

---

135   D. James Kennedy, *Evangelism Explosion* (Wheaton, IL; Tyndale House Publishers, 1977) pp. 16-44.

a. Jesus Christ
    1. The infinite God-man
    2. The meaning of His death
b. The Character of God
    1. Loving and faithful
    2. Just, therefore must punish sin
c. The Character of Man
    1. A sinner
    2. Man cannot save himself
d. Salvation
    1. Trusting Jesus
    2. Result—A new creation
e. The Bible
    1. Prophetic
    2. God is its author

III. The Commitment
a.   The Commitment Question
b.   Clarification of Commitment
c.   Prayer of Commitment
d.   The Assurance

A DETAILED PRESENTATION OF THE GOSPEL

(This presentation is only a model conversation between Paul, the missionary, and Vishwanath, the Hindu. You may use other points of contact, examples, and illustrations as the occasion warrants to present the gospel, always remembering that the Holy Spirit is your guide, and he will break down any barriers of hostility, and use you when you yield yourself to the mighty hand of God.)

I. Introduction

A. Greetings

Paul: Good morning, Mr. Vishwanath. I am Paul from the India Christian Fellowship. May we come in and visit with you for a few minutes?

Vish: Good morning. Please come in.

Paul: Thank you. These are my friends, John Jacob and Samuel Murugan. We are glad you came to our meeting last Saturday.

We wanted to come to your place and become better acquainted with you.

Vish: That is very nice of you. Please be seated. May I give you something to drink?

Paul: Don't bother. Let us just sit and talk.

Vish: It will take only a minute. Tea, or coffee?

Paul: Okay. Tea for me, with sugar and cream. What would you like, John and Sam?

John and Sam: Tea will do, with sugar and cream.

Paul: Where are your wife and kids, Mr. Vishwanath?

Vish: They have gone shopping.

Paul: Shall I come and help you?

Vish: No, no. I will be there in a minute.

(It is customary for Indians to offer something to drink when a distinguished visitor comes to their home, so even if you are not thirsty, it is better to accept at least a glass of water. This custom may have to do with the hot climate of India. Accepting their drink is the sign that you have come as a friend and have accepted his friendship.)

Paul: You have a nice apartment. How long have you been here?

Vish: Four months. We stayed with my brother-in-law at first when we came from Chennai. Then we moved to this apartment.

Paul: So you came from Chennai? I have passed through Chennai several times, but was never there for more than a few hours. It is a nice city, isn't it?

Vish: Yes, it is a nice city, but overpopulated. Flushing is a nicer place to live.

B. Religious Background

Paul: May we inquire about your religious background, Mr. Vishwanath?

Vish: Don't call me mister and all that. A simple Vishwanath, or better, Vish, will do. All my close friends call me Vish. I am a Hindu by birth. However, I did not go to temples except on important days and that because of the insistence of my mother. I have my own doubts about some of the practices and the so-called gurus and priests.

Paul: Why is that?

Vish: Because many of them are self-serving people.

Paul: Does that mean that you don't go to a temple regularly?

Vish: I did not go to a temple regularly even when we were in Chennai. Here, we don't even have the image of our clan god installed in the local temple. So I don't go here at all.

Paul: So you don't worship him at all?

Vish: No, I don't, but my wife does. She has installed a picture of him on the mantle of our living room and lights a lamp every evening in front of that picture.

Paul: What is his name?

Vish: Ganesha. He is a son of Shiva, who is one of the three great gods of Hinduism.

Paul: So he is a son of Shiva, the god who punishes? How is he able to help you?

Vish: I don't know. He has been our family and clan god for centuries. So we continue to do the things our forefathers did.

Paul: You don't seem to have much faith in your clan god. Are you looking for something else? Is that the reason you came to our meeting?

Vish: Yes and no.

Paul: What do you mean, Vish?

Vish: Yes, I am searching. No, I am not planning to change my religion. Our Christian friends invited us to your meeting, and so we came.

C. Our Fellowship

Paul: We are so glad you came. How did you like the meeting?

Vish: It was very nice. The potluck dinner was delicious. I tasted many of the Indian dishes for the first time after coming to the US.

Paul: How was the message?

Vish: It was very good. The music was delightful. People were very friendly, and we felt at home, even though we are not Christians.

Paul: Thank you. We meet every month during the second Saturday. It is a great get-together for Christians of Indian origin from different areas. For two hours, we forget all differences of language, region, and denomination and come together to praise our Lord and Savior, Jesus Christ.

Vish; Yes, I noticed that.

Paul: Do you know how this is possible?

Vish: No, but I would like to know.

D. Testimony

Paul: This is possible only because of Jesus Christ. In spite of our differences in language, customs, region, and denomination, we have the same Lord and Savior, Jesus Christ. We are born-again Christians of Indian origin. Vish, do you know the difference between born-again Christians and nominal Christians?

Vish: Not really. In Hinduism, we have ordinary castes and twice-born castes. Is it anything similar?

Paul: No, it is not. In Hinduism, physical birth determines twice-born status. For example, it you are born in a Brahmin family, you are a Brahmin for life. In Christianity, even if you are born to born-again Christian parents, you do not automatically become born-again unless and until you accept Jesus Christ as your personal Lord and Savior. I was born into and brought up in a Christian family of Kerala and accepted Jesus Christ as my personal Lord and Savior when I was fourteen years old. That is when I became a born-again Christian—born a second time, not physically but spiritually.

Vish: What difference did it make?

Paul: It made a lot of difference. In my case, the difference was slow rather than dramatic because I was brought up in a Christian family. My parents and grandparents were Christians. However, in many cases, the change is dramatic. A person comes to hate the things he once liked and love the things he once hated. There is about a 180-degree turn in his life.

Vish: Does this mean he becomes a perfect man when he is born-again?

Paul: No, he does not become perfect all of a sudden. God alone is perfect. But he does become a new person. Do you know, Vish, how this is possible?

Vish; No, but I am interested.

II. The Good News

A. Jesus Christ
1. The Infinite God-man

Paul: I said earlier that this is possible when a person accepts Jesus Christ as his personal Savior. In order to accept him as your personal Savior, you must know who Jesus Christ is. Let me ask you a question, Vish. You have heard of Jesus Christ, haven't you? What do you think of him?

Vish: I think he was a great man, a great teacher, a miracle worker. He was considered an incarnation, was he not?

Paul: Yes, he was all that you said. You said he was an incarnation. Can you tell me what you understand by that term?

Vish: Well, I believe an incarnation is a god descending from heaven to live among men for a time, a descent. In Hinduism, we call him an avatar.

Paul: So you believe Jesus was an avatar like Rama or Krishna?

Vish: I don't know. From what I understand, he was a better incarnation than Rama or Krishna because unlike them he did not do anything wrong, and yet he was crucified.

Paul: Yes, you are right. Many Hindus believe like you do, Vish. He never did anything wrong. Many are attracted to his moral excellence. While Krishna stole and cheated, and Rama kicked his innocent wife out of his palace on suspicion, Jesus not only led a sinless life, he also helped the needy, the poor, and the sick by his divine power. However, this is not the only difference, even though that is what attracts people to him initially. This is only the surface. When we go deep into his life, we see a fundamental difference. You see, Vish, Krishna came to defeat the wicked Kauravas and restore the kingdom to their cousins, the Pandavas. And Rama came to annihilate the demon king, Ravana. But Jesus did not come to annihilate a few wicked men. He did not come to kill anyone. He came to save people from their sins and to give them eternal life. A lot of people cannot understand this great mystery. Almighty God intervened in history. He left his home in glory and was born not in a palace but in a lowly manger and lived a perfect, spotless life. He taught the great teachings by word and deed and performed the mightiest deeds. Finally, he came to the end of his earthly life, to that hour for which he had come into the world. His crucifixion was not an accident; it was foreordained by God the Father. In that hour, the greatest transaction of the world took place. The infinite God, the almighty God, the all-powerful God died for our sins on the cross of Calvary willingly about two thousand years ago.

Vish: You said God intervened in history. So it must be a historical fact. In what history book is it recorded?

Paul: First of all, it is recorded in the Bible, but the Bible is not a history book, per se. However, it does contain history. The names of kings and rulers like the Roman emperor Augustus Caesar, Syrian governor Quirinius, Roman governor Pontius Pilate, King Herod, and high priests like Annas and Caiaphas were historical people who lived around the time of Jesus. Besides the Bible, a Jewish historian named Josephus and others have recorded many of these things. Jesus stands at the center of history. History before him is known as BC, meaning "Before Christ," and is counted backward. History after him is known by the Latin words, *Anno Domini*, which means "In the year of the Lord," and is counted forward. Thus, he is the central figure of history. The fact that he is the central figure of history is important to us today only if it has existential significance. His incarnation is the final and culminating act of God in a series of revelations to mankind (Hebrews 1:1–2).

(At this point, the evangelist need not quote the Scripture. However, if asked, and the context demands it, he should be ready to point out that the Bible is his authority, and that it is the inspired, inerrant, and infallible Word of God.)

2. The Meaning of His Death

Paul: You see, Vish, almighty God has revealed himself to all mankind in the light of his creation (Romans 1:19–25). In other words, when man sees the wonderful objects of creation, he should be able to see the hands behind that creation. Further, God has placed within each man the light of conscience, as man is made in the image of God, and He has given man a conscience (Romans 2:15). However, in spite of all these resources, man does not acknowledge his Creator. Instead of understanding Him through His creation, man tries to play God and worship created objects instead of worshipping the Creator. Man is vainly trying to understand the nature and person of God through his vain imagination. These attempts of men to know God are sincere, though it is the result of his autonomous thinking. Instead of relying upon God's creation, he relies on his finite understanding. In spite of this, God in His mercy intervened in history and gave special revelation to man. He came down from heaven, lived among men, and died on the cross of Calvary. God's self-sacrifice was absolutely necessary for a couple of reasons:

1. Up to the time of his incarnation, men could worship only an unseen God, hidden behind his incarnation. He had revealed himself through the Old Testament prophets but was seen by none. In Jesus, He revealed himself fully to mankind.

2. He came down to give men an example of holy living. Christ is the only one who set for us the perfect example of a holy life and is the only one who is infallible in his teachings and character. It was necessary that we should have an illustration of what God wants us to be. He is not only our Savior, but he is also our example. On several occasions, the religious leaders of his day tried to find fault with his words and deeds. However, they found none because He was truly God, who came to die for the sins of his people.

People throughout the world have always tried to appease their gods by offerings and sacrifices, such as birds, other animals, and, on occasion, humans. Blood sacrifices were very common. Judaism was no exception. However, birds and animals have very limited value. Their blood is not sufficient to please almighty God. We must remember that he made man in his own image and endowed him with health and wealth and gave him power and dominion over everything on Earth. However, when he disobeyed God and sinned against him, God was displeased, and the blood of birds and animals could not satisfy Him. The infinite God needed to be appeased by an infinite sacrifice. So God in His mercy decided to sacrifice himself to save the most precious of his creation, man, who is made in His own image.

Vish: Yes, I know. Didn't Mahatma Gandhi make use of this idea of self-sacrifice in the freedom struggle for India?

Paul: Yes, Vish, you are right. Mahatma Gandhi made use of this concept of self-sacrifice in a limited way. His *Satyagraha* (search for truth) movement of nonviolence was derived from the gospel. Even before Christ, Gautama Buddha, the founder of Buddhism, had also made use of the concept of *ahimsa* (nonviolence). However, Jesus Christ, the infinite God, the Creator of the universe, sacrificed himself on the cross of Calvary for all mankind, an infinite price paid to appease the justice of God. But He paid it willingly to free us from the bondage of sin. With this infinite price, he satisfied the justice of God so that a just God can show his love for sinners. Now I don't have to pay it any more, because Jesus paid it for me.

We have so far referred only to the wrath and justice of God. However, we have seen that God is loving and merciful. How do we reconcile these opposing qualities?

B. The Character of God
1. Loving and Faithful

Paul: One of the most wonderful things about God is that he loves us in spite of what we are. He loves us not because of what we are, but because of what he is. The love of the holy God is all the more incomprehensible when we know that we are sinners and cannot even approach the throne of grace. His love is not measurable by any yardstick. We saw that he loved man so much that he sent his only begotten Son to this world to die on the cross for us.

2. Just, therefore must punish sin

Paul: On the one hand, he is love, but on the other hand, he is just and holy and therefore must punish sin. This created a problem for God, which he solved by sending his only dear Son to this world to die on the cross of Calvary. So in order to satisfy the justice of God, he sacrificed himself. In other words, God punished himself in order to appease his sense of justice so that without guilt he could love and accept me as a child forever. This is the only way he could accept me because of my sin.

C. The Character of Man
1. A Sinner

Paul: The first thing we must understand about man is that he is a sinner. Why is he a sinner? Here Hinduism and the gospel differ. Sin, according to Hinduism, is the ignorance and imperfections of man, an external accretion that can be removed by prayers and rituals. Man is essentially good, but if per chance he does evil, that is an accidental condition that can be remedied. A real human being could not be a sinner, according to the Vedas.[136] However, this is exactly the opposite of what the Bible says, which is that sin is simply disobedience and rebellion against the holy God, the result of pride and arrogance. Man, who is made in the image of God, considers himself autonomous. He thinks that by reason of his intellect he can be a law unto himself. Sin is want of conformity to and transgression of the law of a righteous and holy God, who is infinite, eternal, and immutable in his perfection. This want of conformity to the law of God embraces want in nature and in conduct. Acts of sin spring from the sinful nature. The Bible tells us: " If we say that we have no sin, we are deceiving ourselves and the truth is not in us" (1 John 1:8).

(At this point it is all right to bring in the Bible, even though a discussion of the Bible itself will come a little later in this discussion because Vish has been adequately prepared for it.)

Paul: According to the Bible, all men have inherited this sinful nature through our first parents, Adam and Eve, when they disobeyed God in the garden of Eden. Individual acts of sin are the result of this sin nature, and the whole human race has inherited this sin nature. The Bible tells us that the sin of Adam is imputed to all his posterity (Romans 5:12; Ephesians 2:3). This imputed sin nature is a pollution that shows itself in a darkened understanding (Romans 1:31), evil and futile imaginations (Romans 1:21), degrading passions (Romans

---

136   Troy Wilson Organ, op. cit. p. 79.

1:26f), unwholesome speech (Ephesians 4:29), a defiled mind and conscience (Titus 1:15), and an enslaved and perverted will (Romans 7:18f). These are symptoms of the corrupt nature. This lack of ability to please God is also called death. Men are said to be "dead ... in transgressions and sins" (Ephesians 2:1) and are totally destitute of spiritual life. However, this does not mean that every man is as thoroughly corrupt as he can become or that every man is absolutely unable to do any good deed. But it does mean that every man is born with a corrupt nature, and that he is unable to change his situation on his own.

Vish: If everyone is born with this corrupt nature and cannot change it, how can any one be saved?

2. Man cannot save himself

Paul: Yes, Vish, a very good question. That is the dilemma. If we all have inherited this corrupt nature and are unable to get rid of it, how can we be saved? That is the most important question. Man is not able to do it himself. However, God Almighty in his mercy has opened a way for us. Remember what I said before. On the one hand, God loves us very much, and on the other hand, he is just and holy and therefore must punish disobedience and sin. In order to find a solution to this vexing problem, he found a way; he punished himself by sending his only begotten son to the cross. Thus his Son, Jesus Christ, became our mediator. He is the only mediator between righteous God and sinful man. A good mediator must represent both sides. No other person could do that except the God-man of the Bible (Galatians 4:12).

Vish: How about Rama and Krishna? They were also god-men, weren't they?

Paul: I have to disagree with you, Vish. Why? Because they never showed the characteristics of God. There is a qualitative difference between God and man. God is holy, righteous, just, good, wise, and true. He is eternal, infinite, and unchangeable. Man is the opposite of all these qualities. One is the Creator; the other is the created. God is perfect; man is imperfect. Imperfect man can never become God. Even in the next life, when righteous men will be with him, they can never become gods. I believe all the mythological stories in Hinduism and other religions are attempts by sincere men to minimize the chasm that exists between God and man. Rama and Krishna were hero-kings in their own right, and later generations ascribed divine status to them because of their heroic acts.

Vish: How was Jesus different?

Paul: Jesus was different because evidence suggests that He was. He was not born in a palace; he did not have the upbringing of a prince. No philosopher taught him. He did not fight any battles. He did not defeat any armies. And yet he lived a perfect and spotless life. He taught the greatest teachings. He performed the mightiest deeds. He was put to death the most heinous way. However, he became the greatest victor, even over death when he rose from the dead. He is the only one who had power over life and death. Therefore, he is the only God-man, the only mediator between God and man.

Vish: Yes, when you think about it deeply, the overwhelming evidence seems to suggest that Jesus was different from all other avatars.

(There seems to be a change in Vish. So far, he has been defensive, if not hostile. However, the barrier seems to be broken. So this is the time to point out his sin and need for the Savior.)

D. Salvation

1. Trusting Jesus

Paul: Yes, Vish, he was different because he was God. There was no sin in him. Many Jewish leaders of his day tried to catch him with his words and deeds; however, no one could. He is the only mediator between God and sinful man. When a sinful man accepts him as his personal Savior by faith, He comes into his life and makes him a new creation. The old life is changed into a new life. The bad things you loved before you come to hate, and the good things you hated before you come to love. Faith is trust in Jesus Christ and his cross for all your needs, physical as well as spiritual, including salvation. By a simple act of faith, you transfer your trust from what you have done to what Christ has done for you. Just as we all acquired a sinful nature through our first parents Adam and Eve when they disobeyed God, we acquire righteousness through Christ when we believe on him because of his obedience. In other words, the righteousness of Jesus Christ is imputed to us when we accept him as our Savior. We are counted righteous when we trust him, and all our sins are blotted out as if we have never committed any sin at all. They are forgiven forever and will not be in our account again.

Vish: Can such a man commit sin again, and if he does, will he be forgiven again?

2. Result—A New Creation

Paul: When he accepts Jesus Christ as his personal Savior, his sins are forgiven, and he becomes a new creation. This new creation is a different man altogether. He does not go back to his old ways. However, this does not mean he has become perfect all of a sudden. Let me explain this by an illustration familiar to you, Vish.

Vish: I am all ears.

Paul: The Indian subcontinent was divided into India and Pakistan in 1947. Since then, the two countries have fought three wars. These border wars did not result in the complete surrender of either country to the other. But suppose for a moment India is the good guy and Pakistan is the bad guy. Now suppose India was defeated in the last war and Pakistan's army was controlling New Delhi. India would then not be free to do anything except what Pakistan dictated. But, thank God, India was not defeated and is still a free country. Now, suppose your heart is India, and Pakistan is the Devil. As long as the Devil controls your heart, you are not free to do good things, as your heart is controlled by the Devil and you must act according to his dictates. But when you accept Jesus Christ as your personal Savior, you are no longer controlled by the Devil but by Christ. You have become a new creation and want to obey Christ and do good things. However, just as Pakistan is on the border of India, the Devil is still lurking on the periphery of your heart. Although he does not have dominion over your heart, he is not far away, so you are still susceptible to small temptations. You do not become perfect all of a sudden, but sin will not have any dominion over you.

Therefore, you will not live in sin nor will you commit the same sin again and again.

Have you read the Sermon on the Mount, Vish? It was a favorite with Mahatma Gandhi. I know it was required reading for English majors in colleges in India.

Vish: Yes, I have read it, although I don't remember all the details now.

Paul: The Sermon on the Mount given in Matthew 5 reveals the characteristics of those who inherit the kingdom of God. It is reserved for the poor, the hungry, the meek, those who mourn, those who are merciful, the peacemakers, and the persecuted for the sake of righteousness. The proud, the arrogant, the adulterer, the murderer, those who look at a woman with lust in their hearts, and those who are angry with their brothers are ineligible for the kingdom of heaven. Jesus asks his followers to love their enemies and bless those who persecute them. It is a tall order, isn't it, Vish?

Vish: Yes, indeed. How can anyone then inherit the kingdom of God?

Paul: Very difficult indeed by man's efforts but possible through the righteousness of Christ. If I depend upon my own efforts, good works, and merits, I will not be able to get there. But when I rely on the merits and righteousness of my Lord and Savior, Jesus Christ, almighty God makes it possible for me in spite of my imperfections.

Vish: I think I understand now. But a person who accepts Jesus will not live in sin again, even if he does not become perfect immediately?

Paul: Yes, Vish, that is right. He does not become a super-saint all of a sudden. However, he will not be slave to sin any more.

Vish: That makes me think. If that is the case, why do we see so much sexual freedom and permissiveness in a Christian country like America?

Paul: Very good question indeed, Vish. Not only do we see this in America, we Indians saw that among the British officials in India before independence. And we see it, the so-called Indian Christians became nominal Christians for a variety of reasons. First of all, my friend, it is a mistake to think that all white people are Christians. Many of them are nominal Christians, meaning, in name only. Very few are born-again Christians. Secondly, no country may be termed Christian, Hindu, or Muslim, because countries are lands within specific borders. But you are right; we call this country "Christian" and that country "Hindu" or "Muslim" because a majority of the people follows a particular religion. It is true that some of the early European settlers in America were Christians, and the framers of the constitution and the laws of America were influenced by Christian principles. However, to call America Christian or think that all Americans are Christians is a gross mistake. And you are right; there are more divorces, permissiveness, and sexual immorality in America and "Christian" Europe than anywhere else in the world. But this is so not because of Christianity but in spite of it. It is the result of sin. The Bible condemns such immorality as perversion and abomination. Those who live in sin shall not inherit the kingdom of God. And this takes us to the Bible itself. In the midst of our conversation, Vish, I referred to the Bible several times. I am sure you have read portions of it. Do you know, Vish, what is so unique about it?

Vish: I have some idea, but let me be certain.

E. The Bible

1. **Prophetic**

Paul: The Bible is self-authenticating; that is, what the Bible says is true because it comes to pass. Of all the religious books in the world, the Bible alone has that characteristic. For example, the writings of Buddhism and Confucianism are totally lacking in any predictive prophecy. So is the *Ramayana*, the *Bhagavat Gita*, the Vedas, and the Quran. However, there are about two thousand specific prophecies in the Bible that have been fulfilled. Whatever it predicted came to pass. The Bible contains science, history, and the future of many nations. No one has been able to contradict what is in the Bible.

Vish: I never knew that.

2. **God is Its Author**

Paul: There are sixty-six books in the Bible that were written by forty different authors over a period of sixteen hundred years in different countries and climates. Yet all the books have an underlying unity. This was possible only if God was the author of these books, as these authors did not know one another. Moses was not alive when God created Adam and Eve, our first parents. So how did he know about the creation of the world? The One who created the world revealed it to him. The Bible is the story of Jesus Christ, and the Old Testament foretold his coming. Almost six hundred years before Christ died on the cross of Calvary for you and me, the prophet Isaiah saw it happening when he wrote: "But he was pierced for our transgressions, he was crushed for our iniquities; the punishment that brought us peace was upon him, and by his wounds we are healed" (Isaiah 53:5). And just as it was foretold, the New Testament describes his birth, life, ministry, death, resurrection, ascension and predicts his second coming in the clouds of heaven to judge the world in righteousness. The Bible is the story of redeeming grace, which is why the Bible is called inspired, inerrant, and infallible. It is inspired by God Almighty; it is inerrant, as it is without error; it is infallible, as it is not likely to fail.

Vish: This makes sense to me for the first time, even though I have read portions of it before.

(Vish seems to be convinced of the truth of the Bible. This is the opportunity you have been waiting for. It is important to lead him to trust in Jesus. Therefore, it is time to get a commitment from him at this time.)

III.   The Commitment
A. The Commitment Question

Paul: That is wonderful, Vish. Oh, I am so glad we came to visit you! Vish, you have heard the good news, the gospel of Jesus Christ. You said it made sense to you for the first time. Now the question almighty God is asking you is this, "Do you want to receive the gift of eternal life?" This is the gift that the Son of God left his throne and came to the earth to die for you on the cross and procure for you life eternal. Would you like to receive it?

Vish: Yes, I would. But may I take some time to think about it? It dawned on me all of a sudden. I want to talk to my wife and convince her also.

Paul: Absolutely. I am not asking you to become another nominal Christian. I am not asking you to change your name or renounce your family. However, I am requesting you to make a decision for Christ in your mind. You know our life on this earth is short. I could die today, and so could you. The Bible does not support the theories of karma and rebirth. Do you believe in them, Vish?

Vish: No, I do not. I did not believe in them before either.

Paul: Why not?

Vish: Because I could not remember anything about my past lives. If I could not recall them, how could anyone else?

Paul: You are right. They are not empirically verifiable. But those theories are the incorrect conclusions of two correct understandings. The first is that God is perfect, and therefore, to dwell with him one must be perfect. The second is that man is sinful and in his present condition cannot even approach God. Therefore, it takes millions of cycles of birth and death to reach perfection. Everyone thinks that one day he will arrive by loving his neighbor and performing filial duties. However, this is contrary to the teaching of the Bible, as it declares: "It is appointed unto men once to die, but after this the judgment" (Hebrews 9:27 KJV). So we have only one life to live, and when we leave this life, we must appear before the judgment seat of Christ. So it is very important to make that decision now, if you are convinced of the truth of the Bible. Do you trust Christ and his righteousness for eternal life, Vish, instead of trusting in your own good works?

Vish: Yes, I do, without a shadow of doubt.

B. Clarification of Commitment

Paul: Let me make clear what this involves. It means that you trust Christ and him alone as your Savior. Remember that God is a jealous God. He does not allow worship of other gods or images. This means that you have to renounce the god of your ancestors and the gods of your village. Are you ready to do that?

Vish: Yes, I am.

Paul: When your relatives hear this, they may ostracize you. You don't have to tell them now. However, eventually they will know. Are you ready to suffer all the consequences?

Vish: Yes, I am ready.

Paul: Let me say one more thing, Vish. When Christ comes into a life as Savior, he comes as Lord, Master, and King. He wants to be accepted as the central figure of your life. He is above all earthly connections because he is the one who made you, redeemed you, and bought you with his own blood shed on the cross of Calvary. Are you willing to surrender and yield your life to him out of gratitude for the gift of eternal life?

Vish: Yes, I am.

Paul: He also commands us to repent of our sins. Are you willing to repent of your sins and follow him? That means you are willing to turn away from what you have been doing that is displeasing to him. Repentance is a complete change of mind about life and death, about God and his world, and is brought about by the Holy Spirit working in us, which leads inevitably to a transformed life. Vish, are you willing to repent of your sins and accept Christ as your personal Lord and Savior?

Vish; Yes, I am.

C. Prayer of Commitment

Paul: Vish, the Lord is right here. The Bible tells us, "Salvation is found in no one else, for there is no other name under heaven given to men by which we must be saved" (Acts of the Apostles 4:12). We can go to this Savior in prayer and tell him that you want to put your trust in him for your salvation and receive him as your personal Lord and Savior. Vish, is this you want?

Vish: Yes, I do want to receive him.

Paul: All right, Vish. If this is really what your heart wants, the Lord will hear your prayer and grant you eternal life. Let us pray. Father, I pray that you would grant Vish the gift of eternal life. He was born and brought up in a Hindu family and has been worshipping the gods of his ancestors. However, he wants to accept you as his personal Savior. May your Spirit draw him to you. Grant him faith to believe in your promises and forgiveness of his sins. Reveal to him the crucified Christ today. Give him boldness to witness to his wife, children, and eventually his parents and extended family. In the name of Christ, we pray. Amen.

Vish: Amen.

Paul: Vish, the Lord has said, "For where two or three come together in my name, there am I with them" (Matthew 18:20). He is right here in our midst and is listening. If you want eternal life, will you say to him out loud after me:

> Lord Jesus, I want you to come in and purify me. Lord, I have been following the gods of my ancestors and other strange gods. I confess before you I am a sinner. I have been trusting in my abilities and in my good works so far, but now on I place my trust in you. I know you died for me, and I accept you as my personal Lord and Savior. Please come into my life. Cleanse me and accept me, even though I am not worthy to be called your servant. I thank you for your love. Please help me to convey your love and grace to my wife, children, and parents. In the name of Jesus, I pray. Amen.

Heavenly Father, You have heard the prayer of my friend, Vish. I pray that in this quiet moment the Holy Spirit will grant him the assurance of salvation. Grant him the certainty that his sins are forgiven. Give him the boldness to witness to his wife, children, and extended family. Lead them also to the knowledge of your Son, Jesus Christ, so that all of them together as a family can rejoice in your salvation. In the name of Jesus, we pray. Amen.

D. The Assurance

Paul: Vish, You have prayed the most important prayer of your life, and I want you to hear what Christ says to you: "I tell you the truth; he who believes has everlasting life" (John 6:47). Vish, a great miracle has taken place in your life. By a simple act of faith, you have placed your trust in Jesus Christ for your salvation and eternal life. Isn't it so, Vish?

Vish: Yes, it is so.

Paul: In whom are you trusting, Vish, for your salvation?

Vish: In Jesus Christ alone.

Paul: If you die tonight, where will your soul go?

Vish: To heaven.

Paul: If God asks you why he should admit you into heaven, what would you say to him?

Vish: Because I trust in Jesus Christ, and I am made righteous through his blood.

Paul: Wonderful, Vish. The angels are rejoicing. There is a great commotion in heaven. They are singing with joy and say to you, "Welcome to the family of God."

Vish: Thank you, my friends, for coming to my house today.

Paul: Don't thank us, Vish. Thank the Lord Jesus for sending us to you today. Vish, you have just begun your new life today, and you need the fellowship of other believers. If you want to come to our church next Sunday, give me a call, and I will pick you up. If you want more time to talk to your wife and children, take as much as you like. They will be upset initially, but be patient and talk to them in love. Witness to them boldly but lovingly. The Lord will give you strength.

Vish: Yes, I am going to talk to my wife first as soon as she comes in. I want her to have the peace I have now.

Paul: Very good. At some point, I would like you to testify publicly in water baptism, which is the external sign and symbol of the new life in Christ. However, take your time. Study the Bible. If you have any questions about any passage, give me a call, and we will find answers together. Talk to your relatives in America before you talk to your parents and others in India. They may not like it and may not welcome you into their homes initially. They may call you names and say that you have betrayed them and your ancestors. But sooner rather than later, they will come to accept you because of your sincerity. Are you ready to face all these consequences, Vish?

Vish: Yes, I am. I am the happiest man on Earth. I do not want to give up my Lord Jesus Christ for the whole world.

Paul: God bless you, Vish. Remember what our Lord said: "And every one who has left houses or brothers or sisters or father or mother or children or fields for my sake will receive a hundred times as much and will inherit eternal life" (Matthew 19:29).

Vish: Thank you, my friends.

Paul: Vish, you need to read the Bible daily and search Scripture diligently. You will find many passages to strengthen your faith. Vish, do you have a Bible in your possession?

Vish: Yes, I do. I got one when I was studying in Chennai. I have read it at times but never clearly understood it until today. I am going to dig it out and devour it. Please pray for me and my family.

Paul: Rest assured, we will. Give us a call if you need anything. We will be in touch with you. May God bless you, Vish.

Chapter 13

ANSWERING COMMON OBJECTIONS

A NUMBER OF QUESTIONS and objections have come from US Hindus when the gospel was presented to them. The most common questions and objections, and how I dealt with them are given below.

1. All religions are the same

One of the most common arguments by US Hindus is that all religions are the same. In the survey I conducted, 83.6% of Hindus made this argument (see Table 15). They maintained that all religions teach the same thing, namely to lead a good, moral life. If you do, you will be blessed not only in this life but also in the life hereafter, they argued.

I did not deny that there are sound moral teachings in other religions, including Hinduism. "Do not steal," "Do not commit adultery," "Do not commit murder," etc. are the basic tenets of all religions, it is maintained. Yes, it is quite true, but it is so because these teachings were written by people who were made in the image of a gracious God. However, that image has been tarnished, and man has become corrupt. This is the reason why, in spite of good basic tenets of various religions, no one can follow them. Hence, sinful man needs a mediator, and the only mediator who can reconcile sinful man to holy God is the God-man of the Bible. We have already noted what Acts of the Apostles 4:12 tells us: "Salvation is found in no one else, for there is no other name under heaven given to men by which we must be saved." Therefore, all religions are not the same, as salvation and eternal life are possible only through Jesus Christ.

2. There is only one God, but He manifests himself in different forms

In the survey, 75.1% of Hindus maintained there is only one God, but that he manifests himself in different forms. Some call him Vishnu, others Allah, and still others Christ, but all these are manifestations of the same God.

The first part of the statement is true. There is only one God, and no one is actually ignorant of this mighty God, as God has revealed himself to all mankind in the light of His creation (Romans 1:19–25) and has placed within each man the light of conscience (Romans 2:15). However, in spite of these revelations, men try to "suppress the truth" (Romans 1:18) and "become vain in their imaginations."(Romans 1:21, KJV) The various manifestations of God originate in the imagination of man and are sincere attempts to understand the nature and person of God. In those attempt, they have devised various names and attributes they assign to this imaginary God. The Bible tells us: "For all the gods of the nations are idols, but the Lord made the heavens. Splendor and majesty are before him; strength and glory are in his sanctuary" (Psalm 96:5–6).

The attempts of men to know God were sincere. However, instead of looking at God's creation and seeing the Creator behind it, man relied on his own understanding and came up with various gods. Therefore, almighty God gave special revelation to man and intervened in history:

> In the past God spoke to our forefathers through the prophets at many times and in various ways, but in these last days he has spoken to us by his Son, whom he appointed heir of all things, and through whom he made the universe. The Son is the radiance of God's glory and the exact representation of his being, sustaining all things, by his powerful word (Hebrews 1:1–3).

The only begotten Son of God not only intervened in history and lived among men, but also died for the sins of many:

> He was in the world, and though the world was made through him, the world did not recognize him. He came to that which

was his own, but his own did not receive him. Yet to all who received him, to those who believed in his name, he gave the right to become children of God—children born not out of natural descent, nor of a human decision or of a husband's will, but born of God (John 1:10–13).

There is only one true God, and he is manifested only in Jesus Christ. All others are the results of sincere attempts of men to know and understand God.

3. All religions will take you to the same place

Seventy point four percent of Hindus surveyed argued that all religions will take you ultimately to the same place. They are referring to two things:

a. The idea of a universal liberation because God is kind and merciful; and
b. The place called "heaven" is the same in every religion.

The answer to (a) will be dealt with later. Here, let us deal with (b), namely that heaven is the same in Hinduism and Christianity.

The argument goes some thing like this: One can achieve liberation by following the precepts of one's religion. So why change the religion of your ancestors in which you were raised? Follow what your ancestors have handed down to you and you will follow them to the place where they have gone before you. Therefore, changing religion is unnecessary and uncalled for.

The question then is this: Do all religions take us to the same place? In the Hindu idea of liberation, the soul of an individual, after millions of births, deaths, rebirths, and re-deaths, is released from the cycle and is absorbed into the Universal Spirit.[137] The condition of the soul, which has been absorbed into the Universal Spirit, is in a state of dreamless sleep from which he will never awaken. Swami Nikhilananda speaks of the "boredom of heaven and the contentless existence of the soul there."[138]

This is not the same as salvation and eternal life in heaven with Christ and in the company of the redeemed in Christianity. The life of the redeemed in heaven is not of boredom and contentless existence, as they will have conscious existence and will not lose their individuality. They do no pass

---

137   See chapter 4 for details.

138   Swami Nikhilananda, *The Upanishads* (New York: Harper and Row, 1949) p. 103.

into nothingness. Look at what the book of Revelation describes about this existence in heaven: "They will see his face, and his name will be on their foreheads. There will be no more night. They will not need the light of a lamp or the light of the sun, for the Lord God will give them light. And they will reign forever and ever" (Revelation 22:4–5).

4. Forsaking Hinduism is betrayal of family and caste

Another objection frequently heard is that forsaking Hinduism is a betrayal of family, clan, and caste, which has agitated the minds of many would-be Hindu coverts. Even after they realize the truth of the gospel, the final break with family, clan, and caste is always painful and is interpreted by relatives as betrayal. As a result, many were excommunicated from their caste. In Indian villages, this has created untold suffering to the new convert, as marriage and other social relations are based on caste. In the United States and other Diaspora communities, this was less of a problem. However, this is a problem in this age of instant communication.

This objection comes from several misunderstandings. The first is that every ethnic group must have its own religion. So if you are an Indian, you must be a Hindu, if you are a Caucasian, you must be a Christian, and if you are an Arab, you must be a Muslim, and so on. But this is a false idea of religion, as religion should have no geographic boundaries. After all, Christ died for all who are redeemed by his blood. The benefits of his death should not be limited to a few based on geographic boundaries and ethnic restrictions.

Every religion should have the freedom to attract people of various national and ethnic origins. The battle is for souls, which are colorless. Christianity does not ask for any exclusivity in witnessing to others. But because it is the only revealed religion by a merciful God, men and women from any ethnic or geographic area of the world are welcome to accept Jesus Christ as their personal Lord and Savior. When one accepts Christ as Lord and Savior, it should not be interpreted as betrayal of anyone but rather acceptance of the truth. He should be allowed to witness to other members of his family, clan, tribe, and caste so they too will come to know the truth that will liberate them from their sins and age-old customs and practices.

5. Forsaking Hinduism is betrayal of dead ancestors

Very closely connected with the previous argument is the argument that forsaking Hinduism is betrayal of dead ancestors. It must be noted that when parents die, children of Hindus are obligated to perform certain rituals for the souls of the departed parents to go in peace to their designated places. Absence of male offspring is considered to be a great shame because then there is no one to perform these rituals. Although a close male relative may perform the ritual, it is not the same as if one's own son performed the ritual. If the son becomes a Christian, the result is the same as if he were dead because he then cannot do anything for the departed soul. Therefore, relatives of the Christian convert feel pity for his parents whether they are dead or living, as their souls now or later will have to suffer in the abode of ancestors, as their Christian son is not able to rescue them from the abode of the departed souls.

While the Christian sympathizes with the living parents of the convert, he has no qualms about the dead ancestors. In evangelical Christianity, there is no ritual, prayer, or penance with which the son can even attempt to help the dead ancestors. They are dead and gone, beyond the curtain. What the son does or does not do will have no bearing on the destiny of the dead ancestors. Forsaking Hinduism is no betrayal of living or dead ancestors.

The converted son should have great concern for his living parents, however. He should want them to enjoy the peace and happiness he enjoys since he accepted Jesus Christ as his personal Lord and Savior.

6. Forsaking Hinduism is selfish

Closely connected with the last two arguments is the one that maintains that forsaking Hinduism and accepting Christianity is purely selfish on the part of the converted man. If all his ancestors who have lived and died as Hindus are going to hell, is it not selfish for the converted man to go to heaven to enjoy the so-called blessings there? Since there is no ritual, prayer, or penance in Christianity by which the converted man can take his dead ancestors with him to heaven, why should he be so selfish to go there without the long line of his ancestors?

A twofold answer can be given to this vexing question. The first is that we do not have to make a judgment regarding the eternal destiny of any ancestor. The Lord is the righteous judge. Before Christ came into this world, a number of people lived and died without having heard the name of the Savior, so it does not mean that all of them went to hell. Men are condemned only for their sin, and even before Christ came into the world, God's marvelous grace was operative in the world. The Bible declares that God has revealed himself to all men through the light of his creation and through the light of conscience before he gave the special revelation.[139] So no one can claim total ignorance of the ways of God. Men get precisely what they deserve in light of what they have done, based on what they know and what their conscience has dictated. God will not be unjust to anyone. He will judge everyone according to his righteous standards.

The second reason should further console the intended convert. In heaven our affections will undergo a revolutionary change, so the affection we have in this world for a father, mother, son, daughter, husband, or wife is limited to this world. In the next world, while we will still recognize others, our affection for them will undergo revolutionary and radical changes. There will not be any husbands, wives, fathers, mothers, brothers, or sisters in heaven, as we will be like the angels in our transformed bodies. Therefore, a Hindu need not hesitate to accept the Lord when thinking about his filial affections and duty toward his dead ancestors.

7. Religion is a crutch

THE MOST COMMON OBJECTION raised by secular Hindus is that religion is simply a crutch for the weak, and that the priests and gurus are simply exploiting the weak to serve their ends. They further say that this phenomena has existed since primitive man, afraid of the lightning and thunder, invented a god to whom he could run for refuge in times of trouble.

Modern man may not be afraid of thunder and lightning, but he is still afraid of the unknown, especially life after death. Hence, the need to cling to an abstract idea of a powerful god. In other words, all men, primitive and modern, have some idea of an almighty God, which is seen not only in the most primitive societies of the ancient past, but also in the most rational societies of the present. Even the atheistic rulers of the Soviet Union and Communist China have not been able to wipe out the idea of God from their people, in spite of their ruthless propaganda against God. The truth is, instead of the believer creating an imaginary God to whom he can flee, the atheist has created an imaginary world in which God does not exist in order to flee from a just God who is angry with him because of his sins.

Christianity is not a crutch; it is the only truth, revealed by a gracious God for saving man from his sins and to give him eternal life.

8. The Bible is a book of fairy tales

---

139   See Romans 1:20 and Psalm 19

This is an objection raised by secular Hindus as well as by others. They have heard from liberal Christians or read portions of Scripture about the virgin birth of Christ, the miracles of our Lord, the resurrection, and the ascension, and their rational mind cannot comprehend these things.

Of all the religious texts in the world, the Bible is the most reliable. To go even further, the Bible is the only reliable scripture because it is revealed by God himself. All other religious books were written by sincere men in their honest attempts to learn about God. However, since they were human attempts, they contain errors.

Almost all religious books of Hinduism, including the *Vedas,* the *Upanishads,* the *Ramayana,* and the *Bhagavat Gita,* contain unbelievable mythological stories, and quite often these stories are contradictory. The scriptures of Confucianism, Taoism, Shintoism, and Buddhism contain good, moral stories. However, none of them contain predictive prophecy but are good attempts to regulate society. Even the Quran rises or falls with the testimony of one man, the prophet Muhammad. Moreover, it contradicts the Bible in several instances, which is the older text. Hence, the Quran and the Bible cannot be truth at the same time. The Bible is self-authenticating, containing over two thousand prophecies, and many of them have already been fulfilled:[140]

> You may say to yourselves, "How can we know when a message has not been spoken by the Lord?" If what a prophet proclaims in the name of the Lord does not take place or come true, that is not a message the Lord has spoken. That prophet has spoken presumptuously. Do not be afraid of him (Deuteronomy 18:21–22).

What the prophets of God foretold has come to pass later, and thus, they are vindicated. Besides, the Bible contains science, history, and predictions of the future of many nations. No one has been able to discredit what the Bible says to be true.

The author of the Bible is God himself. He used forty different human authors who lived over a period of sixteen hundred years in different countries and climates and used at least three different languages. And yet there is an underlying unity in all sixty-six books of the Bible. Many of the authors wrote about things that happened thousands of years before them,

---

140   For numerous Old Testament prophecies and New Testament fulfillments, see D. James Kennedy, op. cit. pp. 86-88.

and some about things that will happen thousands of years afterward. How could they know these things unless they were revealed by the all-knowing God?

To sum it up, the Bible is the inspired, inerrant, and infallible Word of God because God is the ultimate author of the Bible.

9. There is no life after death

There are many skeptics among the Diaspora Hindus, especially in the United States, who, like many Westerners, maintain that there is no life after death. The present life is all there is; after death, there is no life. However, the Bible declares unambiguously that there is life after death. Our souls are indestructible, and after death, the souls end up either in heaven or hell where they will continue forever.

Apart from the declarations of the Bible, a growing number of scientists' and medical personnel's investigations have led them to believe that life goes on beyond the grave. Dr. Elizabeth Kubler-Ross, a noted psychiatrist, recently declared at a national conference on "Death, Dying, and Beyond" attended by over one thousand medical professionals at the University of California in Berkeley: "The evidence is now conclusive: there is life after death."[141] These conclusions were reached after interviews with hundreds of people who had been pronounced clinically dead and later revived. Dr. Raymond Moody of the University of Virginia sums up his findings: "There is a buzz or a ring at the moment of death, followed by a rapid progression through an enclosure or tunnel toward light. There is surprise at being outside the body. Next comes a panoramic view of one's life."[142] People who had been paraplegics for years could move, and those who were blind could see clearly during these experiences. Even atheists described seeing a religious figure at a distance.

The Bible tells us there is one with whom we have to do after death, and that one is none other than Jesus Christ. There is no escaping his judgment. There is life beyond the grave. A Christian is confident about it, not because of the testimony of the "clinically dead" but because the Bible says so.

10. Heaven and hell are right here on Earth

SOME HINDUS MAINTAINED THAT heaven and hell were right here on Earth, meaning, if you live a good, moral life, you will be blessed, but if you lead

141   Ibid, p. 102

142   Ibid, p. 103

a wicked life, you will experience hell right here on Earth. They sought the help of Karma doctrine without associating it with reincarnation. In other words, they maintain that whatever you sow, you will reap the consequences, not in a later life, but right here in this life.

This seems to be at least partially right. Most often, we will suffer the consequences of our actions in this life. The Bible maintains that we have a deposit, of our inheritance here in this world. (2 Corinthians 1:22) However, that is not all. A "Deposit" is simply a portion of what is to follow, so a Christian can indeed experience a "deposit" of heaven here on Earth when he puts his trust in Christ, which is why he can sing and shout praises of joy in the midst of suffering. However, those who do not have Christ and lead wicked lives will have the "deposit" of hell right here and much more in full measure in the next world. "Whoever believes in the Son has eternal life, but whoever rejects the Son will not see life, for God's wrath remains on him" (John 3:36).

Instead of emphasizing punishment and eternal damnation, attempts should be made to assure the prospect of the everlasting promise of God that awaits those who trust in Christ.

11. I believe in karma and rebirth

Almost all Hindus believe in karma and rebirth. They maintain that the belief of the transmigration of the soul after death was also prevalent in people of Aryan origin elsewhere. However, karma seems to be peculiarly Indian in origin, as it was the scholarly Brahmins who combined these two theories into a single one of morality and mortality. As proof, it is absent from the earlier Vedic literature of the Aryans.

Apart from the fact that it is not verifiable, such a theory of mortality is absent in any other religious literature. The Bible says, "Just as man is destined to die once, and after that to face judgment, so Christ was sacrificed once to take away the sins of many people." (Hebrews 9:28) The theory of karma and rebirth is an incorrect conclusion drawn from two correct understandings.[143] The first is that to dwell with God, one must be perfect. The second is that man is at present sinful. Therefore, in order to achieve perfection, one must go through a series of births, deaths, rebirths, and re-deaths. Finally, when one achieves perfection, one may be able to dwell with a perfect God.

---

143   See chapter 4

However, this theory is defective for a very simple, valid reason, apart from many other defects and problems in this theory.[144] The simple reason is that even if man is born a thousand times, as he is constituted today with his body and mind, he cannot become perfect, and the lower animals are even worse. According to Hinduism, the Brahmin is the highest form of man from whom the individual soul merges with the Universal Spirit. However, according to many Hindus, the Brahmin priest is probably as greedy if not more so than members of the three other castes.

A Christian need not become perfect on his own to dwell with God. When he confesses his sins, they are wiped from the slate of his life. "Though your sins are like scarlet, they shall be as white as snow; though they are red as crimson, they shall be like wool" (Isaiah 1:18). The atonement of Christ and his perfect righteousness imputed to the believer are sufficient to make him righteous in the sight of God. Such a man will become perfect on account of the righteousness of Christ and will be able to dwell with holy God forever.

12. God is arbitrary and capricious

Several Hindus maintained that at least one of their gods, Vishnu, the preserver, is merciful and loving, but quite often the God of the Christians appears to be arbitrary and capricious. He threatens with vengeance and hell-fire, on the model of Shiva, the destroyer. In Hinduism, there is at least another god, Vishnu, equally powerful to counterbalance the vengeance of Shiva. But in Christianity, there is no one equal to God. Christ may be coequal to God the Father, but he is subject to his Father. Even if they are both part of the Trinity, how can the same God be cruel and merciful at the same time? This results from not understanding the nature and attributes of the Triune God. The doctrine of the Trinity will be explained a little later in this chapter.

God is our father, as he created us, and the fatherhood of man is modeled after the fatherhood of God. Just as a human father loves and disciplines his children, the heavenly Father does the same with his children. However, this heavenly Father is infinitely more gracious, merciful, and patient with all his children. In his goodness, God has not merely decreed to save some but also to reward those who obey and serve him (Isaiah 63:8–9), which originates in his grace. God is entitled to absolute obedience and is not under any obligation to reward anyone. But he does so because of his grace, not because of his justice. However,

---

144   See chapter 4

because of his absolute holiness and justice, he has decreed to punish the wicked and the disobedient. To a great extent, this punishment is meted out during this life, but the real punishment is postponed until the day of judgment (Revelation 20:11–15).

This God is not arbitrary or capricious. His decrees are just and righteous. What he decreed, he decreed freely and voluntarily, not due to mere caprice or arbitrary will. He does not act from mere emotional impulse. He always acts rationally, mercifully, and righteously. We may not always understand his purposes, but his decrees are based on his most wise and holy counsel. If he punishes sinners, it is punishment they deserve.

13. Accept the Lord later

Some Hindus were convinced of the truth in Christianity. They understood God as gracious and forgiving and therefore will think of God and life in the next world much later in life. For the present, though, they will remain Hindus so as not to alienate their family and friends.

The only problem is no one knows exactly when the Lord will call him or her out of this world. Death can come to anyone at any time. Our Lord Jesus Christ told the parable of the rich fool in Luke 12:16–21. After a bumper harvest, he began to take life easy and subscribed to the philosophy of "eat, drink, and be merry." But God asked him, "You fool! This very night your life will be demanded from you. Then who will get what you have prepared for yourself?" (Luke 12:20)

Death comes to everyone like a thief at the most unexpected time. Therefore, if you postpone the decision to accept Christ, you may never get the chance again. Hence, it is absolutely necessary to make the decision of your life at the earliest opportunity. The Lord is a gracious God, but he is also a strict and just God. It is a terrible thing to fall into his hands after continual disobedience and postponement of accepting him as your personal Savior and Lord.

14. Universal Salvation

Many Hindus maintained that God is gracious and therefore will not allow any soul to go to eternal damnation. Everyone will be saved, although it may take millions of cycles of birth and death. "The firm soul hastes, the feeble tarries. All will reach the summit snows."[145]

The idea of universal salvation is foreign to the Bible, as it clearly tells us, "Man is destined to die once and after that to face judgment"

---

145   Edmund D. Soper, op. cit. p. 136

(Hebrew 9:27). Similarly, the Bible clearly tells us that only a portion of mankind will be saved. "Multitudes who sleep in the dust of the earth will awake: Some to everlasting life and others to shame and everlasting contempt" (Daniel 12:2). The Lord Jesus Christ, in his discourse on the day of judgment, painted this picture: "Then he will say to those on his left, 'Depart from me, you who are cursed, into eternal fire prepared for the devil and his angels' ... Then they will go away to eternal punishment, but the righteous to eternal life" (Matthew 25:41–46).

To sum up, the idea of universal salvation is contrary to the Bible. It is the product of human imagination, borne out of the philosophy of humanism.

15. Son of God and Sons of God

Many Hindus are confused by the term *Son of God* when it is used for Jesus Christ. They question, "How is he different from other people who are also called 'sons of God'?" This is not surprising, for in Hindu mythology not only could gods and goddesses cohabit, they also could have sexual relationships with ordinary mortals. Children born out of such unions were classified as semi-gods and demigods. In addition, ordinary mortals could be called sons and daughters of God, as God is the creator of all human beings.

However, Jesus Christ is not a created being. The Bible tells us, "In the beginning was the Word, and the Word was with God and the Word was God" (John 1:1). He was present in creation as the Word, through whom God the Father created the world and everything in it. Christ, the second person of the Trinity, is called God the Son. God is Father, Son, and Holy Spirit; the Trinity is not three Gods but one God existing in three persons. Christ was born as Jesus, the son of Mary and Joseph in his incarnate state, but he existed as the pre-incarnate Christ and will come again at the end of history as post-incarnate Christ. So there was no time when Jesus did not exist. Therefore, when Christ is referred to as the Son of God, he is qualitatively different from ordinary men because he is God and ordinary men are mortals.

Even in the next world, redeemed men cannot become gods. Even in their transformed bodies, they remain created beings and worship Christ as God. The distinction is permanent. Jesus remains God forever, and men remain created beings forever.

16. The Trinity is Difficult to Understand

> The doctrine of Trinity is a very difficult concept to understand and explain because there is nothing to compare. So it remains as a great mystery. "It may appear to some as an intellectual puzzle or a contradiction. The doctrine of Trinity is not an outgrowth of speculation but of revelation."[146]

> The term *trinity* means that there are three eternal distinctions in the one divine essence, known respectively as Father, Son, and Holy Spirit. These three distinctions are three persons, and one may speak of the tripersonality of God. We worship the triune God. The Athanasian Creed expresses the Trinitarian belief thus, "We worship one God in the Trinity, and the Trinity in unity; we distinguish among the persons, but we do not divide the substance." It goes on to say, "The entire three persons are coeternal and coequal with one another, so that … we worship complete unity in Trinity and Trinity in unity."[147]

Thiessen continues his discussion of the Trinity:

> The doctrine of trinity must be distinguished from both Tritheism and Sabellianism. Tritheism denies the unity of the essence of God and holds to three distinct Gods. The only unity that it recognizes is the unity of purpose and endeavor. God is a unity of essence as well as of purpose and endeavor. The three persons are consubstantial. Sabellianism held to a trinity of revelation, but not of nature. It taught that God, as Father, is the creator and lawgiver; as Son, is the same God incarnate who fulfills the office of redeemer; and as Holy Spirit, is the same God in the work of regeneration and

---

146   Henry Clarence Thiessen, *Lectures in Systematic Theology* (Grand Rapids, Michigan: William Eerdmans Publishing Company, 1949) p. 90

147   Ibid, p. 90

sanctification. In other words, Sabellianism taught a modal unity as distinguished from an ontological trinity. Modalism speaks of a threefold nature of God, in the same sense in which a man may be an artist, a teacher and a friend, or as one may be a father, a son and a brother. But this in reality is a denial of the doctrine of trinity, for these are not three distinctions in the essence, but three qualities or relationship in one and the same person.[148]

Even though the term *trinity* does not appear in the Bible, there are enough hints and suggestions throughout the sixty-six books of the Bible expressing the concept. The triune God has revealed it to us in the Bible progressively. The Old Testament contains hints and suggestions: Genesis 19:24 states, "Then the Lord rained down burning sulfur on Sodom and Gomorrah from the Lord out of the heavens." Hosea 1:7 declares, "Yet I will show love to the house of Judah; and I will save them—not by bow, sword, or battle, or by horses and horsemen, but by the Lord their God." Isaiah 48:16 states, "And now the Sovereign Lord has sent me with his Spirit." Psalm 2:7 reads, "I will proclaim the decree of the Lord; He said to me, 'You are my Son; today I have become your Father.'" Genesis 1:1–2 maintains, "In the beginning God created the heavens and the earth. Now the earth was formless and empty, darkness was over the surface of the deep, and the Spirit of God was hovering over the waters."

The New Testament more clearly sets forth the doctrine of the Trinity. Several times, the three persons of the Godhead are shown together and are seemingly on par with one another: At Jesus' baptism, the Spirit descended on him and a voice from God out of heaven identified Jesus as his beloved Son (Matthew 3:16–17); Jesus prayed that the Father would send another comforter (John 14:16); the disciples were asked to baptize in the name of the Father, the Son, and the Holy Spirit (Matthew 28:19); the three persons of the Trinity are associated together in their work (1 Corinth. 12:4–6; Ephesians 1:13–14; Revelation 14:13); and the apostolic benediction unites the three (2 Corinthians 13:14).

The doctrine of the Trinity is not in conflict with the unity of God. There are three persons in the one essence. There is no perfect analogy in human experience to illustrate this great mystery. The analogy of the psychological unity of the human intellect, affections, and will is the closest with which the Trinity can be explained. But even in this analogy, we have

---

148   ibid,

a certain trinity in unity, but no tri-personality in unity of substance. We as finite human beings are limited in our understanding of the infinite God; our minds cannot grasp the full mystery of the Godhead. However, the doctrine of the Trinity has great practical value for the following reasons:

a. It allows for eternal love. Love was before creation, and yet love needs an object. Love is always flowing among the persons of the Trinity, and thus, love finds fulfillment.

b. Only God can reveal God. The infinite God cannot be explained by finite human reason. God the Father sent God the Son, and God the Holy Spirit reveals all things pertaining to God.

c. Without this Trinity, there could be no incarnation, no objective redemption, and no salvation because no one would be capable of acting as a mediator between holy God and sinful man.

Hindus have difficulty understanding the triune God. While Muslims consider the doctrine of the Trinity as blasphemy, Hindus think of the Trinity as tritheism. In the Hindu triads of gods, there are three distinct and separate gods who have three wills and therefore quite often find themselves at loggerheads with one another. However, in the biblical concept of the triune God, there is only one essence and one will, and therefore, they have perfect accord in all matters.

CONCLUSION

INDIA IS THE TRADITIONAL homeland of the Hindus, and about 850 million Hindus live there today. Even though India is closed to foreign missionaries, the Lord, in his mercy has brought about fifty million Hindus to the outside world and has scattered them all over the world.

It is the duty of every born-again Christian to witness to his Hindu neighbors. He should take the initiative to befriend them. They will consider it a great privilege to be greeted by their Christian neighbors. Hindus want to be accepted and appreciated in the foreign land to which they have migrated for better education for themselves and their children and for better employment opportunities. But what they have faced so far is prejudice and hostility. In a study conducted recently of the East Indian immigrants in Toronto, Canada, it was found that 77% of the sample agreed that there is more hostility against South Asians now than in the past.[149]

The study also revealed a fairly consistent degree of misconception and stereotyping against South Asians and African-Americans. Both groups were thought to be unwilling to work as hard as white immigrants, and nearly 25% believed that both groups were inferior to whites. Even though these prejudices are somewhat mitigated by the influx of highly educated information technology, computer, and medical professionals and other skilled workers from India, the old stereotype still persists at least in the minds of older Caucasians in the United States and Canada. Both the South Asian and African-American groups were thought to make greater use of social and welfare services than do white immigrants, although South Asians were seen as using such services less than African-Americans. South Asians were seen to be arrogant and culturally indifferent to be easily absorbed into North American society. Therefore, middle-class white

---

149   George Kurian and Ram P. Srivastava, *Overseas Indians* (Bombay: Vikas Publishing House, n.d.) p. 45.

Americans hate South Asians more than they hate African-Americans, as the children of South Asians compete for the jobs that are open to middle-class Americans.

Two other factors have somewhat changed the attitudes of the majority community, especially in the United States. First is the addition of Hispanics, legal as well as illegal, especially from Mexico, who are involved mostly in low-paying jobs, such as agricultural labor in the South and the West and cheap menial labor in the North. Second is that after the 9/11 bombing of the Twin Towers of the World Trade Center, Muslims from any country, but especially from Pakistan, Afghanistan, Iran, Iraq, and all of the Mediterranean countries, are hated by all the segments of the US population. Quite often, Hindus and Christians from India are included in this category because of their color and facial features. It is impossible to distinguish between Indian Muslims and Hindus, especially the young ones, as neither use their religious symbols in dress or appearance.

In the midst of this widespread prejudice and hatred, Christian acceptance and appreciation will go a long way in befriending their Hindu neighbors. When the Hindus feel accepted, doors of communication will open, as they will then trust the Christian who befriends them. Once a Hindu lady said, "If your Jesus is like you, I want to know him."[150] The life of the Christian should compel his Hindu neighbor to want to know Jesus. Those who see us should be able to see Jesus, as our words, deeds, gestures, behavior, and everyday life should bear witness to the One who revealed himself in grace and in truth while he lived on this earth.

A Christian must remember that the Hindu living in his neighborhood is a vulnerable person and has many felt-needs. He is away from his natural surroundings, so the village god of his ancestors cannot exert any influence upon him in this foreign land. He is free thus from the taboos and customs that would have been his lot if he were still living in his old ancestral village. He is away from his old religion and has not found anything else worthwhile. Mostly, he is influenced by secular and humanistic ideas he has gathered from his peers at work or school and from the liberal press, but he is not satisfied with those decadent ideas. His mind is groping in the dark for something more substantial, powerful, and lasting.

A Hindu is a deeply religious person. Table 9 shows that 71.1% of Hindus surveyed pray frequently or weekly to their gods. Table 11 shows that many of them feel that their gods are not as powerful here in the US as they are in India. However, they still continue to worship them. They

---

150   Donald W. Carruthers, op. cit, p 9

would like to erect new temples in every urban center and put the image of their deity there. Thus, they want to cling to their old beliefs and customs. They still believe that the *Sanatana Dharma* (eternal religion) is good for them in the foreign land.

The problem is that the old pantheistic thought cannot survive in the new land to which they have migrated, as the new generation of Hindus, who are born and brought up in the new land, cannot accept the age-old beliefs of their ancestors. They cannot believe in the cyclic changes of birth and death, the transmigration of the souls, and the caste system that prevails in India. Modern thought simply will not allow faith in many gods or value idols made of clay and metal. Thinking Hindus will be compelled to form new conceptions of God, man, morality, religion, and the ultimate meaning of life.

So the Hindu religion handed down by their ancestors cannot survive in the new lands to which they have migrated. Something else will have to take its place. As the religion of the wandering Indo-Aryans underwent significant changes after they settled in the fertile farmland of the Ganges River, the Hindu settlers on foreign soil must find a new religion that will satisfy their inner urges again. Only Christianity, with its distinct doctrines of Christ and his Cross, the fatherhood of God, the brotherhood of man, salvation, and eternal life in heaven in the company of all the redeemed, will be able to satisfy the Hindus who are seeking the one true God.

It is in this context that the Christian as his neighbor comes into contact with the Hindu. The Christian neighbor has earned the trust and confidence of the Hindu by his kind words and deeds, and by his life he has made of the Hindus neighbor want to know more about his God. At this time, he must introduce the Hindu to the gentle Savior, Jesus, the God who has come down from heaven, not to annihilate, but to live among men and to die on the cross of Calvary to make reconciliation between holy God and sinful man. This high God is not unapproachable. He is very much involved in the mundane affairs of men.

It is not easy for a Hindu to renounce his religion. We have seen that to him forsaking his religion is tantamount to forsaking everything dear to his heart. He will do so only for something that is far better. If your life is no better than his, why would he forsake his religion, tradition, parents, extended family, and clan gods to join you? If by your words and deeds you do not show that your God is better than his god and that your society is better than his society, he will not come. Unfortunately, the nominal

Christians with whom he has come into contact have not shown that they are any better.

Hindus generally do not pray to their gods extemporaneously unless there is a serious problem. From Table 12, we see that a relative is the problem solver for 67.8% of the participants, and priests, gurus, and religious leaders are problem solvers for only 3.9% of the participants. Not a single Hindu mentioned a favorite god or goddess as the first one he goes to when confronted with a serious problem. Only when all other resources fail do they go to their gods and goddesses. When struck by calamities, such as cholera, plague, earthquake, storm, or lack of rain, there is communal prayer in Indian villages. However, they are not accustomed to having an intimate, personal relationship with a god for their daily sustenance and individual counsel.

However, this does not mean that they are less religious than other groups. They are in the foreign land for education, employment, and financial well-being. They have a lot of felt-needs in the foreign land. As a group, they are vulnerable in the foreign land to which they have migrated and are not sure about the ability of their gods to help them here, where their gods are less powerful. And they have not come across any other gods or philosophic ideas to depend on. The humanistic philosophy of the liberals cannot sustain them here. Fifty-seven point two percent have never visited a church. Even the 42.8% that has been to a church may have gone to a liberal church where the crucified, resurrected, and soon-coming Christ was not proclaimed as Savior and Lord.

Eighty-five percent of them have red the Bible at least once (Table 16). However, they read it because as an English textbook they had to study it in their high school classes. They have known Jesus Christ as an ideal man, a great teacher, or a martyr and may even give him a place of honor equal to that of Krishna or Rama. However, they have not seen Jesus Christ as personal Lord and Savior.

To the question, "Does your religion satisfy you?" none of the participants said that it satisfies him completely (Table 14). 15.1 % said to a great extent and 38.8 % to some extent. 31.6 % said poorly and 9.2 % not at all. Thus, a great majority of them are not at all satisfied with Hinduism, which is distant and contradictory. In India, he could not get out of it because of various family, caste, and social obligations. However, in this foreign land, he is not under such pressures and obligations.

This is the context in which the evangelical Christian meets his Hindu neighbor, who is more open to the gospel than before. Friendship evangelism is the most effective method of witnessing to the Hindus. Bible study, prayer meetings, neighborhood campaigns, tract distribution, street corner meetings, radio and television evangelism, etc. are less effective and more costly. Friendship evangelism requires time and effort but is worthwhile.

Every born-again, evangelical Christian must show that he is indeed redeemed by the blood of the Lamb shed on the cross of Calvary through his words and deeds. The Christian churches and communities must show that they are a new people, separated from the world, called out by the risen Lord, and that their lives are marked by compassion and sacrificial love to the Hindu neighbors in their midst. They should be able to see Jesus Christ as the answer to all their felt-needs and problems in the foreign land through the lives and testimonies of their Christian friends.

The Lord in his wisdom has brought more than fifty million Hindus to the outside world from India. May the Hindu Diaspora be able to see Jesus Christ as the all-sufficient God who came down from heaven to redeem mankind, not to kill a wicked king but from the wicked ruler of the world, Satan himself. The risen Lord is the only Savior who can save Hindus from their sins and give them not only liberation from the cycles of birth, death, and re-birth, but also eternal salvation in the company of the redeemed forever.

Appendix

Questionnaire to Diaspora Hindus

This questionnaire was used to survey the opinions of Diaspora Hindus in Flushing, New York City. The questions are in three categories:

    i.   Personal Background
    ii. Religious/Social Background
    iii. Knowledge of Christianity

i. Personal Background

1. Your name (optional): _____
2. Age: _____
3. Gender: _____ Male _____Female
4. Caste/sub-caste (optional):
5. Employment (What do you do for a living in the US?)
6. Education (Highest general and professional/technical qualification) _____
7. Where did you come from? _____

Born in the US _____

Directly from India _____

After living elsewhere at least one year _____

8. Generation in the US

    _____ First Generation: How old were you when you came to the US?

    _____ Second Generation

    _____ Third Generation or more

ii. Religious/Social Background

9. How often do you go to a temple?

    _____ Daily

    _____ Weekly

_____ Frequently
_____ Rarely
_____ Never

10. How often do you pray/chant/read scripture/worship your favorite deity?

_____ Daily
_____ Weekly
_____ Frequently
_____ Rarely
_____ Never

11. Who is your favorite god/goddess:

_____ Shiva or one of his associates
_____ Vishnu or one of his associates
_____ Brahma or one of his associates
_____ Other (Mention Name): _____
_____ Don't Know
_____ None in particular

12. Do you think your favorite deity is as powerful in America as he/she is in your ancestral place in India?

_____ More Powerful
_____ Less Powerful
_____ The Same
_____ Don't know

13. When you are faced with a difficult problem, to whom do you go first?

_____ Relative
_____ Friend
_____ Neighbor
_____ Priest/Guru/Religious Leader
_____ Favorite god/goddess
_____ Other (Mention Relationship) _____

14. What are your priorities here? (Put 1 for the most important, 2 for the next
Important, and so on to 6 for the least important)

_____ Education for you and/or your children

_____ Good Employment

_____ Finance

_____ Housing

_____ Religious Life

_____ Social/Cultural Life

15. Does your religion satisfy you?

_____ Completely

_____ To a Great Extent

_____ Fairly

_____ Poorly

_____ Not at all

_____ No Comment

iii. **Knowledge of Christianity**

16. Have you been to a church?

_____ Never

_____ Once

_____ More than Once

_____ Many Times

17. Hove you read the Bible or any portion of it?

_____ Never

_____ Once

_____ More than Once

_____ Many Times

18. Have you heard the name of Jesus?

_____ Yes _____ No

19. What do you think of Jesus Christ? (Choose one only)

_____ Almighty God

_____ An Incarnation

_____ Great Teacher

_____ Martyr

_____ Don't know

_____ Other (Please name) _____

20. How would you rate him in comparison to Krishna, Rama, or any other god in Hinduism?

_____ The Same

_____ Better Incarnation

_____ Worse Incarnation

_____ Don't Know

_____ No comment

21. What do you like about Christianity? (Mention as many things as possible)

22. What do you dislike about Christianity? (Mention as many things as possible)

23. What arguments can you give in defense of Hinduism? (Mention as many as possible)

24. Any other comments to help me to understand Diaspora Hinduism?

BIBLIOGRAPHY

Akhilananda, Swami. *Hindu View of Christ*. New York: Philosophical Library, 1949.

Albrecht, Mark C. *Reincarnation, a Christian Appraisal*. Downers Grove, Ill.: InterVarsity, 1982.

Aldwinckle, Russell F. *Jesus: A Savior or the Savior*. Macon, GA: Mercer University Press, 1982.

Allen, Roland. *Missionary Methods: St. Paul's or Ours*. London, U.K.: World Dominion Press, 1960.

———. *Missionary Principles*. Grand Rapids, MI: William B. Eerdmans, 1964.

———. *The Spontaneous Expansion of the Church*. London, U.K.: World Dominion Press, 1927.

Alphonse, Martin. *The Gospel for the Hindus*. Chennai, India: Mission Educational Books, 2001.

Anderson, Gerald H., ed. *Asian Voices in Christian Theology*. Maryknoll, NY: Orbis Books, 1976.

——— ed. *Sermons to Men of Other Faiths and Traditions*. Nashville, TN: Abington Press, 1966.

———, and Thomas F. Stransky, eds. *Christ's Lordship and Religious Pluralism*. Maryknoll, NY: Orbis Books, 1981.

Anderson, J. N. D., *Christianity and Comparative Religion*. Downers Grove, IL: InterVarsity, 1970.

———. *Christianity: The Witness of History*. London, U.K.: Tyndale Press, 1969.

———. *Christianity and World Religions*. Downers Grove, IL: InterVarsity, 1984.

Anderson, Sir Norman. *The World's Religions*. Grand Rapids, MI: William B. Eerdmans, 1976.

Appasamy, A. J. *The Gospel and India's Heritage*. London, U.K.: SPCK Press, 1942.

Appasamy, A. J. "Christian Theology in India." *International Review of Missions* 38, no. 150 (1949): 149–155.

Asirvatham, Eddy. *Christianity in the Indian Crucible*, 2nd rev. ed. Calcutta, India: YMCA, 1957.

Aswametham, New York, 9, no. 10 (1987): 19

Athyal, Saphir, ed. *Church in Asia Today*. Singapore: Asia Lausanne Committee for World Evangelization, 1996.

Athyal, Saphir P. "Israel Among the Nations— A Confrontation of Faiths." *Religion and Society* 14, no. 1 (1967): 21–30.

Auboyer, Jeannine. *Daily Life in Ancient India*. London, U.K.: Phoenix Press, 1965.

Ayrookuzhiel, A. M. Abraham. *The Sacred in Popular Hinduism*. Madras, India: Christian Literature Society, 1983

Baago, Kaj. *Pioneers of Indigenous Christianity*. Madras, India: Christian Literature Society, 1967.

Bandopadhyaya, Hari B. *Hindu Religion and Cultures: A Scientific Discussion*. Calcutta, India: Sahitya Sree, 1972.

Barrett, David B., ed. *World Christian Encyclopedia*. New York, NY: Oxford University Press, 1982.

Basham, A. L. *The Wonder That Was India*. New York, NY: MacMillan, 1954.

Barttacharya, Haridas. *The Foundations of Living Faiths*. Calcutta, India: University of Calcutta, 1938.

Bavinck, J. H. *The Church between the Temple and Mosque*. Grand Rapids, MI: William B. Eerdmans, 1981.

———. *An Introduction to the Science of Missions*. Translated by David Hugh Freeman. Philadelphia, PA: P & R Publishing, 1960.

Berger, Peter L. *The Sacred Canopy*. New York, NY: Anchor Books, 1969.

Berkhof, Louis. *Systematic Theology*, 4th ed. Grand Rapids, MI: William B. Eerdmans, 1974.

Beyerhaus, Peter. *Bangkok 73: The Beginning or End of World Mission?* Grand Rapids, MI: Zondervan, 1973.

———. *Missions: Which Way?* Grand Rapids, MI: Zondervan, 1971.

———. *Shaken Foundations*. Grand Rapids, MI: Zondervan, 1972.

———, and Henry Lefever. *The Responsible Church and the Foreign Mission*. Grand Rapids, MI: William B. Eerdmans, 1964.

Blauw, Johannes. *The Missionary Nature of the Church*. Grand Rapids, MI: William B. Eerdmans, 1974.

Boa, Kenneth. *Cults, World Religions, and You*. Wheaton, IL: Victor Books, 1986.

Bockmuehl, Klaus. *The Challenge of Marxism*. Downers Grove, IL: InterVarsity, 1980.

Boer, Harry R. *Pentecost and Missions*. Grand Rapids, MI: William B. Eerdmans, 1975.

Bonino, Jose Miguez. *Doing Theology in a Revolutionary Situation*. Philadelphia, PA: Fortress Press, 1975.

Bose, Ashish. *India's Urbanisation, 1901–2001*. New Delhi, India: Tata McGraw Hill, 1978.

————. *Population of India, 2001 Census Results and Methodology*. Delhi, India: B. R. Publishing, 2001

Bose, Abinash Chandra. *Hymns from the Vedas*. Bombay, India: Asia Publishing House, 1966.

Bouquet, A. C. *Hinduism*. London, U.K.: Hutchinson University Library, 1969.

Boyd, R. H. S. *India and the Latin Captivity of the Church*. London, U.K.: Cambridge University Press, 1974.

————. *An Introduction to Indian Christian Theology*. Madras, India: Christian Literature Society, 1969.

Bradley, David G. *A Guide to the World's Religions*. Englewood Cliffs, NJ: Prentice-Hall, 1963.

Braybrooke, Marcus. *The Undiscovered Christ*. Madras, India: Christian Literature Society, 1973.

Brockington, J. L. *The Sacred Thread*. Edinburgh, U.K.: University Press, 1981.

Brown, Brian, ed. *The Wisdom of the Hindus*. New York, NY: Garden City Publishing, 1938.

Brown, L. W. *The Indian Christians of St. Thomas*. London, U.K.: Cambridge University Press, 1956.

Burkle, Horst, Wolfgang Horst, and M. W. Roth, eds. *Indian Voices in Today's Theological Debate*. Lucknow, India: Lucknow Publishing House, 1972.

Carey, George. *A Tale of Two Churches*. Downers Grove, IL: InterVarsity, 1985.

Carruthers, Donald W. *How to Share Your Faith*. Atlanta, GA: Lay Renewal Publications, 1968.

Cave, Sydney. *Redemption, Hindu and Christian.* London, U.K.: Oxford University Press, 1919.

Chambers. Margaret. *Reaching Asians Internationally,* Wayne, NJ: International Missions, 1984.

Chandler, Paul Gordon. *Divine Mosaic.* London, U.K.: SPCK, 1997.

Chandran J. Russell. "Baptism—A Scandal or a Challenge." *Religion and Society* 19, no. 1 (1972): 51–58.

Chang, Lit-Sen. *Strategy of Missions in the Orient.* Philadelphia, PA: P & R Publishing, 1968.

Chetthimattam, John Britto, ed. *Unique and Universal: Fundamental Problems of an Indian Theology.* Bangalore, India: Center for the Study of World Religions, 1972.

Clark, Gordon H., et al. *Can I Trust the Bible?* Chicago, IL: Moody Press, 1963.

Clasper, Paul. *Eastern Paths and the Christian Way.* Maryknoll, NY: Orbis Books, 1982.

Clements, R. D. *God and the Gurus.* Downers Grove, IL: InterVarsity, 1975.

Clowney, Edmund P. *Preaching and Biblical Theology.* Nutley, NJ: P & R Publishing, 1973.

Clowney, Edmund P. "Contextualization and the Biblical Theology of Culture." *Contextualization Study Group,* Jan 29–31, 1976. Abington, PA: Partnership in Mission, 1976.

Coggins, Wade T., and E. L. Frizen, eds. *Evangelical Missions Tomorrow.* Pasadena, CA: William Carey Library, 1977.

Cole, T. F. "The Expression of Alienation in Indigenous Indian Theology." *Theology and the Church* 9, no. 4 (1971): 20–40.

Coleman, Robert E. *The Master Plan of Evangelism.* Old Tappan, NJ: Revell, 1963.

Conn, Harvie M. *Evangelism: Doing Justice and Preaching Grace.* Grand Rapids, MI: Zondervan, 1982.

_____. *Reaching the Unreached.* Philipsburg, NJ: P & R Publishing, 1984.

_____, ed. *Theological Perspectives on Church Growth.* Nutley, NJ: P & R & P Publishing, 1976

Corduan, Winfried. *Pocket Guide to World Religions.* Downers Grove, IL: InterVarsity, 2006.

Costas, Orlando E. *The Church and Its Mission: A Shattering Critique from the Third World.* Wheaton, IL: Tyndale House, 1974.

———— *The Integrity of Mission*. New York, NY: Harper & Row, 1979.

Coward, Harold, John R. Hinnells, and Raymond Brady, eds. *The South Asian Religious Diaspora in Britain, Canada, and the United States*. Albany, NY: State University of New York Press, 2000.

Cox, Harvey. *Many Mansions*. Boston, MA: Beacon Press, 1988.

————. *The Secular City*. New York, NY: Macmillan, 1965

Cragg, Kenneth. *Christianity in World Perspective*. New York, NY: Oxford University Press, 1968.

Crooke, W. *The Popular Religion and Folklore of Northern India*, 2 vols. Delhi, India: Munshiram Manoharlal, 1968.

Crow, G. R. *The Guru*. Bombay, India: Gospel Literature Service, 1972.

————. *The Guru and You*. Bombay, India: Gospel Literature Service, 1972.

Culver, Robert Duncan. *A Great Commission: A Theology for World Missions*. Chicago, IL: Moody Press, 1984.

Danielou, A. *Hindu Polytheism*. New York, NY: Bollingen Foundation, 1964.

David, George. *Communicating Christ among Hindu Peoples*. Chennai, India: CBMTM Publications, 1998.

Dayton, Edward R., and Samuel Wilson. *The Future of World Evangelization: Unreached Peoples '84*. Monrovia, CA: MARC, 1984.

DeRidder, Richard R. *Discipling the Nations*. Grand Rapids, MI: Baker Book House, 1974.

Deshpande, P. Y. "Genesis—A Hindu Reflection on the Bible." *Journal of Ecumenical Studies* 8, no. 3 (1971): 575–580.

Devanandan, P. D. *The Concept of Maya*. London, U.K.: Lutterworth Press, 1951.

————. *The Gospel and Renascent Hinduism*. London, U.K.: SCM Press, 1959.

————. *Presenting Christ to India*. Madras, India: Christian Literature Society for India, 1957.

————. "The Christian Attitude and Approach to Non-Christian Religions." *International Review of Missions* 41, no. 162 (1952): 177–184.

————. "The Nature of Ultimate Truth: The Christian Understanding." *Religion and Society* 9, no. 3 (1962): 7–13.

Devaraja, Nand Kishore. *Hinduism and Christianity*. Bombay, India: Asia Publishing House, 1969.

Dhavamony, Mariasusai. *Classical Hinduism*. Rome: Gregorian University Press, 1982.

D'souza, Joseph. *Dalit Freedom—Now and Forever*. Secunderabad, India: OM Books, 2004.

Dubois, J. A., and H. K. Beauchamp. *Hindu Manners, Customs, and Ceremonies*. Oxford, U.K.: Clarindon Press, 1906.

Dyck, Paul I. *Emergence of New Castes in India*. Winnipeg, Canada: University of Manitoba, 1970.

Elkholy, Abdo A. *Religion and Assimilation in Two Muslim Communities in America*. Ann Arbor, MI: University Microfilms, Inc., 1960.

Elwell, Walter A., ed. *Evangelical Dictionary of Theology*. Grand Rapids, MI: Baker Book House, 1984.

Elwood, Douglas J., ed. *Asian Christian Theology: Emerging Themes*. Philadelphia, PA: The Westminster Press, 1980.

Fallon, P. "A Critical Evaluation of the Hindu Interpretation of Christ." *India Journal of Theology* 15, no. 4 (1966): 150–153.

Farquhar, J. N. *The Crown of Hinduism*. London, U.K.: Oxford University Press, 1971.

———— *A Primer on Hinduism*. New Delhi, India: Bharatiya Book Corporation, 1976.

Fife, Eric S., and Arthur F. Glasser. *Missions in Crisis*. Chicago, IL: InterVarsity, 1961.

Firth, C. B. *An Introduction to Indian Church History*. Madras, India: Christian Literature Society, 1961.

Fleming, Bruce C. E. *Contextualization of Theology*. Pasadena, CA: William Carey Library, 1980.

Fleming, Robert L. *India, Past and Present*. Mysore City, India: Wesley Press and Publishing House, 1949.

Forman, Charles W. "Freedom of Conversion: The Issue in India." *International Review of Missions* 45, no. 178 (1956): 180–193.

Freud, Sigmund. *Totem and Taboo*. New York, NY: Vintage Books, 1918.

Gandhi, M. K. *An Autobiography*. Ahmedabad, India: Navajivan Publishing House, 1927.

Geehan, E. R., ed. *Jerusalem and Athens*. Philadelphia, PA: P & R Publishing, 1971.

Geisler, Norman L. *From God to Us*. Chicago, IL: Moody Press, 1974.

————, and William E. Nix. *A General Introduction to the Bible*. Chicago, IL: Moody Press, 1968.

George, Sam. *Understanding the Coconut Generation*. Niles, IL: Mall Publishing, 2006.

Gerber, Virgil. *God's Way to Keep a Church Going and Growing*. Pasadena, CA: William Carey Library, 1973.

_____. *Missions in Creative Tension*. Pasadena, CA: William Carey Library, 1971.

Gerstner, John H. *The Theology of the Major Sects*. Grand Rapids, MI: Baker Book House, 1960.

Gidoomal, Ram, and Mike Fearson. *Karma 'n' Chips*. London, U.K.: Wimbledon Publishing Company, 1994.

_____, and Margaret Wardell. *Lions, Princesses, Gurus*. Godalming, Surrey, U.K.: Highland Books, 1996.

Glasser, Arthur F., and Donald A. McGarran. *Contemporary Theologies of Mission*. Grand Rapids, MI: Baker Book House, 1983.

Greenlee, David, ed. *Global Passion*. Waynesboro, GA: Authentic Lifestyle, 2003.

Greenway, Roger S., ed. *Guidelines for Urban Church Planning*. Grand Rapids, MI: Baker Book House, 1976.

_____. *An Urban Strategy for Latin America*. Grand Rapids, MI: Baker Book House, 1973.

Griffiths, Bede. *Christ in India—Essays towards a Hindu-Christian Dialogue*. New York, NY: Charles Scribner's Sons, 1966.

The Hymns of the Rig Veda. Translated by Ralph T. Griffiths. Banares, India: E. J. Lazarus and Co., 1896.

Guha, Ramachandra, *India after Gandhi*. New York, NY: HarperCollins Publishers, 2007.

_____, ed. *Makers of Modern India*, Cambridge, MA and London, England, The Belknap Press of Harvard University Press, 2011

Guinness, O. S. *The Dust of Death*. Downers Grove, IL: InterVarsity, 1973.

Gupta, S. M., *Vishnu and His Incarnations*. Bombay, India: Somaiya Publications, 1974.

Gutierrez, Gustavo. *A Theology of Liberation*. Translated by Sister Caridad and John Eagleson. Maryknoll, NY: Orbis Books, 1973.

Haigh, Henry. *Some Leading Ideas of Hinduism*. London, U.K.: Charles H. Kelley, 1903.

Hardwick, Charles. *Christ and Other Masters*. London, U.K.: MacMillan, 1874.

Hedlund, Roger E. *Church Growth in the Third World*. Bombay, India: Gospel Literature Service, 1977.

Hendricks, Howard G. *Say It with Love*. Wheaton, IL: Victor Books, 1974.

Hendry, George S. *The Gospel of the Incarnation*. Philadelphia, PA: Westminster Press, n.d.

Herman, A. L. *An Introduction to Indian Thought*. Englewood Cliffs, NJ: Prentice-Hall, 1976.

Hesselgrave, David J. *Communicating Christ Cross-Culturally*. Grand Rapids, MI: Zondervan, 1978.

———, ed. *Theology and Mission*. Grand Rapids, MI: Baker Book House, 1978.

Hick, John. *God Has Many Names*. London, U.K.: MacMillan, 1980.

———, and Brian Hebblethwaite. *Christianity and Other Religions*. Philadelphia, PA: Fortress Press, 1980.

Hierbert, Paul G. *Cultural Anthropology*. Grand Rapids, MI: Baker Book House, 1983.

Hinnells, John R., and Eric J. Sharp. *Hinduism*. New Castle upon Tyne, England: Oriel Press, 1972.

Hiriyana, M. *The Essentials of Indian Philosophy*. London, U.K.: George Allen and Unwin, 1932.

Hoffman, Mark S., ed. *World Almanac 1987*. New York, NY: Barrows Books, 1987.

Hogg, A. G. *The Christian Message to the Hindu*. London, NY: SCM Press, 1947.

———. *Karma and Redemption*. Madras, India: Christian Literature Society, 1970.

Hoke, W. R. *Each One Win One*. Allahabad, India: Allahabad Bible Seminary, 1972.

Holland, Barron. *Popular Hinduism and Hindu Mythology*. Westport, CT: Greenwood Press, 1979.

Hollis, A. M. "The New Testament and the Christian Ministry in India." *Southeast Asia Journal of Theology* 2, no. 1 (1960): 6–11.

Hopkins, Thomas J. *The Hindu Religious Tradition*. Encins, CA: Dickinson Publishing Co., 1971.

Howells, George. *The Soul of India*. London, U.K.: James Clarke & Co., 1910.

Hutton, J. H. *Caste in India: Its Nature, Function, and Origins*. London, U.K.: Oxford University Press, 1963.

Irudayaraj, X. "An Attempt at an Indian Christology." *Indian Ecclesiastical Studies* 9 (1971): 125–131.

Immanuel, R. D. *The Influence of Hinduism on Indian Christians*. Jabalpur, India: Leonard Theological College, 1950.

International Missionary Society. *The Growing Church*. Vol. 2. The Madras Series. New York, NY: International Missionary Council, 1939.

Jaisingh, Herbert. *My Neighbors: Men of Different Faiths*. Bangalore, India: CISRS, 1966.

Jaisingh, Herbert. "Christian Conversion in a Hindu Context," *Ecumenical Review* 19, no. 3 (1967): 302–306.

Jha, D. N. *The Myth of the Holy Cow*. New York, NY: Verso, 2002.

John, Mathew P. "The Idea of Grace in Christianity and Hinduism," *Indian Journal of Theology*, Vol. XIX, No. 2 (1970), 59-73.

Jones, E. Stanley, *The Christ of the Indian Road*. New York, NY: The Abingdon Press, 1925.

Jung, C. G. *Psychology & Religion*. London, U.K.: Yale University Press, 1938.

Kane, Herbert J. *A Global View of Christian Missions*. Grand Rapids, MI: Baker Book House, 1971

———. *Winds of Change in the Christian Mission*. Chicago, IL: Moody Press, 1973.

Kelly, J. N. D. *Early Christian Doctrines*. New York, NY: Harper & Row, 1960.

Kennedy, D. James. *Evangelism Explosion*. Wheaton, IL: Tyndale House, 1977.

Kirk, James A. *Stories of the Hindus*. New York, NY: MacMillan, 1972.

Knitter, Paul. *No Other Name*. Maryknoll, NY: Orbis Books, 1985.

Koshy, Ninan. *Caste in the Kerala Churches*. Bangalore, India: Christian Institute for the Study of Religion and Society, 1968.

Koshy, T.E. *Brother Bakht Singh of India*. Secunderabad, India: OM Books, 2003

Kraemer, Hendrik. *The Christian Message in a Non-Christian World*. Grand Rapids, MI: Kregel Publications, 1969.

———. *Why Christianity of All Religions?* London, U.K.: Lutterworth Press, 1962.

Kuiper, R. B. *God-Centered Evangelism*. Grand Rapids, MI: Baker Book House, 1961.

Kulandran, S. Grace. *A Comparative Study of the Doctrine in Christianity and Hinduism*. London, U.K.: Lutterworth Press, 1964.

Kurian, George, and Ram P. Srivastara. *Overseas Indians*. Bombay, India: Vikas Publishing House, n.d.

Kurian, V. T. "A Strategy for Theological Education in an Era of Ecumenism." *The Indian Journal of Theology* 22, no. 2 (1973): 58.

Kuruvilla, K. K. *A History of the Marthoma Church and Its Doctrines*. Madras, India: Christian Literature Society, 1951.

LaBrack, Bruce Wilfred. *The Sikhs of Northern California: A Socio-Historical Study*. Ann Arbor, MI: University Microfilms, 1980.

Lamb, C. A. *Jesus through Other Eyes*. Oxford, U.K.: Latimer Press, 1982.

Latourette, Kenneth Scott. *A History of the Expansion of Christianity*, Vol. 1, *The First Five Centuries*. New York, NY: Harper & Row, 1937.

———. *A History of the Expansion of Christianity*. Vol. 2, *The Thousand Years of Uncertainty*. New York, NY: Harper & Row, 1938.

———. *A History of the Expansion of Christianity*. Vol. 3, *Three Centuries of Advance*. New York, NY: Harper & Row, 1939.

———. *A History of the Expansion of Christianity*. Vol. 4, *The Great Century: Europe and the United States*. New York, NY: Harper & Row, 1941.

———. *A History of the Expansion of Christianity*. Vol. 5, *The Great Century: The Americas, Australasia, and Africa*. New York, NY: Harper & Row, 1943.

———. *A History of the Expansion of Christianity*. Vol. 6, *The Great Century: North Africa and Asia*. New York, NY: Harper & Row, 1944.

———. *A History of the Expansion of Christianity*. Vol. 7, *Advance through Storm*. New York, NY: Harper & Row, 1945.

———. *History of Christianity*. New York, NY: Harper & Row, 1953.

Lausanne Committee for World Evangelization. *Christian Witness to Hindus*. Lausanne Occasional Papers. Wheaton, IL: Lausanne Committee for World Evangelization, 1980.

Lazerberg, H. "Background and Future Perspectives of Indian Mission." *Church Growth Bulletin* 58 (1969): 172–180.

Little, Paul E. *How to Give Away Your Faith*. Downers Grove, IL: InterVarsity, 1966.

Luke, P. Y., and John B. Carman. *Village Christians and Hindu Culture*. London, U.K.: Lutterworth Press, 1968.

Lum, Ada. *A Hitchhiker's Guide to Missions*. Downers Grove, IL: InterVarsity, 1984.

Lutz, Lorry. *Destined for Royalty*. Pasadena, CA: William Carey Library, 1985.

Luzbetak, Louis J. *The Church and Cultures*. Pasadena, CA: William Carey Library, 1970.

Macaulay, J. C., and Robert H. Belton. *Personal Evangelism*. Chicago, IL: Moody Press, 1965.

Mahadevan, T. M. P. *Outlines of Hinduism*. Bombay, India: Chetana Ltd., 1956.

Maharaj, Rabindranath R., and Dave Hunt. *Death of a Guru*. Burlington, Ontario: Welch Publishing Company Inc., 1977.

Majumdar, D. N. *Caste and Communication in an Indian Village*. Bombay, India: Asia Publishing House, 1962.

Malinowski, Bronislaw. *Magic, Science, and Religion*. Garden City, NY: Anchor Books, 1954.

Mangalwadi, Vishal. *India: The Grand Experiment*. Farnham, Surrey, U.K.: Pippa Rann Books, 1997.

————. *Missionary Conspiracy: Letters to a Postmodern Hindu*. Mussoorie, India: Nivedit Good Books Distributors Pvt. Ltd., 1996.

————. *Truth and Social Reform*. New Delhi, India: Nivedit Good Books Distributers Pvt., 1986.

————. *When the New Age Gets Old*. Downers Grove, IL: InterVarsity, 1992.

————. *The World of Gurus*. New Delhi, India: Vikas Publishing House, 1977.

Manikam, Rajah B. *Christianity and the Asian Revolution*. New York, NY: Friendship Press, 1955.

Mathew, C. P., and M. M. Thomas. *The Indian Churches of Saint Thomas*. Delhi, India: ISPCK, 1967.

Mathew, C. V. *The Saffron Mission*. Delhi, India: Indian Society for the Promoting Christian Knowledge, 1999.

Mayers, Marvin K. *Christianity Confronts Culture: A Strategy for Cross-Cultural Evangelism*. Grand Rapids, MI: Zondervan, 1974.

Mozoomdar, P.C. *The Oriental Christ*. Boston, MA: George H. Ellis Co. 1883.

McGavran, Donald A. *The Bridges of God*. London, U.K.: World Dominion Press, 1955.

————, ed. *Church Growth and Christian Mission*. New York, NY: Harper & Row, 1965.

_____. *The Clash between Christianity and Cultures*. Washington, DC: Canon Press, 1974.

_____, ed. *Cultural Issues in Missions Tomorrow*. Chicago, IL: Moody Press, 1972.

_____. *Ethnic Realities and the Church: Lessons from India*. Pasadena, CA: William Carey Library, 1979.

_____, ed. *Eye of the Storm*. Waco, TX: Word Press, 1972.

_____. *How Churches Grow*. New York, NY: Friendship Press, 1966.

_____.*The Satnami Story*. Pasadena, CA: William Carey Library, 1990.

_____. *Understanding Church Growth*. Grand Rapids, MI: William B. Eerdmans, 1970.

_____. "New Methods for a New Age in Mission." *International Review of Missions* (1955): 402.

McKenzie, J. *Hinduism and Christianity*. London, U.K.: Lutterworth Press, 1950.

McQuilkin, J. Robertson. *Measuring the Church Growth Movement*. Chicago, IL: Moody Press, 1973.

Miller, Calvin. *Transcendental Hesitation*. Grand Rapids, MI: Zondervan, 1977.

Minz, Nirmal. *Mahatma Gandhi and Hindu-Christian Dialogue*. Madras, India: Christian Literature Society, 1970.

Monier-Williams, Sir M. *Religious Thought and Life in India*. New Delhi, India: Oriental Books Reprint Corporation, 1974.

Moraes, George Mark. *A History of Christianity in India*. Bombay, India: Manaktalas, 1964.

Morgan, Troy Wilson. *The Hindu Quest for the Perfection of Man*. Athens, OH: Ohio University, 1970.

Mott, John R. *Liberating the Lay Force of Christianity*. New York, NY: MacMillan, 1932.

Motwani, Kewal. *India, a Synthesis of Cultures*. Bombay, India: Thacker & Co., 1967.

Mulholland, Kenneth B. *Adventure in Training the Ministry*. Nutley, NJ: P & R Publishing, 1976.

Muller, F. Max. *India: What Can It Teach Us?*. New York, NY: Funk & Wagnalls, 1883.

Muller, Jacobus J. "The Epistle of Paul to the Philippians and to Philemon." In *The New International Commentary on the New Testament*. Grand Rapids, MI: William B. Eerdmans, 1955.

Murray, Andrew. *Key to the Missionary Problem*. Fort Washington, PA: Christian Literature Crusade, 1979.

Naranjo, Claudio, and Robert E. Ornstein. *On the Psychology of Meditation*. New York, NY: Penguin Books, 1976

Neill, Stephen. *Christian Faith and Other Faiths*. London, U.K.: Oxford University Press, 1961.

———. *A History of Christian Missions*. Grand Rapids, MI: William B. Eerdmans, 1965.

———. *Salvation Tomorrow*. Nashville, TN: Abington Press, 1976.

———. *The Story of the Christian Church in India and Pakistan*. Grand Rapids, MI: William B. Eerdmans, 1970.

———, Gerald Anderson, and John Goodwin, eds. *Concise Dictionary of the Christian World Mission*. Nashville, TN: Abington Press, 1976.

Nelson, Amritharaj. *A New Day in Madras*. Pasadena, CA: William Carey Library, 1975.

Nevius, John L. *The Planting and Development of Missionary Churches*. Grand Rapids, MI: Baker Book House, 1958.

Newbigin, Lesslie. *The Finality of Christ*. London, U.K.: SCM Press, 1969.

———. *The Open Secret*. Grand Rapids, MI: William B. Eerdmans, 1978.

Nida, Eugene A. *Custom and Cultures*. New York, NY: Harper & Row, 1959.

———. *Message and Mission*. New York, NY: Harper & Row, 1960.

Nikhilananda, Swami. *Rama Krishna: Prophet of New India*. New York, NY: Harper & Bros., 1948.

———. *The Upanishads*. Vol. 1. New York, NY: Harper & Row, 1949.

———. *The Upanishads*. Vol. 2. New York, NY: Harper & Row, 1952.

———. *Vivekananda: A Biography*. New York, NY: Rama Krishna-Vivekananda Center, 1953.

Niles, Daniel T. *Upon the Earth*. London, U.K.: Lutterworth Press, 1962.

Ninan, M. M. *Hinduism: What Really Happened in India?* San Jose, CA: Global Publishers, 2004.

Noss, John B. *Man's Religions*. New York, NY: MacMillan, 1963.

O'Malley, L. S. S. *Popular Hinduism*. London, U.K.: Cambridge University Press, 1935.

Organ, Troy Wilson. *Hinduism: Its Historical Development*. New York, NY: Barron's Educational Series, 1974.

Orr, J. Edwin. *Evangelical Awakening in India*. New Delhi, India: Masihi Sahitya Samasta, 1970.

———. *Mysticism, East and West*. New York, NY: MacMillan, 1932.

Otto, Rudolf. *The Idea of the Holy*. New York, NY: Oxford University Press, 1950.

Packer, James I. *Evangelism and the Sovereignty of God*. Chicago, IL: InterVarsity, 1961.

Padilla, Rene. "Evangelism and the World." In *Let the Earth Hear His Voice*, edited by J. D. Douglas. Minneapolis, MN: Worldwide Publications, 1975.

———, ed. *The New Face of Evangelism*. Downers Grove, IL: InterVarsity, 1976.

Panikkar, K. M. *Asia and Western Dominance*. London, U.K.: Allen & Unwin, 1959.

———. *The Foundation of New India*. London, U.K.: Allen & Unwin, 1963.

Panikkar, Raimundo. *The Unknown Christ of Hinduism*. London, U.K.: Danton, Longman, & Todd, 1964.

Parrinder, Geoffrey. *Avatar and Incarnation*. London, U.K.: Faber and Faber, 1970.

Pathickal, Paul. *The Cross and the Cow Belt of India*, Enumclaw, WA, WinePress Publishing, 2011

Pearson, Nathaniel. *Sri Aurobindo and the Soul Quest of Men*. London, U.K.: George Allen and Unwin Ltd., 1952.

Pentecost, Edward C. *Reaching the Unreached*. Pasadena, CA: William Carey Library, 1974.

Percival, H. C., and E. R. Hambye. *Christianity in India*. Alleppy, India: Prakasam Publications, 1972.

Pereira, Peter, and Mary Lou Wilson. "Responding to the Presence of Asian Indians in North America, Houston '85." n.p.: Evangelizing Ethnic America, 1985.

Pickett, J. Waskom. *Christian Mass Movements in India.* Lucknow, India: Lucknow Publishing House, 1969.

————. *Christ's Way to India's Heart.* Lucknow, India: Lucknow Publishing House, 1938.

————. *The Dynamics of Church Growth.* Nashville, TN: Abington Press, 1963.

————, A. L. Warnshuis, G. H. Singh, and D. A. McGavran. *Church Growth and Group Conversion.* Lucknow, India: Lucknow Publishing House, 1962.

Pitt, Malcolm. *Introducing Hinduism.* New York: Friendship Press, 1955.

Ponraj. S. D. *The Mark of a Missionary.* Chennai, India: Mission Educational Books 1990.

Pothen, S. G. *The Syrian Christians of Kerala.* New York, NY: Asia Publishing House, 1963.

Potter Karl H. *Presuppositions of India's Philosophies.* Westport, CT: Greenwood Press, 1976.

Prabhavananda, Swami, and Christopher Isherwood. *The Song of God: Bhagavad-Gita.* New York, N.Y.: Mentor Books, 1944.

Prabhupada, A. C. Bhaktivedanta. *Bhagavat Gita as It Is.* New York, NY: Collier Books, 1972.

Presler, Henry H. *Introducing Strangers to Hinduism.* Allahabad, India: North India Christian Tract and Book Society, 1987.

Radhakrishnan, S. *The Bhagavat Gita.* New York, NY: Harper & Bros., 1948.

————. *The Hindu View of Life.* Bombay, India: George Allen & Unwin (India) Private, 1971.

————. *The Principal Upanishads.* London, U.K.: George Allen & Unwin, 1953.

Raj, Sunder. *The Confusion Called Conversion.* New Delhi, India: TRACI publications, 1986.

Ramachandra, Vinoth. *Gods That Fail.* Downers Grove, IL: InterVarsity, 1996.

Read, Hollis. *India and Its People:* Columbus, Ohio: Osgood & Pearce, 1858.

Renou, Louis. *The Nature of Hinduism.* Translated by Patrick Evans. New York, NY: Walker and Co., 1962.

Report of the Christian Missionary Activity Enquiry Committee, Madhya Pradesh. Nagpur, India: Government Printing Press, 1956.

Richard, H. L. *Following Jesus in the Hindu Context.* Pasadena, CA: William Carey Library, 1998.

Ridderbos, Herman. *The Coming of the Kingdom.* Philadelphia, PA: P & R Publishing, 1962.

_____. *Paul.* Grand Rapids, MI: William B. Eerdmans, 1975.

_____. *Paul and Jesus.* Philadelphia, PA: P & R Publishing, 1974.

Rommen, Edweard, and Harold Netland, eds. *Christianity and the Religions.* Pasadena, CA: William Carey Library, 1995.

Samartha, S. J. *Courage for Dialogue.* Maryknoll, NY: Orbis Books, 1981.

_____. *Dialogue between Men of Living Faiths.* Geneva: World Council of Churches, 1971.

_____. *The Hindu Response to the Unbound Christ.* Madras, India: Christian Literature Society, 1974.

Sanders, Frank K. *The Presentation of Christianity to Hindus.* New York, NY: Board of Missionary Preparation, 1917.

Sargunam, M. Ezra. *Multiplying Churches in Modern India.* Madras, India: Federation of Evangelical Churches in India, 1974.

Schaeffer, Francis A. *The Church at the End of the Twentieth Century.* London, U.K.: Hodder and Stoughton, 1975.

_____. *The God Who Is There.* Downers Grove, IL: InterVarsity, 1968.

Scherer, James A. *Missionary Go Home!* Englewood Cliffs, NJ: Prentice-Hall, 1964.

Schulberg, Lucille. *Historical India.* New York, NY: Time-Life Books, 1968.

Scott, Waldron. *Bring Forth Justice.* Grand Rapids, MI: William B. Eerdmans, 1980.

Sen, K. M. *Hinduism.* Harmondsworth, England: Penguin Books, 1961.

Seunarine, James Forbes. *Reconversion to Hinduism through Suddhi.* Ann Arbor, MI: University Microfilms International, 1975.

Shah, Douglas, *The Mediators.* Plainfield, NJ: Logos International. 1975.

Sharma, R.S., *Material Culture and Social Formations in Ancient India.* Delhi, India: Macmillan, 1983

Sharpe, Eric J., *The Theology of A. G. Hogg.* Madras, India: CLS-CISRS, 1971.

Shaw, Robert, *An Exposition of the Confession of Faith of the Westminster Assembly of Divines.* Philadelphia, PA: Presbyterian Board of Publication, 1846.

Shearer, Roy E. *Wildfire: Church Growth in Korea.* Grand Rapids, MI: William B. Eerdmans, 1966.

Shenk, Wilbert R., ed., *The Challenge of Church Growth, a Symposium.* Elkhart, IN: Institute of Mennonite Studies, 1973.

Shrinivas, M. N. *Caste in Modern India.* New York, NY: Asia Publishing House, 1962.

Smith, Huston. *The World's Religions.* New York, NY: HarperCollins, 1991.

Sookhdeo, Patrick, ed. *Jesus Christ, the Only Way.* Exeter, England: Paternoster Press, 1978.

Soper, Edmund Davison. *The Inevitable Choice: Vedanta Philosophy or Christian Gospel.* Nashville, TN: Abington Press, 1957.

_____, *The Philosophy of the Christian World View.* Nashville, TN: Abington Press, 1943.

Spear, Percival, *A History of India.* Vol.2. Hammondsworth, U.K.: Penguin Books, 1965.

_____, *India, Pakistan, and the West.* London, U.K.: Oxford University Press, 1967.

Spittler, Russell P., *Cults and Isms.* Grand Rapids, MI: Baker Book House, 1962.

Spradley, James P., *The Ethnographic Interview.* New York, NY: Holt, Rinehart and Winston, 1979.

Sproul, R. C., *The Psychology of Atheism.* Minneapolis, MN: Bethany House, 1974.

Srivastava, Dayawanti, ed. *India-2008, a Reference Manual.* New Delhi, India: Publication Division, Ministry of Information and Broadcasting, Government of India, 2008.

Stock, Frederick and Margaret Stock, *People Movement in the Punjab.* Pasadena, CA: William Carey Library, 1975.

Stott, John R. W. *Basic Christianity.* London, U.K.: InterVarsity, 1958.

_____, and Robert Coote, eds. *Down to Earth: Studies in Christianity and Culture.* Grand Rapids, MI: William B. Eerdmans, 1980.

Street, T. Watson, *On the Growing Edge of the Church.* Richmond, VA: John Knox Press, 1965.

Stroup, Herbert, *Like a Great River: An Introduction to Hinduism.* London, U.K.: Harper & Row, 1972.

Subbamma, B. V. *Christ Confronts India: Indigenous Expressions of Christianity.* Madras, India: Diocesan Press, 1973.

————, *New Patterns for Discipling Hindus.* Pasadena, CA: William Carey Library, 1970.

Sundkler, Bengt. *The World of Mission.* Grand Rapids, MI: William B. Eerdmans, 1965.

Taylor, John C. *India: Dr. John Taylor Remembers.* Wilmington, DE: World Presbyterian Missions, 1971.

Thapar, Romila, *A History of India.* Baltimore, MD: Penguin Books, Inc. 1966.

The Thirteen Principal Upanishads, Translated by R. E. Hume. London, U.K.: Oxford University Press, 1934.Thiessen, Henry C. *Lectures in Systematic Theology.* Grand Rapids, MI: William B. Eerdmans, 1981.

Thirumalai, Madasamy, *Sharing Your Faith with a Hindu.* Minneapolis, MN: Bethany House, 2002.

Thoburn, James M., *The Christian Conquest of India.* Philadelphia, PA: Westminster Press, 1906.

Thomas, M. M., *Salvation and Humanisation.* Madras, India: Christian Literature Society, 1971.

————. "The Gospel and the Quest of Modern Asia." *Union Seminary Quarterly Review* 22, no. 3 (1967): 229–241.

Thomas, P., *Christians and Christianity in India and Pakistan.* London, U.K.: George Allen & Unwin, 1954.

Thompson, E. W., *The Word of the Cross to Hindus.* Madras, India: Christian Literature Society, 1956.

Tinker, Hugh. *A New System of Slavery: The Export of Indian Labour Overseas, 1830-1920.* London, U.K.: Oxford University Press, 1974.

Tippett, Allan R., *Church Growth and the Word of God.* Grand Rapids, MI: William B. Eerdmans, 1970.

————, ed. *God, Man and Church Growth.* Grand Rapids, MI: William B. Eerdmans, 1973.

————, *Verdict Theology in Missionary Theory.* Pasadena, CA: William Carey Library, 1973.

Tisserant, Cardinal Eugene, *Eastern Christianity in India.* Bombay, India: Orient Longmans, 1957.

Tonna, Benjamin, *Gospel for the Cities.* Maryknoll, NY: Orbis Books, 1978.

Unger, Merrill F., *Archaeology and the Old Testament*. Grand Rapids, MI: Zondervan, 1954.

Van Baalen, Jan Karel, *The Chaos of Cults*. Grand Rapids, MI: William B Eerdmans, 1938

Van Til, Cornelius, *The Defense of the Faith*. Philadelphia, PA: P & R Publishing, 1955.

————, *In Defense of the Faith*. Vol.3. Philadelphia, PA: Den Dulk Christian Foundation, 1974.

Vedic Hymns, Translated by Edward J. Thomas. London, U.K.: John Murray, 1923.

Venugopal, C. T. *Witness to Christ*. Madras, India: Christian Literature Society, 1972.

Vertovec, Steven, *The Hindu Diaspora*. London, U.K.: Routledge, 2000.

Visser't Hooft, W. A., *No Other Name*. Philadelphia, PA: Westminster Press, 1963.

Vos, Geerhardus, *Biblical Theology*. Grand Rapids, MI: William B. Eerdmans, 1948.

————, *The Pauline Eschatology*. Grand Rapids, MI: William B. Eerdmans, 1972.

Vos, Johannes G. *A Christian Introduction to Religions of the World*. Grand Rapids, MI: Baker Book House, 1965.

Wagner, C. Peter, ed. *Church/Mission Tension Today*. Chicago, IL: Moody Press, 1972.

————, *Frontiers in Missionary Strategy*. Chicago, IL: Moody Press, 1972.

Wallbank, T. Walter, *A Short History of India and Pakistan*. New York, NY: Mentor Books. 1958

Warfield, B. B., *The Person and Work of Christ*. Philadelphia, PA: P & R Publishing, 1950.

Warnack, Gustav, *Modern Missions and Culture*. Translated by Thomas Smith. Edinburgh, U.K.: James Gemmell, 1883.

Warneck, Johannes. *The Living Christ and Dying Heathenism*. Grand Rapids, MI: Baker Book House, 1954.

Weber, Max, *The Protestant Ethic and the Spirit of Capitalism*. Translated by Talcott Parsons. New York, NY: Charles Scribner's Sons, 1958.

Whaling, Frank, *An Approach to Dialogue with Hinduism*. Lucknow, India: Lucknow Publishing House, 1966.

Wheeler, Sir Mortimer, *Civilizations of the Indus Valley and Beyond*. London, U.K.: Thomas and Hudson, 1961.

Wild, Wayne and D. A. McGavran, *Principles of Church Growth*. Pasadena, CA: William Carey Library, 1924.

Williams, Raymond, "Hinduism in America." *The Christian Century*, March 11, 1987: 247.

Wilson, H. H. *The Vishnu Purana: A System of Hindu Mythology and Tradition*. Calcutta, India: Punthi Pustak, 1961.

Winslow, Jack C., *The Christian Approach to the Hindu*. London, U.K.: Edinburgh House Press, 1958.

Winter, Ralph, ed., *The Evangelical Response to Bangkok*. Pasadena, CA: William Carey Library, 1973.

_____. *The 25 Unbelievable Years, 1945–1969*. Pasadena, CA: William Carey Library, 1970.

_____. *The World Christian Movement, 1950-1975: An Interpretive Essay*. Pasadena, CA: William Carey Library, 1975

_____, and Steven C. Hawthorne, eds. *Perspectives on the World Christian Movement: A Reader*. Pasadena, CA: William Carey Library, 1981.

Witzel, Michael. ed. *Inside the Texts and beyond the Texts: New Approaches to the Study of the Vedas*. Cambridge, U.K.: Harvard Oriental Series, 1997

Wong, James, Peter Larson and Edward Pentecost. *Missions from the Third World*. Singapore: Church Growth Study Center, 1973.

Wood, Michael. *India*. New York, NY: Basic Books, n.d.

Wysham, William Norris. *Christians, Claim Your Heritage*. New York, N.Y.: World Horizons, 1967.

Yamamori, Tetsunao, Bryant Myers and David Conner, eds. *Serving with the Poor in Asia*. Monrovia, CA: MARC, 1995.

Yohannan, K. P., *The Coming Revolution in World Missions*. Altamonte Springs, FL: Creation House, 1986.

Young, Robert D. *Encounter with World Religions*. Philadelphia, PA: Westminster Press, 1970.

Zachariah, Mathai, ed. *The Indian Church: Identity and Fulfillment*. Madras, India: Christian Literature Society, 1971.

Zacharias, Ravi, *The Lotus and the Cross*. Sisters, OR: Multnomah, 2001.

———, *Walking from East to West*. Grand Rapids, MI: Zondervan, 2006.

Zaehner, R. C. *Hinduism*. London: Oxford University Press, 1962.

GLOSSARY OF SELECT HINDU WORDS

Acharya—Great spiritual leader

Advaita—Non-dualism; the Monistic system of Vedanta philosophy

Agni—The god of fire

Ahimsa—Nonviolence; non-injuring in thought, word, or deed

Akbar—Mogul Emperor of India, 1542–1605 AD

Amrith—Nectar of immortality

Ananda—Bliss, extreme happiness

Ashoka—A great Hindu king who embraced Buddhism, 259–222 BC

Atharva Veda—The fourth Veda dealing with magical spells and incantations

Atman—The Eternal Self

Avatar—A divine incarnation

Avidya—Ignorance

Banyan Tree—*Ficus Indica*; a holy tree whose branches drop roots to the ground to become new trunks

Bhagawat Gita—"The Holy Song"; the advice of Krishna on the historic battlefield at Kurukshetra

Bhagawan—A title of god; literally "possessor of all powers"

Bhakti—Intense devotion

Bhakti Marga—The way of devotion to attain Nirvana or Moksha

Bhakti Yoga—Union with the Divine through devotion

Bramacharya—Chastity in thought, word, and deed

Bramacharin—One who has devoted himself to continence and the pursuit of spiritual wisdom

Brahma—The Creator; one of the three great gods directly under Brahman

Brahman—The One Existence, the Absolute, the Supreme God, the Universal Spirit

Brahmana—A member of the priestly caste

Brahmin—Anglicized form of Brahmana; "A twice- born man"; one who is born into the priestly caste. This term has become the standard.

Brahmanas—Those portions of the Vedas that state the rules for chanting hymns at various ceremonies

Buddha—The name of the founder of Buddhism, whose full name is Siddharta Gautama; Buddha literally means "the enlightened one"; one of the ten avatars in Hinduism

Dharma—Religious duty

Gopis—Milkmaids, worshippers of Krishna

Guru—A religious teacher

Hanuman—The monkey-god who helped to rescue Sita from Ravana of Lanka

Indra—A great god

Ishwar, Isvar—The Supreme Ruler

Jnana—Pure intelligence; knowledge

Kama—Lust; sexual desire

Karma—Work or action; the law of cause and effect in the moral world

Karma Marga—The way of action to attain Nirvana or Moksha

Karma Yoga—Union with the divine through unselfish performance of duty

Krishna—The latest incarnation of Vishnu

Madhva—A commentator of the dualistic school of the Vedanta philosophy

Mahatma—Great soul; a title usually reserved for Mohandas K. Gandhi

Mantra—A prayer or chant; a magical chant to affect the desired result

Maya—Illusion; mistaking the unreal and the phenomenal for the real and eternal

Mlecha—Uncivilized person

Moksha—Liberation; freedom from the sensory world

Mukti—Emancipation from the cycles of birth and death; liberation

Muni—A religious sage; one who has renounced the pleasures of life

Nirguna—Without attributes or qualities

Nirvana—Extinction from the cycles of birth and death; liberation

Nyaya—The science of logical philosophy; the school of Indian logic

Om—The most holy word of the Vedas; symbolic word meaning "the Supreme Being"

Para-Brahman—The Supreme Being

Para-Bhakti—Supreme devotion

Parameshwar—Supreme God; One who is above all gods

Patanjali—Founder of the Yoga School of Philosophy

Purana—Ancient story

Quran—the holy scripture of Islam

Ramanuja—A noted scholar of Advaida philosophy

Ram, Rama—An incarnation of Vishnu; the hero king of the epic poem *Ramayana*

Ramayana—One of the two great epics written by Valmiki based on the life of Rama

Rig Veda—the oldest of the four Vedas, comprised of hymns in praise of and petition to nature gods

Rishi—A holy man possessed of supersensory knowledge

Rudra—The name of a fierce and destructive Vedic god

Sama Veda—The portion of the Veda containing chants sung during ceremonies

Samadhi—The state where one achieves super-consciousness

Samsara—The visible world where the endless cycle of life and death occurs

Sankara, Sankaracharya—The founder of the non-dualistic school of Vedanta

philosophy; sometimes called Adi-Sankara to distinguish him from his successors, who are also called Sankaracharyas

Sankya—A system of philosophy founded by the great sage Kapila

Sanyasa—Complete renunciation of all worldly pleasures, property, and fame

Sanyasin—One who makes *Sanyasa* and renounces all worldly pleasures

Sastra—Sacred scriptures; science

Sat—Existence; absolute

Satyam—Truthfulness

Sayujya—Unity with Brahman

Siva, Shiva—One of the three great gods of Hinduism; one who destroys or punishes

Smriti—That which is remembered; non-Vedic authoritative scripture

Soma—nectar from certain plants capable of hallucination

Sri—Holy or blessed

Sruti—That which is uttered; non-Vedic hymns chanted from other holy scriptures

Sutra—Ancient aphorisms; sacred verse; literally "thread"

Tamas—Darkness; inertia

Tantras—Sacred books of certain sects

Tapas—Deep meditation by fasting

"Tat tvam asi"—"That thou art"

Tulsidas—The name of a great sage who translated *Ramayana* into Hindustani

Upanishad—That which sits beside; the group of treatises written after the Vedas

Varuna—The Aryan god of the sky; the god of cosmic and moral order

Vayu—Air

Veda—Wisdom or revealed knowledge

Vedas—Ancient Hindu scriptures

Vedanta—The end of Veda; the final philosophy of the Vedas as expressed in the Upanishads; encompasses the monistic, the mono-dualistic, and the dualistic philosophies

Vidya—Knowledge

Vishnu—One of the three great gods under Brahman; the god who incarnated himself to save mankind from the wicked

Vyasa—The sage who wrote the epic poem *Mahabharata*

Yaga—Any kind of sacrifice with which to placate gods

Yajur Veda—The ritualistic portion of the Vedas containing sacred formulae

Yama—The god of Death so called by his power of self-control; the internal purification through intense training, preparatory to yoga

Yoga—Joining; union of the lower self with the higher self by means of self-control

Yogi—One who practices yoga

Yuga—A cycle or age of the world; the present Yuga is called the Kali Yuga to mark the end of the world

INDEX

A

Adam 45, 126, 128, 132, 154, 156, 160
Adharma 48
Adi-Sankara 215
Advaita 29, 31, 213
Agamas 19, 23, 28
Agni 213
Ahimsa 213
Akbar 213
Alexander 15
Allah 95, 168
Allen, Roland 193
America iv, xii, 3, 5–8, 58, 90, 158–159, 164, 190, 198–199, 207, 212
  United States iv, xii, 3, 5–8, 58, 90, 158–159, 164, 190, 198–199, 207, 212
Amrith 26, 213
Animism 17, 88, 105
Apostle Paul 46, 100
Apostle Peter 124
Arjuna 22, 27
Aryan 12–15, 19, 31, 33–34, 38–39, 105, 175, 216
  Aryanism 12–15, 19, 31, 33–34, 38–39, 105, 175, 216
Arya Samaj 44
Asceticism 29, 49, 86, 116
Asia 3, 19, 87, 194–195, 200, 202–203, 206, 207, 209–210, 212
Asian 3, 19, 87, 194–195, 197, 200, 202–203, 206–207, 209–210, 212
Atharva Veda 15, 20, 213
Athens 198
Atman 24, 213
Avatar 22, 27, 30, 69, 74, 98, 130, 150
Avidya 48
Ayodhya 26–27
  Oudh 26–27
Ayurveda 20

B

Babar 27
Bajrang Dal xii, 17
Banares 199
  Kashi 199
    Varanasi 199
Bangladesh xii, 4
Beef 88
Bengal 28–29, 62
Bethlehem 74, 75, 131
Bhagawan 9, 21, 24, 69, 213
Bhagawat Gita 213
Bhajens 6, 113
Bhakti 30, 49
  Bhakti Marga 30, 49
Bharat 1
Bharata 1, 27
Bharatiya Janata Party xii, 17

BJP xii, 17
Bible 19, 45, 68, 70, 76, 78–80, 83,
    93–95, 98, 100, 103, 107,
    115–117, 124–127, 140, 146,
    151, 154–155, 159–162,
    164–165, 167–168, 171–175,
    177–178, 180, 186–187, 191,
    196–198, 200
Bihar 28, 62
Bombay 54, 183, 195, 197, 199–200,
    202–204, 207, 210
Brahma 25, 28, 44, 63, 80, 190, 213
Brahman 21–22, 24–25, 50, 63, 69,
    94–95, 213–216
Brahmanas 19, 21, 23, 214
Brahmin 1, 8, 17–18, 21, 24–26,
    39–41, 43, 47, 74, 80, 89–90,
    106, 140, 149, 176, 214
British 2–4, 12, 15, 55, 73, 79, 84–85,
    88, 158
    British Empire 2–4, 12, 15, 55, 73,
        79, 84–85, 88, 158
    British Raj 4, 12
Buddha 26, 30, 69, 74, 77, 95, 153,
    214
    Gautama 26, 30, 69, 74, 77, 95, 153,
        214
Buddhism xi, 16–17, 26, 29–31, 43,
    105, 153, 159, 173, 213–214

C

Calcutta 54, 88, 194, 212
Carey, William 88, 96, 128, 140, 196,
    198–199, 203–206, 208–210,
    212
Caspian Sea 13
Caste ix, xii, 2–3, 7, 10, 15–16, 20,
    23–24, 26, 31, 37–48, 56–57,
    60, 72, 78, 80, 85, 88–90, 103,
    105–106, 112, 118–120, 138,
    170, 185–186, 189, 214
Caste system 15, 38, 41, 43–45, 89,
    185
Celts 13

Ceylon 26
Chattisgarh 62
Chennai 54, 147–148, 165, 193, 197,
    207
    Madras 54, 147–148, 165, 193, 197,
        207
China 88, 172
Christians xii, 3–4, 10, 42, 45–46,
    53, 55, 61, 63, 68, 69, 71–72,
    74, 76–78, 80–85, 87–90, 96,
    98, 101, 105, 117–122, 135,
    148–149, 158, 158–159, 173,
    176, 184, 186, 195, 201–202,
    207, 210, 212
Conn, Harvie M. ix, 196
Cow xii, 36, 201, 206
Creator 25, 28, 178–179

D

Dalit 198
Darsanas 19, 23
Das 34
    Seth Govinda 34
David 20, 86, 194–195, 197, 199–
    200, 212
Deccan Plateau 14
Deity 8, 17–18, 21, 25, 27, 29, 32,
    111, 113–114, 119, 138, 185,
    190
Delhi 22, 33, 54, 81, 90, 157, 195,
    197–198, 203–204, 206–209
Demigods 25, 178
Demonolatry 17
Demons 17–18, 25
    Demonism 17–18, 25
Devanandan 197
Devil 102, 140, 157
Dharma 185, 214
Dispersion 1
Dravidianism 14
Dravidians 14–15, 23–24, 34, 38–39
Dutch 15

E

East India Company 88
Epic 15, 22, 26–27, 30, 215–216
Esther 15
Eurasian Plateau 12–13
Europe 3, 13, 44, 81, 90, 159, 202
Evangelical v, xii, 61, 171, 186–187
Extermination 42
Extinction 50

F

Farquhar 33, 198
Festivals 5
Fetishism 17
Firth, C.B. 90
French 15

G

Gama, Vasco da 87
Gandhi 5, 17, 44, 73–75, 79, 96–97,
    153, 158, 198–199, 204, 214
  Mahatma 5, 17, 44, 73–75, 79,
    96–97, 153, 158, 198–199, 204,
    214
    Mohan Das 5, 17, 44, 73–75, 79,
    96–97, 153, 158, 198–199, 204,
    214
Ganges River 2, 185
Gita 22, 27, 30–31, 40, 50, 84, 102,
    159, 173, 207, 213
God 12, 20–23, 25–27, 29–32, 33,
    37, 40, 42, 47, 49, 60–63, 69,
    77–80, 94, 100, 114, 130,
    138–139, 148, 150, 155, 161,
    172, 176, 184–186, 190, 192,
    213–216
Goddess 6, 23, 32, 37, 49, 61–63, 138,
    186, 190
Goddesses 15, 17, 24–25, 32, 42,
    63–64, 80, 111, 138–139, 178,
    186
God-man 98, 100, 131, 146, 150,
    155–156, 167
Gods 14–18, 20–26, 28, 30–32, 37,
    41–42, 62–64, 74, 77, 77–79,
    83, 88, 96, 103, 111, 128–130,
    138–139, 148, 152, 156,
    161–163, 168, 176, 178, 181,
    184–186, 213, 215–216
Government of India xi, 4, 112
Great Commission xii, 45, 197
Greece 39
Greek 13, 17, 19, 24, 46, 77
Greeks 12–13, 34
Greenway, Roger ix, 199
Gujarat 28, 32
Gupta, Sir K.G. 42, 199
Guru 64, 190, 197, 203, 214

H

Hanuman 22, 26, 214
Harappa 12, 14
Harappans 14
Harmonization 42–43
Haryana 12
Henotheism 63
Herod 151
High-castes 89–90
Himalayas 2, 13, 20
Hind 12
Hindi 7, 62, 134
Hindu Kush 12–13
Hindu Mahasabha xii, 17, 44
Hindustan 1–2, 17
Hindustani 216
Hiriyana, M 34, 200
Hittites 13
Hogg, A.G. 36, 200, 208
Hollis, A.M. 200, 207
Holy Cow 201
Holy Spirit 25, 80, 125, 134, 139–140,
    142, 145–146, 162–163,
    178–181

I

Identification 6, 42
Incarnation 26, 191–192, 200, 206
India ix–xii, 1–10, 12–20, 27–32,
    33, 35–39, 42–46, 53–57, 59,

62–64, 73–75, 77, 81–82, 84,
86–89, 100, 102, 112–113,
118, 121–122, 128, 131, 135,
140, 146–147, 153, 157–158,
164, 183, 183–187, 189–190,
193–213
Indigenization 84
Indo-Aryan 185
Indo-European 14, 23
Indra 12, 214
Indus River 12, 14
Iran xii, 13, 184
Islam xi, 11, 16–17, 30, 43, 88, 97,
102, 215

J

Jainism 16, 29, 31
Jati 38
Jerusalem 1, 131, 198
Jesus, Jesus Christ ix–x, xii, 11, 27, 45–
46, 55, 68–70, 73–74, 77–79,
82–86, 88, 90, 95–99, 101, 105,
107–108, 114, 116–119, 124,
126, 131–136, 139–140, 142,
146, 148–153, 155–158, 160,
163–164, 167, 169–171, 174,
178–179, 180, 184–187, 191,
193, 202, 208–209
Jews 1, 42, 107, 125
Jha, D.N. 201
Jharkhand 62
Jnana Marga 47–49
Judea 1
Judge 75, 84, 99, 107–109, 116, 160,
171–172

K

Kali 29, 32, 216
Kali Yuga 216
Kalki 27
Kamsa 30
Karachi 12
Karma 33–38, 40, 47–48, 99, 128,
131, 175, 199–200, 214

Karma Marga 214
Karnataka 28
Kassites 13
Kauravas 22, 27, 30, 150
Kerala x, 32, 81, 87, 89, 149, 201, 207
Kraemer, Hendrik 201
Krishna 3, 9, 22, 26–27, 30, 50, 62,
69–70, 74, 78, 83, 98–99, 116,
130, 150, 155–156, 186, 192,
205, 213–214
Krishnaism 98
Kshatriya 26, 40
Kurma 26
Kurukshetra 22, 27, 30, 213

L

Lanka 4, 26, 214
Latin 3, 137, 151, 195, 199
Liberation 22, 24, 31, 33, 36–37, 41,
46–51, 98, 100–101, 124, 169,
187, 214
Low-castes 45, 72, 88–90

M

Madhva 214
Madhya Pradesh 62, 84, 208
Mahabharata 15, 22, 26, 30, 48, 61,
216
Mahasabha xii, 17, 44
Mandara 26
Mangalwadi, Vishal 203
Manu 1, 19, 23, 26, 37, 47–48
Marga 37, 47–49, 78, 213–214
Marthoma Church 202
Matsya 26
McGavran, Donald 203
McQuilkin, Robertson 204
Mediator 75, 83, 95, 98–100, 117,
131–132, 139, 155–156, 167,
181
Medicine 5, 20, 58, 76
Mediterranean 13, 38, 184
Messiah 28, 30
Mohammed 11

Moksha 24
Monier-Williams, Sir 204
Muhammad 94, 173
Mumbai 54
Muslim 27, 159, 170, 198
Myth 201

N

Narasimha 26
National Christian Council 84
Negro 38
Nehru, Jawaharlal 79, 81, 87
Nevius, John 205
New Delhi 33, 54, 81, 157, 195, 198,
   203–204, 206–207, 209
New Testament 74, 83–84, 94, 99,
   108, 160, 173, 180, 200, 204
Nikhilananda, Swami 205
Niles, D.T. 199, 206
Nirvana 213–214
Non-violence 26
Nyaya 214
Nyogi Commission 84

O

Old Testament 15, 30, 84, 94, 102,
   107, 115, 152, 160, 173, 180,
   211
Organ, Troy Wilson 206
Orissa xii

P

Packer, J.I. 206
Pakistan xii, 4, 12, 16, 87, 157, 184,
   205
Pandavas 22, 27, 30, 150
Panikkar, K.M. 87–88, 206
Pantheon 17, 25, 31–32, 74
Para-Brahman 24, 215
Paramatman 24
Parasurama 26
Persecution xi, 4, 44
Philosophy 10–11, 14, 21, 23, 25–26,
   28–31, 49, 105, 116, 177–178,

186, 213–216
Plato 39
Portuguese 15, 38
Punjab 12, 209
Puranas 11, 19, 22, 30, 80, 105, 113

R

Radhakrishnan, Sarvepalli 35, 41–43,
   207
Rai, Lala Lajpat 43
Rajah 203
Rajanya 40
Rama 1, 22, 26–27, 30, 62, 69, 74, 78,
   150, 155–156, 186, 192, 205,
   215
Ramakrishna Mission 34, 97
Ramanuja 49, 215
Ramayana 15, 22, 26, 30–31, 61, 159,
   173, 215–216
Rashtriya Swayamsevak Sangh xii, 17
Ravana 22, 26–27, 74, 150, 214
Rebirth 33–36, 40–41, 46–48, 50–51,
   89, 100, 161, 175
Reconversion 2, 208
Re-death 36, 46
Redeemer 179
Redemption 31, 181
Reincarnation 193
Rice Christians 89
Rig Veda 15, 19–20, 40, 199, 215
Rishi 215
Rome 198
RSS xii

S

Salvation 47, 51, 95–96, 100–101,
   105, 107–108, 131–132, 143,
   156, 162–164, 167, 169,
   177–178, 181, 185, 187
Samaritan 45
Samartha, Stanley 97, 208
Sama Veda 15, 20, 215
Samkhya 48
Samsara 215

Sankara 215
Sanskrit 8, 14, 18, 23, 28–29, 38, 134
Satan 102, 187
Savior ix–x, 76, 84, 88, 95, 102, 109,
    115–116, 124, 126, 129–131,
    134, 141, 143, 148–150, 152,
    156–158, 161–163, 170–171,
    177, 185–187, 193
Self 21–22, 25, 48–50, 70, 75, 83, 89,
    137, 140, 147, 152–153, 159,
    173, 213, 216
Sepoy Mutiny 12
Serampore 88
Shaivism 28–29, 31
Shakti 29
Shamanism 17
Shiva 17, 25, 28–29, 31–32, 62–63,
    80, 95, 111, 148, 176, 190, 215
Shiva Sena 17
Sikh 53
Sikhism xi, 16–17, 128
Sin 45, 48, 74, 83, 98, 125, 125–128,
    130–132, 146, 153–159, 171
Sind 12
Sindhu, See Indus River 12
Sita 22, 26, 74, 214
Smriti 215
Soma 215
Spear, Percival 209
Spirit 21, 24–25, 38, 46, 50, 63, 69,
    76, 80, 94, 100, 125, 134, 139–
    140, 142, 145–146, 162–163,
    169, 176, 178–181, 211, 214
Sri Lanka 4, 26
Staines, Graham xii
Subordination 42
Sudra 40
Supernatural beings 25
Supreme deity 21, 25
Supreme Soul 24
Sutra 216

T

Tagore, Rabindra Nath 43

Tamil 28–29, 31, 128
Tamil Nadu 28, 31, 128
Tapas 216
Tat tvam asi 216
Testament 15, 30, 74, 83–84, 94, 99,
    102, 107–108, 115, 152, 160,
    173, 180, 200, 204, 211
Teutons 13
Trinal 25
Trinity 25, 75, 80, 116, 176, 179–182
Twice-born 39, 41, 44–45, 49, 80, 149

U

Ultimate Reality 21, 24, 48–49
Universal Spirit 21, 24–25, 38, 46, 50,
    63, 69, 94, 100, 169, 176, 214
Upanishads 11, 17, 19, 21, 23–24, 30,
    33, 35, 50, 105, 169, 173, 205,
    207, 210, 216
Upper Caste 56
Uttar Pradesh 28, 32, 62

V

Vaishnavism 28–31
Vaisya 40
Vamana 26
Varaha 26
Varna 38
Varuna 216
Vasco da Gama 87
Vedanta 20–21, 49, 105, 209, 213–216
Vedas 8, 11–12, 15, 17, 19–21, 23,
    26, 30, 39, 47, 77, 94, 105,
    113, 154, 159, 173, 195, 212,
    214–216
Vedic 15, 20, 23, 30–31, 33, 175, 211,
    215
Vid 19
Vidya 35
Vindhya Mountains 14
Vishnu 6, 22, 25–32, 62–63, 69, 74,
    80, 95, 98–99, 130, 168, 176,
    190, 199, 212, 214–216
Vishwa Hindu Parishad 17

Vivekananda, Swami 34–35, 97, 128,
    205

W

Weber, Max 211
West Bengal 28
Wilson, Troy Organ 6, 11–12, 14,
    29–30, 115, 154, 197, 206–207,
    212

Y

Yajur Veda 15, 20, 216
Yoga 3, 216